LEGAL AND HEALTHCARE ETHICS FOR THE ELDERLY

LEGAL AND HEALTHCARE ETHICS FOR THE ELDERLY

George P. Smith, II
Columbus School of Law
Catholic University of America
Washington, D.C.

Taylor & Francis
Publishers since 1798

USA	Publishing Office:	Taylor & Francis
		1101 Vermont Ave., N.W., Suite 200
		Washington, DC 20005
		Tel: (202) 289-2174
		Fax: (202) 289-3665
	Distribution Center:	Taylor & Francis
		1900 Frost Road, Suite 101
		Bristol, PA 19007-1598
		Tel: (215) 785-5800
		Fax: (215) 785-5515
UK		Taylor & Francis, Ltd.
		1 Gunpowder Square
		London EC4A 3DE
		Tel: 071 538 0490
		Fax: 071 538 0581

LEGAL AND HEALTHCARE ETHICS FOR THE ELDERLY

1 2 3 4 5 6 7 8 9 0 BRBR 9 8 7 6 5

This book was set in Times Roman by Harlowe Typography, Inc. The editors were Holly Seltzer and Joyce Duncan. Cover design by Michelle Fleitz. Prepress supervisor was Miriam Gonzalez. Printing and binding by Braun-Brumfield, Inc.

A CIP catalog record for this book is available from the British Library.
∞ The paper in this publication meets the requirements of the ANSI Standard Z39.48-1984 (Permanence of Paper)

Library of Congress Cataloging-in-Publication Data
Smith, George Patrick, date
  Legal and healthcare ethics for the elderly/George P. Smith, II.
    p. cm.
  Includes bibliographical references.

  1. Aged—Medical care—Law and legislation—United States.
2. Aged—Medical care—Moral and ethical aspects. I. Title.
KF3821.S64   1996
344.73′0326—dc20
[347.304326]   95-40599
                                                                      CIP

ISBN 1-56032-452-X (cloth)
ISBN 1-56032-453-8 (paper)

TO

*Jonathan Z. Friedman, Esquire, and Michael F. Colligan, Esquire,
great teachers, valued friends, and unfailing
sources of support over the years.*

"There comes a point in nearly everybody's life when he must accept the fact that he is old; from that moment onwards all that is left is a melancholy process of decay; sometimes mitigated by remissions or apparent recoveries, sometimes proceeding headlong to total degeneration. With one victim the mind decays more quickly than the body, with another the physical collapse comes first, but always the path leads the same way, only the pace is different. . . ."

Philip Ziegler, King Edward VIII, 554, (Collins, 1990)

Contents

Preface

Within the vortex of the three central bioethical issues of autonomy, justice, and beneficence, which permeate modern healthcare ethics, is also to be found the fundamental or paradigmatic dilemma: Can legal and ethical decision making preserve justice, advance autonomy and promote beneficence?[1] As to the delivery and maintenance of healthcare for the elderly, this dilemma can be reshaped or restated to embrace three essential themes: paternalism, costs, and death.[2] Within the central dilemma and principal themes will emerge dynamic, subissues of competency, informed consent, healthcare financing, the ethics of rationing, admission to and life within assisted care environments, refusing, withdrawing or withholding life-sustaining medical treatment and death with dignity.

Tragically, growing old in the United States is all too often tantamount to losing control. For the elderly, then, autonomy or self-determination, with all of its permutations, and the countervailing force of paternalism in healthcare decision making, is the core consideration and focus for evaluation. If dignity in self-determination is maintained, all actions flowing from this can be seen as both beneficent and just. A paramount value to recognition and maintenance of this perspective is that the boundaries of life, and thus the ultimate reality of death, is accepted both at the *micro* and *macro* levels of healthcare administration. More and more an articulated question is being posited: Should a personal moral duty to die in the most economically efficient manner be enforced by society on terminal or dying people, not so much as a consequence or need for rationing, but as merely recognition of an intergenerational obligation to die?[3]

The process of aging has been around as long as life has been recorded.[4] Indeed, the central concern of virtually all social orders throughout recorded history has been longevity. Even though in most societies the *average* length of human life did not extend into "old age" until the twentieth century, old people have inhabited the earth for thousands of years. Yet, in spite of these facts, the systematic study of aging—especially its social aspects—traces its formal beginnings to the organization, in 1945, of the Gerontological Society of America.[5]

As a discipline, gerontology is defined as "the use of reason to understand aging."[6] Drawing upon the methods of study and evaluation from other disciplines including the humanities, social policy, human services, and professional practice, the phenomenon of aging is examined from multiple, yet interlinking, perspectives. Social gerontology, as a subset, seeks to analyze how individuals maintain or defend their concepts of self over a broad portion of the human life cycle rather than how such concepts developed initially. And, one most interesting conclusion drawn from the work in this field is that a positive relationship exists between the degree of activity and the level of life satisfaction one finds among older individuals.[7]

The base of current knowledge for studies of social gerontology derives primarily from studies of aging in the United States. Other sources of study derive from information regarding social policies affecting older people that have been enacted into governmental action either through formal lawmaking or administrative processes.[8] Interestingly, no unifying set of legal principles can be found in modern gerontology. Rather, the current interest in or linkage between law and aging is said to be but a simple reflection of the enhanced numerical positions (i.e., demographically, economically, and medically) of the elderly in America.[9]

While research into aging has, then, been focused traditionally on the biological and psychological causes of aging, by contrast, longevity research focuses on the biological and the psychosocial potential of the human species not only to achieve an extended life expectancy but to remain in optimum health.[10] As a phenomenon, it is seen that longevity involves an inextricable interaction between three influences: biochemical, psychological and socioeconomic. When retirement occurs, a complex microcosm of biological, psychosocial, financial, social, and public policy issues are grouped around longevity—for it is in retirement that an 80% increase in the risk of coronary mortality occurs as well as an increase in financial concerns, loneliness,and boredom and a plethora of other personal and ethical issues arise.[11]

Today, the older population is divided into the young-old (65 to 74 years old), the middle-old (75 to 84 years old), and the old-old (85 years old and above). While the good news is that Americans are living longer, the bad news is that they are sick longer as well.[12] Seventy-one percent of all deaths in the United States occur among people age 65 or older.[13] In 1960, approximately two thirds of the older population was found to be under 75 years of age. By the year 2000, however, one study suggests the young-old will have dropped to 50.5% of the older population while at the same time, the old-old will have increased from 6% of the older population in 1960 to 14.7% in 2000. The entire older population will, in absolute numbers under this projection, more than double over the entire 40-year period, while the old-old will nearly quintuple. Thus, of the 68.5 million older people projected to be living in 2050, they will represent 22.9% of the total population projected for that year.[14]

For those individuals dying at the oldest ages, more disability than disease is found prior to death than for those dying at younger ages. Predictably, as death approaches, the rates of disease and disability rise; and those destined to die have higher disease and disability rates than those of the same sex and age who survive.[15] Every added year of life translates only into about 6 or 7 weeks of disease-free life expectancy. Thus, most of the gerontological gains made in additional years of life are not evidenced in healthy states of existence; rather, they are in additional years of disability of frailty.[16]

The goal of the healthcare system in the United States is to conquer all diseases and thereby postpone the finality of death—this, in spite of the costs involved. Driven by overall national patterns of improved health, societal expectations for even better health are set that in turn require improved medical technology.[17] Thus, what is seen is that the health care industry generates, through its successes, its own market and, furthermore, one that is generally oblivious to the need for meeting standards of cost-effectiveness.[18] In 1993, for example, one in every seven dollars was estimated to have been spent for the healthcare delivery system—compensating not only physicians and hospitals, but insurance and drug companies as well as equipment makers, bureaucrats and other "partners" in the health system.[19]

Instead of mounting a frontal attack on all disease and the avoidance of death, greater achievement could be sustained if efforts were directed toward developing strategies to accommodate living within accepted boundaries of a finite body and of finite resources and of civilizing the whole process of dying.[20] This, in turn, would assist in reducing the level of expectation that people have about the parameters of healthcare delivery.[21] Physicians would then be enabled to act, in the management of their cases, in a more medically responsible way[22] and in a way that actualized the biomedical principle of nonmaleficence which commands that physicians minimize patient risk and do them no harm.[23] Once this goal or redirection is achieved, the task becomes one of finding a good balance or point of equilibrium that supports measured medical progress, yet seeks to enhance the quality of life instead of postponing death and similarly seeks to prevent illness and reduce the debilities of old age rather than promote high-technology cures that in truth are but palliatives. Enhancing the overall level of public health is a more admirable and coherent national healthcare goal than continuing to pursue the special curative needs of one segment of society.[24]

Acknowledgments

I began in earnest the research for this book in July 1991, when I was a Visiting Professor of Research at the Faculty of Law, University of Auckland, New Zealand. To Professor R. Grant Hammond, who was then the Dean of the Law Faculty (he is now Associate Justice of the New Zealand High Court) and his colleagues—especially Ronald J. Paterson and Warren J. Brookbanks—I express my very sincere thanks for their exceedingly gracious hospitality and support during my visit. In August 1991, I continued work at the University of Sydney Law Faculty, Australia, as a Visiting Professor. To Professor James R. Crawford, then-Dean and current Whewell Professor at Cambridge University, England, I acknowledge my heartfelt thanks for his many kindnesses and friendship during my visit. And, to Professor Ivan A. Shearer, who was, at the time of my visit, with the University of New South Wales Faculty of Law (he is now Challis Professor at the University of Sydney Law Faculty), I record my gratitude for his warm friendship and continuing support.

My clinical perspectives for this book were provided as a consequence of my participation in the Medical Institute for Law Faculty of the Cleveland Clinic Foundation's Center for Creative Thinking in Medicine at the Cleveland-State University College of Law in Ohio during June 1991, and my subsequent association with the Center for the Study of Aging and Human Development at the Duke University Medical Center, Durham, North Carolina in May 1994, as a Senior Visiting Fellow. To Dr. Shattuck W. Hartwell, Jr., Director of the I. H. Page Center at the Cleveland Clinic Foundation, Dr. William M. Michner, Chairman of the Division of Education at the Clinic and to Dean Steven R. Smith of the Cleveland-State University College of Law, I record my very sincere appreciation for their support and friendship during my stay in Cleveland. To Dr. Harvey Jay Cohen, Director of the Aging and Human Development Center at Duke, I express equal appreciation and gratitude to him for his very gracious hospitality and support during my visit.

During the fall of 1991, I continued my appointment as a Visiting Research Fellow at the Center for the Advanced Study of Ethics at Georgetown University in Washington, D.C. To its then-Director, Professor Edmund D. Pellegrino, M.D., I record my lifetime debt of gratitude for his guiding influence and, indeed, inspiration.

In December 1991, I was a Visiting Scholar at the Center for Biomedical Ethics, University of Minnesota Medical School, and I thank Professor Arthur L. Caplin, then-Director of the Center, for his kind assistance, support and creative cross-fertilization of ideas. An equal debt of gratitude goes to Professor Rosalie A. Kane, Director of the Long-Term Care Decisions Resource Center in the School of Social Work and the School of Public Health at the University of Minnesota for her stimulating ideas, insightful approaches, and rich scholarship in aging and geriatrics. Dr. Jeanne E. Bader, Coordinator of the Minnesota Area Geriatric Education Center at the University of Minnesota was especially helpful in assisting me in my efforts to develop a comprehensive bibliography in the field of elder law and senescence. Steven Miles, M.D., of the Hennepin County Medical Center's Division of Geriatrics and Extended Care in Minneapolis, was kind enough to listen to my ideas for developing this book and to offer constructive criticisms; I thank him most sincerely.

January 1992 found me as a Visiting Fellow at the Working Center for Studies in German and International Medical Malpractice Law at the Free University of Berlin. To the Director of the Center, Professor Dr. Dieter Giesen, I record my appreciation for his most gracious hospitality and strong support of my research.

In February 1992, I was a Visiting Professor of Research at the University of Victoria in British Columbia and I thank Professor Donald G. Casswell for his support and friendship over the years and during that visit especially. In April, I was a Visiting Professor of Research at the Faculty of Law Trinity College, University of Dublin, Ireland, and I acknowledge the many kindnesses shown me by Professor William R. Duncan during that visit.

The spring term of 1992 found me as a Visiting Fellow at Wolfson College, Cambridge University, and as a visiting member of the law faculty. The President of the College and Vice Chancellor of the University, Professor Sir David G. T. Williams and his wife, Lady Sally, were very gracious and supportive of my research and writing and provided me with a most conducive atmosphere for genteel living as well. I thank them both most sincerely. Keith J. A. McVeigh, the Squire Law Librarian, was, as always, an indispensable ally for this research project leading to the completion of my book.

In June 1992, I was a Visiting Fellow at the Centre of Medical Law and Ethics at King's College, London, England, and I take this occasion to thank Professor I. M. Kennedy, the Executive Director of the Centre, and Mr. Andrew Grubb for their continuing support and friendship during that visit. I continued my research and writing in July 1992, at the Centre for Socio-Legal Studies at Wolfson College, Oxford University, England, and acknowledge with pleasure the support of its Director at that time, Dr. Donald Harris.

I continued research and began initial writing in May, 1993, as a Visiting Scholar at the Center for Clinical Medical Ethics, Pritzker School of Medicine, University of Chicago, Illinois, in July as a Visiting Scholar at the Princeton

Theological Seminary, Princeton University, New Jersey, and in August, as a Visiting Professor of Research, at the University of Queensland, Brisbane, Australia. In December of that year, I held a research appointment as a Visiting Scholar at the Columbia University in New York City. Dr. David J. Rothman, the Center's Director, was most considerate and helpful during my stay.

During the summer of 1994, I began to complete the final wiring of this book—first as a Visiting Scholar in June at the Poynter Center for the Study of Ethics and American Institutions, Indiana University, Bloomington, where I profited greatly from the continuing friendship and support of the Center's Director, Professor David H. Smith. The Director of the Law School Library, Colleen K. Pauwells, and Associate Director, Linda K. Fariss, were also most obliging during my stay at the university. Then, in July, I accepted affiliations with the Faculty of Law of the University of Otago, Dunedin, New Zealand, and the University Bioethics Center. To Dean J.S. Anderson and Professors Alastair Campbell and Peter Skegg, I express my gratitude for their hospitality and support. Finally, in August, I renewed my affiliation at Hughes Hall, Cambridge University, England, as the Visiting Fellow in Law and Medicine, and, again, profited from the indefatigable spirit of assistance of my friend, Keith J. A. McVeigh, the Librarian of the Squire Law Library.

Some ideas presented in Chapters 7 and 9 of this book were developed originally from various law review articles and papers I authored. They have been tested, elaborated upon and revised over time and may be found in: Reviving the Swan, Extending the Curse of Methuselah or Adhering to the Kevorkian Ethic?, 2 Cambridge Quarterly of Healthcare Ethics 49 (1993); Recognizing Personhood and the Right to Die with Dignity, 6 Journal of Palliative Care 24 (1990); and All's Well That End's Well: Toward A Policy of Assisted Rational Suicide or Merely Enlightened Self-determination, 22 University of California-Davis Law Review 275 (1989).

The papers include: "Medical Futility: Safeguarding the Constitutional Protection Against Cruel and Unusual Punishment," Center for the Study of Aging and Human Development, Duke University Medical Center, Durham, North Carolina, May 1994; "Medical Futility or Human Compassion," Center for the Study of Society and Medicine, College of Physicians and Surgeons, Columbia University, New York, New York, December 1993; and "Quiet Desperation or Heightened Living: The Plight of the Elderly," University of Victoria Faculty of Law, British Columbia, Victoria, Canada, February 1992.

I also participated in a Colloquy on Palliative Care at the National Institutes of Health in Bethesda, Maryland, in April 1994, that afforded me an opportunity to test certain of my ideas concerning death with dignity.

Several of my former students assisted me in my research efforts, first and foremost being Marc F. Jaffan-Letts, as well as Eric J. Pelletier, Bernard M. Raiche, Susan Carletta, and Patricia J. Chupkovitch, and Todd Gazda. Finally, to Julie A. Ruhling, my secretary, I express my gratitude for her high level of efficiency, diligence, and absolute wizardry at the word processor in the preparation of this book.

Chapter 1

Aging as a Phenomenon

Aging is inescapable because—simply—individual cells are mortal.[1] Perhaps the real shock of growing old is not that it happens, but that it occurs before most people are ready for it.[2] If pathologies of aging were ranked by the degree to which they are feared, perhaps disorders of the brain that lead to dementia would be at the top. Indeed, this is the single most dreaded disease of all. The next most feared are cancer, bone weaknesses, fractures, arthritis, incontinence, muscular wasting, Parkinsonism, ischemic heart disease, prostatic hypertrophy, and pneumonia together with a generally increased vulnerability to infection. These assaults to the immune system represent disease states that are both discrete and sharply identified. They are superimposed on the natural aging process; each is capable of turning an otherwise normal stage of life into a chronic pattern of illness, incapacity, or even premature death.[3]

In nature, aging is not a universal phenomenon. Indeed, it is not even a common occurrence; for, in the wild, most creatures either die off or are killed at the first loss of physical or mental power.[4] Aging, advanced through the continuation of a long period of senescence, is a relatively recent human invention. In the past, aging relatives were probably dealt with in a manner similar to that of primitive cultures today—namely, by some form of euthanasia. Many thousands of years and the development of a workable economy were needed before civilized societies concluded that healthy and intelligent older individuals were assets to an evolving human culture.[5]

Aging has, over the years, been viewed as a "neglected stepchild of the human life cycle."[6] Indeed, it has been viewed as a nearly unmanageable problem—much more so than even death. Although death is a dramatic, one-time crisis in a lifetime; old age is a day-to-day, year-by-year confrontation with powerful external and internal forces.[7] Aging should not be viewed as a disease but as an inherent part of human life. Yet in the modern era it is all too often seen as a tragic social and economic problem. It has become a serious "problem" simply because people are living longer today than they did previously. Thus, at the turn of the century, the aged were not a socioeconomic problem because relatively few attained the age of 65.[8]

In the United States, few people like to consider old age because it reminds them of their own mortality; it frightens with illness and deformity and is all too often viewed as a disease or illness itself.[9] A contradictory pattern of attitudes is all too often seen here. For, although many pay lip service to idealized images of wise and tranquil white-haired elders, opposite images predominate that, although not disparaging the elderly, see them as a source of decay and undignified dependency. Indeed, the mass media present few if any positive images of aging.[10] Sadly, in the past, national social policies have mirrored these conflicting attitudes[11] and not allowed for or promoted the conceptualization of extended objective and humane discussion of this topic.

The various experiences of old age have truly become inseparable from cultural representations of aging.[12] Western cultures, aging, old age, and death are all so inextricably related that it becomes nearly impossible to separate individual, phobic responses from social constructions and aging practices from ageism.[13] Gerontophobia (or an irrational fear of aging) and ageism as cultural fears and social practices can only be attacked by producing new, positive representations of aging.[14] Perhaps a modest beginning in this direction may be seen in the very language of gerontology wherein a change in phraseology leads to a more positive connotation associated with the phrase "old age." Accordingly, "late life," "later life," and even "growing older" are beginning to be used more frequently in order to de-emphasize the idea of a prospective or fixed stage. And, "life course" underscores this shift in attitude over terms such as "life cycle" or "life span."[15]

In 1969, Dr. Robert Butler coined a word—"ageism"—to explain precisely what was occurring then and, in reality, still exists today. It is seen

> as a systematic stereotyping of a discrimination against people because they are old just as racism and sexism accomplish this with skin color and gender. Old people are characterized as senile, rigid in thought and manner, old fashioned in morality and skills . . . ageism allows the younger generation to see older people as different from themselves; thus they subtly cease to identify with elders as human beings.[16]

Interestingly, during the past several years, "intergenerational equity" has become a watchword and contemporary metaphor for ageism for such lobbying groups as the Americans for Generational Equity (AGE), which have asserted that because older persons already consume more than their proportional share of available public resources, it is unreasonable as well as socially and economically foolish to allow the nation to divert more and more public funds for healthcare for the elderly from services (e.g., healthcare, housing, and education) for the young.[17]

THEORIES OF AGING

Although the true nature of the aging process and the pathogenesis of senescence still count, two lines of reasoning or theories are advanced to explain the process: one focuses on extrinsic factors, or the continued progressive damage done to cells and organs as a consequence of their normal environmental functions; the other evaluates intrinsic factors and stresses genetically designed or predetermined life spans that control development not only of cells but of organs and entire organisms.[18] Both theories conduce to Isaac Newton's Second Law of Thermodynamics or the "increasing entropy" law thought to apply to all systems. Accordingly, it is held

> that all systems tend to become more disorganized as time passes, unless energy is expended to generate order. Unless molecules are stored at absolute zero and shielded from all forms of radiation, they will gradually deteriorate to less ordered arrangements of their constituent atoms.[19]

It is seen, then, that although the law of entropy remains invariant—except in the instance of subatomic particles—the duration of time during which order is maintained is highly variable. Thus, it has been suggested that aging can be interpreted as but a complex variant of Newton's basic law.[20]

Old age should not be viewed as either solely biological or a cultural fact. Rather, it should be understood as a whole; as a process halfway between illness and health and as a status imposed by society.[21] Although at any age, the way conditions supporting attainment and maintenance of life satisfaction vary, for older people they remain virtually the same as those faced by younger adults—with only the context within which solutions are sought being different. Thus, all age groups suffer a decline in the level of life satisfaction without sufficient food, clothing, shelter, and social relations.[22] The four dimensions of the individual—physical, psychological, social, and spiritual—all interact differently from a contextual standpoint as age progresses and they should be integrated into a balanced plan of both care and intervention in order to assist the individual in finding a sense of reality and meaning or satisfaction in daily living.[23]

SOCIAL DEMOGRAPHICS

Increased Longevity

When this century began, fewer than 1 in 10 Americans were more than 55 years old, and 1 in 25 were more than 65 years old. In 1987, statistics showed that 1 in 5 Americans were at least 55 years old and 1 in 8 was at least 65.[24] The "baby boom" generation (those between the ages of 22 and 40), which spawned as a result of increased fertility since World War II, from 1946–1964, will dominate the age distribution of this country well into the next century. Thus, by the early part of the 21st century when this group starts collecting the Social Security benefits that it earned during its productive years, it will swell the ranks of the 65-plus generation to the point where at least 1 in 5 Americans will in fact be a part of that age group. Although increased longevity will continue to swell the ranks of older Americans, that explains only part of this demographic reality. The central reason is the increase in the annual number of births before 1920 and after World War II.[25]

It is expected that the median age of the U.S. population will rise—because of the projected growth in the older population—from 32.8 years old in 1987, to 36 years old by the year 2000, to age 42 by the year 2030, and then to 46 years in 2050. The 65-plus population, then, in this study, is expected to more than double between 1985 and 2030, making it the only age group to experience significant growth in the next century.[26] One statistical projection finds 86.8 million persons over age 65 in the year 2040; another places the population of 85-year-olds and older in the range of 23.5 million by that year.[27] By the turn of the century, half of the elderly population is expected to be age 65 to 74 and half will be 75 years old or older.[28] Although growth and longevity in the age 85 and older population may be recognized as a major achievement in combating disease and improving healthcare, it has major implications for public policy because of the high probability of health problems for this age group and of their need for health and social services.

The Support Ratio

The whole shape of the "elderly support ratio" or, the number of 65-plus persons relative to the number of persons of working age (18 to 64 years) is changing because people are living longer and families are having fewer children. In the early 1900s, the average family had four children. Today, the average family has fewer than two children. When this factor is combined with a 27-year increase in life expectancy since 1900, it is clear that the ratio of elderly persons compared to persons of working age has increased. In 1900, there were approximately 7 elderly persons for every 100 persons of working age. In 1990, the ratio was about 20 elderly persons per 100 of working age; and by 2020, that ratio will rise to about 29 per 100—with an expected rapid increase to 38 per 100 by the year 2030.[29]

In economic terms, the support ratio is important because the working population can be viewed as supporting nonworking age groups. Yet such a support or dependency ratio is only a crude measure because a significant number of younger and older persons are in the labor force and not dependent whereas others of labor force age may not be working at all. Although it is expected that during the next century the total support ratio (young and old combined) will increase, a substantial decline has occurred since 1990.[30] All this suggests that, currently, fewer economic demands are placed on Americans of working age for supporting the young and the old. This decline in the total support ratio—caused as such by a significant decline in the number of children—masks, from a public policy standpoint, the actual rise in the elderly support ratio. This is an important distinction because this ratio is funded primarily by public programs that serve the elderly whereas, contrariwise, most private (i.e., family) funds are directed toward support of the young. The increasing demands on public programs caused by a growing elder population are nonetheless in large measure offset by declining demands on private funds for supporting children.[31]

A Shifting Ratio

When society records a shift from a high ratio of young to a high ratio of the elderly, profound political, economic, and legal implications will be seen. For one, the flow of public expenditures, as observed, will be altered dramatically because these occur typically for the young at the local levels primarily for schools and recreation. The elderly, however, draw their primary source of public expenditures from the federal government with a somewhat lesser expenditure by state government.

This decline in the number of children and a diminished proportion of children relative to the total population will affect, far beyond complex issues of intergenerational transfer payments, local versus federal expenditures or the maintenance of a strong, adequate labor force to provide a consistent level of goods and services necessary to sustain society. Indeed, this shift in ratio will force a fundamental question to be answered: namely, what are the consequences of a societal attitude that sees fewer and fewer adults taking an interest or making a sustained commitment to both quality and quantity in the delivery of services to the young? Under these circumstances in which a growing proportion of the young live in abject poverty, it can be anticipated that support for children will decline. Ultimately, such a decrease in investment in the children of tomorrow will surely exacerbate serious shortages in creating and maintaining not only a skilled, but a compassionate future work force.[32]

Physician Care and Institutionalization

A greater demand for physician care will come with an aging population. On the basis of 1986 physician contact rates and projections for the noninstitutionalized elderly population, the demand for physician contacts will increase by 22%, from 250 million to 304 million contacts by the year 2000. By 2030, physician contacts will increase by 129%, producing more than 570 million visits.[33]

Older people are generally admitted to a hospital for acute episodes of a chronic condition—the most common being diseases of the circulatory system, digestive diseases, respiratory diseases (including pneumonia), and neoplasms. Nursing home admissions present an altogether different picture; for although only approximately 5% of the elderly are, at any given time, in nursing homes, a considerable number will live there during their lifetimes.[34]

The risk of institutionalization at age 65 is an issue of wide debate—with estimates ranging anywhere from 36% to 65%. One fact not subject to debate is that women are more likely than men of comparable ages to enter a nursing home, with the lifetime risk of institutionalization for women at age 65 being estimated at 52% and that for men at 30%.[35] The residents of nursing homes are elderly, female, and white; nearly 84% of them are without a spouse compared to the noninstitutionalized elderly, 45% of whom are without their spouses. Only 63% of older nursing home residents have children, whereas 81% of noninstitutionalized older people have children. This statistic, when added to profiles that show nursing home residents tend to have health problems significantly restricting their ability to care for themselves, lead to a tentative, but almost inescapable, conclusion that the absence either of a spouse or other family member who can provide at least a level of informal support for health and maintenance requirements is the most critical factor in the decision to institutionalize an older person.[36]

In a 1992 survey by the Families and Work Institute, it was found that on average, women spend more time than men caring for elders. Indeed, the time spent by women to meet these responsibilities is equivalent to a half-time job. Of the elderly who receive care, 92% of them receive it from family members and 8% receive it from friends and neighbors.[37]

This material shows that the real consequences of being old in the United States are tied in no small part to demographic considerations and the changing values emerging from them. Indeed, what is done (or not done) today, in many ways, will define what new crises will exist 10 years from now.[38]

Chapter 2

A Full or Limited Right of Access to Healthcare Services

TOWARD BUREAUCRATIC MEDICINE

Today, most healthcare is delivered by physicians within institutions—whether they be health maintenance organizations, hospitals, or clinics.[1] This care is paid for by employers, government insurance, or by third-party insurance—thus subjecting the physician to a range of not only direct pressures, but indirect incentives to maintain costs in patient management—a practice that 30 years ago was unknown. This shift from patient-centered beneficence to cost containment promotes fears that the long-prized fiduciary relationship between doctor and patient will be weakened to such a degree that contemporary physicians will no longer be viewed as trusted counselors because their economic ties to profit-seeking businesses force them to consider their patients as customers.[2]

Although not the dominant factor in healthcare delivery decision making, it is nonetheless reasonable to give priority to consideration of providing limited services and resources to the young over the old, the poor over the rich (especially those participating in government programs), family members over unmarried individuals and—barring exceptions—life-saving care over other forms of healthcare. Economic tools—such as cost-benefit calculations—are also perfectly legitimate mechanisms for decision making. The extent of their use and ultimate value is shaped directly, however, by a recognition that society alone makes the political decision on the nature and extent of healthcare delivery.[3] Yet a lethargic, uneducated society becomes easy prey for the economic forces of cost containment and efficiency.

DELIVERY BIAS

Regrettably, modern medicine appears to have a bias against old people. Old and infirm patients suffering from cancer and other nontreatable illnesses are all too often written off—with the classic attitude exemplified in a typical physician's comment such as, "At his age, what does he expect?" The elderly patient's best interest has in the past often been in conflict with the family's interest to see the patient through any medical crisis at all costs.[4]

Both diagnostically and from standards of treatment, more and more individuals, upon reaching the age of 65, are routinely neglected or undertreated by primary care physicians. Failure to encourage such tests as regular mammograms for women over 65 and cholesterol, colorectal, and prostate screenings for men occurs frequently despite statistics showing 80% of all fatal heart attacks and 60% of all cancer deaths strike Americans who are 65 or older.[5]

Although depression in the elderly is readily diagnosed, in 1989 the National Institute of Mental Health estimated more than 60% of older people are depressed yet receive inadequate therapy.[6] Interestingly, recent medical studies show overtreatment in some areas of healthcare to be another serious problem for the elderly—especially certain surgical procedures. Excesses were recorded commonly in the widespread use of coronary angiographies (x-rays of the blood vessels that nourish the heart), carotid endarterectomies (cholesterol-cleaning operations on blood vessels in the neck), upper GI endoscopies (visual inspections of the gastrointestinal tract), and coronary bypasses. Inappropriate drug prescriptions are also of serious concern.[7]

A fair number of physicians appear to use chronological age as a the most important factor in the decision-making process to deliver or withhold medical treatment for conditions the patient may have. Stated otherwise, negative characteristics including, for example, poor prognosis, cognitive impairment, limited life expectancy, decreased social worth, and decreased quality of life are attributed to the elderly because of their age. On the basis of such factors, decisions may be made to withhold efficacious treatment, which may result in additional suffering and unnecessary morbidity as well as mortality.[8]

A recent study of critically ill cancer patients shows that hospital treatment buys so little extra quality time and costs so much that physicians should seek a truly informed consent from the patients and their families before putting them through this arduous procedure.[9] The study revealed the average hospital costs in intensive care units of a 1-year survival for patients with solid tumors (most non-blood cancers) were $82,845. For patients with hematologic cancers (e.g., leukemia or lymphoma) the cost of survival for 1 year averaged $189,339.

As has been observed, with age the quality of life among the elderly drops dramatically. Indeed, as life is extended and death occurs at older ages, individuals are more likely to spend greater time in disabled or severely restricted states with mental impairment before they die. The result of this life extension means a considerable use of healthcare resources is expended for a growing number of individuals.[10] The long-term care associated with these states of living is not covered by Medicare.[11] The average annual Medicare costs per person increase substantially with age—rising from $2,017 for those aged 65 to 74 years to $3,215 for those 85 years old and above. By the year 2020, it is estimated the total projected costs of Medicare expenditures will have nearly doubled—with the greatest proportional increases coming in the oldest age groups, 75 to 85 years of age.[12]

As the elderly—especially those over 85—continue to grow even older, assuming stability in the level of disability and utilization of nursing home beds as well by this group—a large increase in the need for nursing home beds will be seen. In fact, by 2040, one estimate has the number of nursing residents aged 65 and above reaching between 3.6 and 5.9 million—2.0 to 3.8 million of whom will be aged 85 years and above.[13]

Two age-dependent disorders contribute significantly to disability, long-term care, and healthcare expense: dementias and hip fractures.[14] Alzheimer's accounts for 50% to 60% of the cases of dementia, yet it afflicts only 1% of the population between the ages of 65 and 70. Of the population over age 65, 25% are diagnosed with it, however.[15] Dementia of depression includes memory loss, difficulty with language, diminished concentration, and delusions of illness and poverty.[16]

The average yearly costs for a dementia patient are $22,458 for nursing home care, and $11,750 for home care. Using projections for the year 2040, anywhere from 6.1 to 9.8 million Americans with moderate to severe dementia could require between $92 and $149 billion for care.[17] By the year 2000, it is projected that hip fractures will increase to approximately 330,000 (from 220,000 in 1987) and to between 530,000 and 840,000 by 2040. The costs are projected to increase approximately $1.6 billion from 1987 to over $2 billion in 2000—rising in 2040 to as much as $6 billion.[18]

How should society deal with these projected increases in healthcare costs? A reduction in reimbursement for healthcare by setting specifically fixed prospective payments for diagnosis-related groups might at first glance seem attractive. Yet, imposing caps on the costs for diagnosis-related funds (DRFs) that cover dementias and hip fractures would not be able to prevent massive increases in overall cost because of the rapid anticipated increases in the number of affected individuals. Rationing of healthcare by age, with medical care provided only to relieve suffering at the conclusion of a natural life span, has also been proposed. However, it is difficult to agree on a definition of natural life span that does not subject itself to a charge of age discrimination by being tied to chronological age.[19] Perhaps the most direct approach to reducing healthcare costs would be realized through aggressive research aimed at preventing or curing the common diseases and disorders leading to long-term disability. If tuberculosis and polio can be conquered, why not Alzheimer's disease?[20]

THE NATURE OF HEALTHCARE "RIGHTS"

In 1983, the President's Commission for the Study of Ethical Problems in Medicine and Biomedical and Behavioral Research concluded that access to healthcare should be framed in terms of "ethical obligations":

1. [Society] has an ethical obligation to ensure equitable access to healthcare for all.
2. The societal obligation is balanced by individual obligations.
3. Equitable access to healthcare requires that all citizens be able to secure an adequate level of care without incurring excessive burdens.
4. When equity occurs through the operation of private forces, there is no need for government involvement, but the ultimate responsibility for ensuring that society's obligation is met . . . rests with the Federal government.
5. The cost of achieving equitable access to healthcare ought to be shared fairly.
6. Efforts to contain rising healthcare costs are important but should not focus on limiting the attainment of equitable access for the least well-served portion of the public.[21]

The "rights" to healthcare in the United States do not derive in any general sense from the Constitution. Rather, they are more properly characterized as political rights or entitlements than constitutional rights.[22] For older adults, the principal national goal—or what has been perceived as an entitlement—has, since 1979, been the prevention of functional disability.[23] Yet, a particular dilemma is presented to an aging society whose healthcare system seeks to foster technological progress and also to meet expansive public demands not only to prevent disability but to ensure an expanded right to control all illnesses and death itself. If this direction is sustained, an eventual depletion of healthcare resources and a distortion of overall social priorities will occur.[24] If, rather, the nation curtails its aspiration toward increasing entitlements and returns to what has been termed "old-fashioned fatalism" (e.g., the acceptance of death and unavoidable suffering), then some may charge that healthcare delivery has turned back the clock and become unfair and, indeed, cruel to those individuals who become ill and die subsequently because of medical omissions.[25]

TOWARD A NEW HEALTHCARE DELIVERY ETHIC

In order to resolve this vexatious dilemma and redirect the force of medical technology, and thereby escape its coercive control, a new contemporary medical ethic is needed that assures patients that they will be allowed to die when they determine it is appropriate and reasonable.[26] This proposal runs counter to the present medical norm for decision making—namely, prolonging life—that "is positively affirmed, liberally espoused, or instinctively assumed" by physicians who face clinical decision without the clear benefit of medico-legal guidelines for terminating care.[27] Aggressive treatment without much, if any, concern for the "whole patient" has, unfortunately, become the new standard of care.[28]

The new healthcare delivery ethic for the elderly that is proposed here would modify the present treatment norm by stressing the need to withhold curative, or life-extending technologies for the critically ill, likely terminal, or irreversibly declining patient, unless two conditions were met simultaneously: namely, a good probability the treatment will modify in a significant way the direction of the underlying illness by arresting or reversing its course of development and a positive long-term patient outcome is achievable.[29] The ultimate effect of these suggestions is the use of a positive presumption before use of medical technology that the specific treatment proposed will confer a *real benefit* on the welfare of the patient and not merely forestall death or sustain faltered organ systems.[30]

PATIENT PREFERENCES AS CONSTRUCTS FOR DECISION MAKING

Obviously, because patient preferences are consistent with principles of autonomy or self-determination, they should be central to medical decisions to withhold treatment. Sadly, in many cases —indeed, the vast majority—these preferences are not made known before intervening crises (e.g., incompetency) occur. And, under present standards of good medical practice as observed, life will be prolonged. Absent a declaration of preferences—and consistent with the new nontreatment ethic or presumption proposed here—the task to be undertaken is determining when most people would prefer to have certain treatments not initiated or withdrawn. National public opinion polls reveal the following situations in which treatment should not be given:

1. Patients who are on life-support systems and have no hope of recovery.
2. Comatose patients who have no brain activity and who are being kept alive by feeding tubes.
3. Patients who are either terminally ill or irreversibly comatose and who are on life-support systems, including food and water.
4. Patients suffering from illnesses that make them totally dependent on family members or others for all of their care (a situation in which they would not want their doctors to do everything possible to save their lives).
5. Patients with incurable diseases who are suffering a great deal of physical pain.
6. Comatose patients who are in no pain, but for whom their is no hope of recovery.

   7. Hopelessly ill or comatose patients who are on life-support systems, if their families request the withdrawal of life support.
   8. Permanently unconscious patients receiving food and water.

Following are other situations, evolving specifically from experiences of the elderly, retirees, nursing home residents, and physicians, in which at least some treatment should be withheld:

   9. Patients with terminal illnesses that have progressed and caused their hearts to stop beating.
   10. Mentally incompetent patients with terminal illnesses that have progressed and caused their hearts to stop beating.
   11. Permanently unconscious patients who are in persistent vegetative states and unable to eat on their own, needing artificial feedings.
   12. Nursing home patients, no matter what the level of cognitive functioning at the time of treatment, who need resuscitation, amputations, or tube feedings (either temporary or permanent).
   13. Nursing home residents who are about to die of natural causes and who need drugs, fluids, food by tubes, breathing machines, or heart massages.
   14. Terminally ill retirees who need cardiopulmonary resuscitation, respirators, nasogastric feeding tubes, or intravenous fluids.[31]

   However, polls showed two situations in which therapy should be initiated: resuscitation and hospitalization for AIDS patients. Interestingly, these findings run counter to the actual preference of AIDS patients, themselves, who appear to wish no ventilation or resuscitation in those cases where the disease has progressed to severe loss of memory and severe pneumonia. Early treatments do seem to be desired for other terminal illnesses, but extreme levels of treatment are not desired.[32]
   The value—professional or persuasive—of the information from national polls depends upon how it is used as an aid or even construct to facilitating a level of informed decision making for incompetent patients. In advising a family or other surrogate of the medical condition of a patient, a physician could explain that ''most patients would want treatment withdrawn.''[33] If the family then chose what most families would, to let the patient die, that knowledge might well have had a positive effect by lessening anxiety and economic costs as well.
   Using the statistical patient-preference results from these national polls, physicians could present another statistical basis for shaping a reasonable course of medical action or inaction, depending on the individual case—much as is done presently by physicians when they base medical advice on the statistical prognosis for various conditions. Thus, for example, when facing end-of-life situations, the families of those patients could be told simply that statistics reveal between 73% and 85% of the adult population in the United States have expressed a preference that treatment be withdrawn in such cases and, furthermore, that

between 86% and 93% of all attending physicians would, under such circumstances, prefer no treatment for themselves. Again, anxiety should be lessened dramatically, guidance and support obtained, and expeditious action helped by making families or other surrogate decision makers aware of the preference of most other similarly situated people.[34]

Chapter 3

Healthcare Financing

COST CONTAINMENT AND QUALITY ASSURANCE

For older Americans, the healthcare delivery system is financed by a complex structure that makes delivery and reimbursement not only perplexing, but intimidating and even infuriating.[1] The central ethical issues arising from the complexities of healthcare financing are today, and will be tomorrow, regardless of "new" healthcare initiatives, the extent to which quality of care can be assured and a level of cost efficiency maintained within the system itself. This issue or dilemma affects the degree of geriatric care and management that must be assumed by the afflicted individual, the concerned family, healthcare service providers, as well as the entire healthcare system.

Although the complexities and, indeed, defects of healthcare financing may be viewed by some as "assaults on autonomy," others might choose to see these actions as nothing but benevolent paternalism. Whatever the actions and programs are called, their difficulties find ready focus in common ethical issues such as failure to discuss fully with older persons the range of clinical options available for delivery of healthcare services; the older person's exclusion altogether from clinical decision making; establishment of lower treatment priorities for the aged patient; and allowing children to assume more comprehensive rights and superior status over their parents when the parents, themselves, may be fully competent to make medical care decisions for themselves.[2]

Particularly germane to a treatment of the economics of healthcare are those value judgments that impact on the system's level and provide the framework for social policy. For example, they influence the allocation of resources within the health-care system and affect the enactment and enforcement of laws and regulations governing the health-care system.[3]

MEDICAID AND MEDICARE

Currently five sources of funding are used to support the healthcare financing needs of the elderly: Medicare provides funding for 45% of all these needs; another 11% is covered by private insurance programs, including Medicare supplements; Medicaid covers 13%; the Veterans Administration covers 6%; and patients and their families fund 26%.[4]

Since its creation in 1965, the Medicaid program has sought to provide a modest level of long-term care insurance for the country's poor.[5] Although the program is administered by the Health Care Financing Administration within the Department of Health and Human Services, the states bear the central responsibility for the operational units of the program itself.[6] The Medicaid program used welfare delivery as a model and, as such, is financed by both state and federal general revenues with eligibility for participation tied to a means test. Essentially, healthcare professionals are paid for rendering enumerated medical services to groups of very specific poor people. Thus, subscribers to Medicaid who are unable to pay for their health services from their own resources and who are not reimbursed through Medicare receive substantial funding for these services from Medicaid. State participation in the program is optional.[7]

Interestingly, despite the generous two-tiered benefit programs of Medicaid covering a mandated level of inpatient hospitalization, skilled nursing facilities, outpatient services, physician care, etc., and an elective level of state services triggered at the option of each state that may include prescription drugs, adult day-care, physical therapy, and intermediate-care facilities, it is estimated that of poor older Americans, 64% are not even eligible for Medicaid. Further, 20% of all aged have no health insurance coverage beyond Medicare.[8]

Medicare, also established in 1965 by Congress, was designed as a program to provide assistance to the country's elderly in meeting the escalating costs of healthcare. For Medicare, a social insurance model was developed that is characterized by federal administration of the program financed through a separate wage tax—with eligibility based on contributions made by employee-beneficiaries during their working years. Most elderly persons, together with some categories of disabled persons, are covered by this federal program. Divided into two sections, Hospital Insurance Benefits (Part A) and Supplementary Medical Insurance Benefits (Part B), the Medicare program seeks a reimbursement balance for hospital and skilled nursing care, home health agency services, and hospice services with physician-related care. Presently, Medicare is the primary source of public funding for medical care of the nation's elderly.[9]

In 1983, Medicare reimbursement for inpatient services policies was changed by Congress through legislation that moved from one of direct cost containment to a prospective payment system (PPS). This effort was directed toward curtailing the high costs associated with administering the Medicare program. Whereas under the direct cost-reimbursement system the federal government would reimburse hospitals for actual dollar amounts of Medicare patient cost regarded as reasonable, under PPS, hospital reimbursements are tied to a fixed, predetermined sum for treatment services rendered.[10] The computation of this sum of money is determined by the "average cost of treating a patient in a particular Diagnostic-Related Group" (DRG)—regardless of actual cost to the hospital of the treatment for the Medicare patient. Accordingly, in the event that a Medicare patient's cost of hospitalization exceeds the prospective payment, the hospital will lose money.[11] The amount of payment depends primarily on the disease groups to which a patient is assigned; initially 20 sets of rates for 467 DRGs were authorized. By 1988, hospitals were reimbursed using a national DRG system.[12]

In order to forestall, or at least lessen, the prospects of losing money under the system, hospitals have undertaken to increase their revenue base and profit margins—all in the name of greater efficiency.[13] Yet assessing and achieving efficiency in the management of hospital services is exceedingly difficult; these difficulties are not totally solved by a DRG patient classification scheme. One major difficulty is failure to differentiate variations in the severity of illness and quality of care in DRG patient groups; because of this, observable cost differences among hospitals for a single DRG simply are not sound indicators of differences in efficiency.[14]

Clinical practices have been altered significantly in some cases in order to contain costs, with greater emphasis being placed on preadmission testing, same-day surgery with follow-up care after discharge, and outpatient services. Although there is no doubt that total healthcare costs are decreased by such actions, there is evidence "that the frail, elderly population is at risk for compromised quality of care, difficulty in accessing care and critical decisions with respect to the allocation of resources."[15] All too often, these patients have been discharged from hospitals in sicker conditions and with more unresolved health problems than when they initially sought hospital care.[16]

Patients covered by Medicaid often have great difficulty finding medical treatment in their neighborhoods because many physicians refuse to accept Medicaid because it does not reimburse them for the same amount they can receive from private patients. In New York, for example, the basic Medicaid payment for a routine doctor's visit by an adult ranges from $7 to $25. With this rate, Medicaid business is sought by few and those who do accept it will spend little more than a few minutes with each patient.[17]

Additional discrimination against "very old" Medicare beneficiaries can be seen in this system when it is realized that the prospective payment system fails to take into account that, with age, the average length of hospital stay increases, which has an additional impact on direct costs. Still another discriminatory weakness is seen with PPS's failure to consider either multiple clinical problems or severity of illness. "Since the 'oldest' elderly often exhibit serious, multiple problems, hospital administrators may view them as undesirable revenue losers."[18]

CONTROLLING HOSPITAL STAYS

Because of the federal government's power to compel reductions in inpatient days and achieve other cost cuts in hospitals, Medicare has been able to restrain its payments to hospitals far more than other payers, such as insurance companies and individuals. As a direct consequence of this power, the private sector is forced to bear a disproportionate share of the hospital burden, and in effect is forced to subsidize the Medicare programs.[19] Under the old system before the institutionalization of DRGs, even after hospital patients were no longer in need of daily care, they were nonetheless allowed a few extra days in the hospital to rest and fully recover. Now, they are released even if they are weak and in considerable pain from surgery. The end result of early discharge of patients in unstable condition is longer recovery periods, continuing complications, and sometimes premature death.[20]

Typically, in the past, if a physician had an older bedridden patient with swollen legs and shortness of breath, he or she would send that patient to a hospital for a routine cardiogram. Now that patient will be required to stay at home until pulmonary edema (fluid in the lungs) develops at which time he or she will be admitted through the emergency room. The first sign of pulmonary edema is often a swelling of the legs. Early detection not only helps prevent respiratory failure but saves lives as well.[21]

The Older Americans Act and Noninstitutionalized Long-Term Care

In 1965, Congress passed the Older Americans Act (OAA) and thereby proclaimed broad policy objectives for the nation to meet with respect to older persons. More specifically, older Americans are now entitled to adequate income; the best possible physical and mental health; suitable housing; full restorative (rehabilitative) services; opportunity for employment without age discrimination; pursuit of meaningful activity; and retirement with health, honor, and dignity.[22] The Older Americans Act was part of President Lyndon B. Johnson's "Great Society" and today has much the same mandate it had when enacted originally: to foster maximum independence, thus avoiding unnecessary and costly institutionalization. The specific services supported under the act include congregate and home-delivered meals, community service and employment programs, nursing home ombudsman activities, and senior centers.[23]

Regrettably, public programs promoted by the OAA as well as noninstitutional services by Medicaid have failed to develop and maintain a coordinated noninstitutional program for long-term care. Across the whole long-term care system, no one organization emerges as having sole responsibility for healthcare delivery. If more nursing home beds were available, a considerable number of hospital patients could be cared for more appropriately. If healthcare providers could be reimbursed for home services, patients admitted to a hospital from home often could be cared for at home.

The underdevelopment of home- and community-based chronic care services is due to economic fears by government and the private insurance industry that reimbursing a broader range of services will increase costs significantly. Rightly or wrongly, this fear arises from concern over what has been termed the "add-on effect," under which the creation and extension of new long-term care cases a community receives brings with it additional formal services, even if nursing home care is not needed.[24]

ROUTINE AND LONG-TERM CARE FINANCING

For those individuals who need long-term care and can afford it, it is readily available.[25] Most Americans, as many as four out of five, believe Medicaid will cover nursing home care and rely upon it to aid them.[26] Under Medicare A, or hospital insurance, inpatient room and board, nursing care, as well as other hospital services, are provided for an unlimited period of time. Under Medicare B, a provider or patient will be reimbursed for up to 80% of what are determined to be "reasonable" charges for physician services after the patient has met a $100 calendar-year deductible.[27] Inpatient deductibles are required and by 1993, the adjustments had grown to $676. The full coverage for inpatient care under Medicare is capped at 60 days—after the deductible charge—and then 30 days of coverage at 75% is provided. A substantial daily copayment is required if any of the 60 extra or "lifetime reserve days" are used subsequently; and a maximum limit of 190 days is imposed for inpatient care in a mental health hospital.[28]

For posthospital rehabilitation requiring a high level of skilled care, Medicare A will also provide coverage for up to 100 days of confinement if the care is provided in a properly designated and certified skilled nursing home. For the first 20 days of this period, an initial coinsurance charge equal to one eighth of the inpatient deductible is required. This type of rehabilitative care is substantially different from those less intensive services given by custodial care facilities. Indeed, although many of these custodial or intermediate facilities, referred to commonly as nursing homes, provide what patients or their families recognize as skilled nursing care, Medicare does not cover them. In order to qualify for home health benefits provided under Medicare A, a patient is required to show a need for skilled nursing care or for specified therapeutic services under the direction of a physician. Because of strict medical eligibility requirements and equally strict reimbursement policies, many patients having long-term and chronic care needs are unable to qualify for these benefits.[29]

SUPPLEMENTAL MEDICAL INSURANCE

Medicare beneficiaries also enroll in what is termed supplemental medical insurance (SMI) or simply Medicare B. Although this includes a broad range of physician services for diagnosis and treatment,[30] it excludes routine checkups and physical examinations. Generally, the level of patient-provider reimbursement is 80% of reasonable charges after a $100 calendar-year deductible is applied. A substantial copayment of up to 50% is required for mental health services. Also excluded generally from Medicare coverage are prescription medications prescribed outside the hospital—except for cases where immunosuppressant or injectable drugs are prescribed for cases of osteoporosis. Outpatient physical therapies—including speech therapy—are capped.[31]

MEDIGAP COVERAGE

In order to meet the various Medicare gaps in coverage, "Medigap" supplementary insurance is available from 10 nationally approved and standardized Medigap plans. Accordingly, although premium costs will vary among insurers, the Medigap plans are consistent in benefit structure. Two thirds of all aged Americans, in fact, have Medigap coverage that generally allows for the initial inpatient deductible together with a reimbursement for the 20% co-insurance charges under Medicare B.[32]

Because many of the elderly neither distinguish between Part A and Part B benefits under Medicare, nor comprehend the inherent complexities of the 20% co-insurance provisions or the reduced mental health coverage, great confusion and misunderstanding results for them in executing the various claim forms. Even though Medigap insurance claims for the hospital deductible, co-insurance, and other expenses are processed by most inpatient facilities, Part B reimbursement responsibilities for obtaining the beneficiary share of medical services frequently fall upon patients themselves.[33]

MEDICAID TRUSTS

Although Medicare excludes from its coverage most forms of routine care and other frequent expenses either too costly or difficult to control, Medicaid acts as a final "safety net" to protect the aged from living without necessary care. This level of care is not to be made available until most of an individual's financial resources are depleted, however.[34]

Although allowed by law, asset transfer or Medicaid Trusts are viewed by many as fraud.[35] Under federal legislation, a Medicaid qualifying trust is one established—other than by will—by an individual or his or her spouse that allows the individual to be the beneficiary of all or part of these payments from the trust—with the distribution of payments being determined by one or more trustees who are permitted to exercise discretion with respect to distribution to the individual.[36] Accordingly, those individuals expecting to need long-term care may transfer their assets into an irrevocable Medicaid trust for the purpose of excluding those funds from making the initial determination of eligibility for Medicaid. These asset transfers must be made 30 months before an application for Medicaid benefits is processed.[37]

Whether a state can take a trust of this nature into account for the purposes of determining eligibility of an individual for benefits or for the purpose of reimbursement for Medicaid services already expended depends primarily upon whether the trust is characterized as a support trust or a discretionary trust. In the case of a discretionary trust, the trustee has the sole discretion to either make or withhold benefits and, further, to decide the amount of those payments. Contrariwise, in a support trust, the trustee is required to make payments from the trust to provide for the beneficiary's educational support. Consequently, the beneficiary of a support trust (or the creditors of the beneficiary) can force payment from the trustee, whereas the beneficiary of a discretionary trust cannot.[38] Generally, courts have held that the assets in a support trust can be taken into account for the purposes of determining eligibility and for reimbursing the state for Medicaid expenses, where as those from a discretionary trust cannot.[39]

PEER REVIEW ORGANIZATIONS

After Congress created Medicare in 1965, beneficiaries of the program were to be monitored for quality assurance by experimental medical care review organizations and professional standards review organizations (PSROs). In 1982, Congress replaced the PSROs with designated peer review organizations (PROs) that are designed to confront issues relating to rising costs, over-use of services, and quality of patient care. Housed within the Health Care Financing Administration (HCFA), this program was to provide a means of monitoring and implementing Medicare's DRG-based prospective payment system, which began in 1983. Statewide organizations with which HCFA contracts may qualify as PROs if they are composed of at least 10% of the practicing physicians in the area or, alternatively, have available for PRO review at least one physician in every recognized specialty within a given area. Instead of meeting its stated goal of ensuring quality care, the PRO program has concentrated on the use of services and costs or, simply, cost containment in hospital care and monitoring implementation.[40]

PROs serve the older person by reviewing whether hospital treatment is appropriate and whether quality care is provided. A modest record of enforcement is being developed whereby physicians have been disciplined mostly for poor care and hospitals have been disciplined for costly and unnecessary treatments.[41] Yet, because the sanctioning process is focused not on average providers but on ''outliers'' that are taking exceptionally costly cases requiring more hospital days for recuperation, enforcement has been judged to be largely ineffective in attacking the more pervasive or systematic problems. Generally, PROs are regarded as being adversarial and punitive in their mission and as imposing considerable burdens on the network of healthcare providers.[42]

HEALTH MAINTENANCE ORGANIZATIONS

Although the concept of a prepaid health system began to take roots in the 1920s as a way to contain medical costs, it has only been since 1971 that these systems have taken form in what is now known as health maintenance organizations (HMOs).[43] These organizations operate on fixed budgets that seek to contain costs by strict incentives or controls—the principal method of enforcement is strong control over the allocation of hospitalization and expensive medical resources.[44] Further cost containment is achieved by placing greater emphasis on preventive health through health promotion and early disease detection. In fact, many HMOs provide coverage or referral not only for routine physical examinations but exercise classes, nutrition education, self-care instruction, and weight control classes.[45]

In order for Medicaid recipients to access HMOs, these organizations must be either near low-income neighborhoods or in them. This fact, however, acts as a serious obstacle for non-Medicaid recipients enrolling in HMOs. Because the HMOs earn a profit by seeking to enroll low-risk consumers, and non-Medicaid recipients are generally acknowledged as being a lower healthcare risk than actual Medicaid recipients, HMOs must locate where they can attract the Medicaid and non-Medicaid consumer. Despite federal efforts to provide monetary subsidies for locating HMOs in low-income areas, as observed previously, they continue to prefer locations in middle-class areas.[46]

Until recently, HMOs have played an insignificant role in healthcare for the aged because, until 1985, Medicare reimbursement policies were considered inadequate to the HMO industry. In that year, however, the federal government issued regulations allowing HMOs nationwide to offer, consistent with federal contracting standards, Medicare programs.[47] Interestingly, no more than about 3% of the aged population have Medicare enrollment through HMOs. Perhaps the greatest source of dissatisfaction with the HMOs, and the greatest deterrent to their growth, is the level of federal reimbursement to Medicare programs.[48] Here, again, although cost containment remains the central focus of healthcare delivery, it is placed or balanced within a framework, albeit a weak one at times, of the delivery of quality care.[49]

PREFERRED PROVIDER ORGANIZATIONS

The preferred provider organization (PPO) is a system akin to the HMO, but with less administrative complexity. Under the PPOs, agreements are made with fee-for-service providers willing to deliver services at discount rates in exchange for significant numbers of patients and prompt payments. Cost control is maintained by dropping physicians from the system if their costs of delivery are excessive. Because of a surplus of physicians competing for patients, doctors are more willing to adhere to lower rate schedules. Similarly, patients are attracted to the PPOs because not only of the greater freedom in choice they have to determine their healthcare providers than with HMO programs, but because of the ease in payment arrangements. Because of the fact that PPOs are essentially agreements with providers covering utilization controls, claim procedures, etc., and not organizations as such, the operation costs for their operational procedures are considerably less than for HMOs.[50]

HEALTH COMPETITION?

Competition between healthcare delivery systems such as HMOs and PPOs is useful, even though it has been recognized that structural weaknesses in both have led to the development of large administrative bureaucracies. In some programs, this has caused a proliferation of smaller systems, leading not only to the growth of administrative bodies but to the duplication of services as well.[51]

In some states, managed care systems for the poor are being tested and developed as a method of providing coordinated care to recipients under Medicaid. These systems may be operated by either HMOs or by health-insuring organizations. Before managed care systems can claim any sustained degree of success in controlling Medicaid expenditures, they first need to have greater controlled success with inpatient utilization through careful selection. One case study in the state of Washington discovered, for example, contrary to expectations, that there was much higher use of inpatient services for Medicaid recipients in an HMO than that of its counterparts in the fee-for-service sector.[52] In managed care systems, HMOs and other groups manage each case carefully in order to ensure patients are not admitted to a hospital unnecessarily and do not stay longer than necessary.[53]

OVERALL EFFECTIVENESS OR INHERENT WEAKNESSES?

Cost-containment regulations under the Medicare and Medicaid programs have succeeded in achieving a reduction in the number of people being served. They have also succeeded in increasing the portion of care that the elderly recipients must pay. But these regulations have had little real effect on the spiraling inflation of healthcare costs. Although many older individuals successfully satisfy their healthcare needs within this system, those who have long-term care needs and the unemployed poor find the system wanting if not totally exclusionary.[54] Indeed, it has been suggested that there are more failures with cost-containment policies than sustained successes. Some cite the number of HMOs that are poorly managed and in financial difficulty as well as the failure of the DRGs to bring down health costs significantly rather than merely shift costs from one sector to another with no apparent net gain in savings.[55] Perhaps an inherent flaw or contradiction in the whole policy goal of cost containment prevents it from ever being a totally realizable or implemented policy. That weakness may be that, although the national healthcare goal is to control costs, the companion goal is to improve the quality, extent of, and access to healthcare.[56] Both simply cannot be done simultaneously. In the final analysis, it must be underscored that cost containment is not an unethical motive. Rather, the point of contention is who decides what costs are to be contained and under what circumstances they are contained.[57]

Additional concerns over cost containment were raised by a new report of the Health Care Financing Administration, which noted a cost crisis was developing for Medicare, that is, that under this program, lifetime expenses for those who turn 65 in the year 2020 would be $98 billion more than those who turned 65 in 1990. Although total Medicare spending will record this huge increase because, simply, more individuals will be covered by this program the estimated lifetime Medicare expenses for a person who turned 65 in 1990 are set at $53,256 while in the year 2020 it is expected the rise will reach only $54,326.[58]

Two interesting suggestions designed to curb Medicare costs bear further study. One calls for a reduction in Medicare payments in the last 2 years of life through the greater use of advance directives and hospice care and less aggressive interventions (e.g., do not resuscitate orders). The second suggestion points to a bold reform in healthcare financing that would encourage the use of long-term and primary care services designed to maintain functional independence and an avoidance of hospitalization. In order to implement this idea, Medicare financing for acute care should be integrated with financing for long-term care.[59]

Chapter 4

Economic Efficiency, Prioritizing, and Rationing

Ideally, the delivery of medical care resources should be shaped by standards both of economic efficiency and of commitment to individual patient needs. In reality, however, these two principles are having a disrupting influence on the health profession. Although physicians, abiding by the Hippocratic oath, are bound to provide that level of professional assistance that will help improve the conditions of their patients, the physician—as the initial gatekeeper to the health-care delivery system—must also try to maximize the efficiency of each healthcare resource or, in other words, obtain the greatest value from finite resources.[1] Opportunity costs are minimized by obtaining from healthcare dollars as much value as possible.[2]

Despite widespread differences among countries in the world community in their financing and organization of healthcare delivery systems, a common observation has been that all countries have a similar problem maintaining efficiency. This problem entails meeting cost inflation in healthcare expenditures.[3] Efficient use of resources in medical care (or in any other field for that matter) requires that the benefit from the last dollar spent in any activity be no lower than the benefit obtainable from spending an additional dollar on some other procedure or from some other patient. Stated another way, if allocations of healthcare resources were totally efficient, it would be impossible to increase total medical benefits by diverting any money away from one service, for example, chemotherapy, and spending it on another, such as radiology.[4] Thus, most economists hold that treatments should cease when marginal benefits equal marginal cost.[5]

Interestingly, in Britain, countless patients with chronic renal failure die earlier than necessary due to lack of dialysis treatment facilities. Yet large expenditures are routinely made to prolong the lives of metastic cancer patients for brief periods.[6] Thus, a rationing of care, to some stated or unstated degree, is seen in all health systems, and a conflict of approach as well.[7] For at one level of analysis is the outright denial of economic efficiency as any valid factor in medical practice and, at another level, a recognition that there is a moral impetus behind efficiency. Those with the second view conclude correctly that it would be unethical, and indeed fanatical, to foster an approach that allows one person to consume healthcare resources regardless of benefits conferred while totally ignoring other more valuable and directly beneficial uses of the resource.[8]

Rationing policies encounter the most difficulties in the area of marginally beneficial healthcare. The reason for this is simple: it is quite difficult and distasteful to fine-tune rationing policies to the degree that they select the treatments, diseases, and people for whom marginal benefits are as great as opportunity costs.[9]Quite often age is a quotient in determining success of treatments and, at the same time, a factor in discrimination of healthcare delivery.[10]

RATIONING AS A FACT

Rationing has been in effect for quite some time and may be seen in three particular settings. First, it is implicit in all systems where limited amounts of money are available for healthcare and it is practiced daily by clinical physicians who must decide how resources will be used as each case is presented. This is the method of practice in prepaid health insurance programs, and so long as there are sufficient funds, the front-line physicians will have few challenges made to their clinical judgments. When third parties fail to fund specific treatments medically indicated, explicit rationing occurs. Even though physicians may be of the mind that certain medical procedures or surgical interventions are indicated, these treatments cannot be undertaken unless the patient can either fund them privately or prevail upon the doctor to complete them free of charge. A system of this design eliminates totally physician discretion for all items explicitly prohibited.[11]

For those individuals who have both money and health insurance, the market place itself structures methods of rationing that include copayments and deductibles, which force upon patients the ultimate decision whether they are willing to expend additional monies in order to obtain specific care. Consequently, for those citizens who are strained economically or without funds at all and are ineligible for public assistance, rationing of health services is not even an operable issue. There is no access to it at all! Sadly, it has been estimated that somewhere between 30 and 37 million Americans have no health insurance of any type available to them—either public or private.[12]

Those individuals qualifying the income criteria for Medicaid programs have few problems with access to the healthcare delivery programs or the costs thereunder because virtually everything their physician recommends is available—so long as the monies allocated within the program last. It has been thus suggested that—to the extent health problems can be regulated—serious illnesses should be presented at the first part of each fiscal year. Many families that are not wealthy still find that their income levels exceed the qualifying levels for membership in public health programs and are consequently denied even a minimum level of the most critical care because they simply cannot pay. It has been suggested further that by eliminating some of the available benefits of the Medicaid program not judged to be as important as others, funds could then be released so more people could become eligible for coverage even though overall fewer benefits would be available.[13]

Prioritization

The pressing question, if such a change as this is advanced, is how to determine those benefits that could be retained. The clearest and most direct approach to resolving this question would be to assemble—as the state of Oregon did recently—a group of experts to develop a list, in order of importance to health, of medical procedures and surgical interventions. This, then, is labeled *prioritization*. A cut-off level could be set by the legislature or even by a private insurance company. Although a legislature would simply make the cut-off, the limit for present or even future funding—determined actuarially for the number of citizens eligible in the state—private insurance companies would probably use this priority list by writing policies at different rates and then offering them for various cut-off points on the list.[14]

In the event a legislature chose a cut-off point on the priority list where the population covered by the program was being denied beneficial healthcare, this could be termed properly *rationing*. Similarly, the private insurance company could be thought of as rationing according to the levels private citizens could afford to pay for themselves. Certainly it is not unfair in any sense of the word to expect some limit for a public health program of this design—especially if the program were not unconscionably restricted.[15]

It can be argued persuasively that because public funds are expended on healthcare in recognition of the social good attached to health maintenance, society has every right to administer and control the monies expended in order to assure their wise and just allocation.

Those who oppose prioritization because of the possible rationing which could result do not appear to recognize the rationing already in existence which eliminates care for those without money or who are not eligible for public support. However, none of them could object to eliminating useless treatments, or choosing less expensive treatments with proven equal outcome . . . [or] to using outpatient facilities rather than the more expensive hospital facilities. . . .[16]

It is now time to determine which medical interventions are effective.

Necessary Healthcare Need Variables

Rationing can be avoided as a national policy if an agreement can be reached in identifying "really necessary" healthcare interventions and a process then designed to ensure all patients equitable access to them. Thus, objective criteria, which could possibly take the form of clinical guidelines, must be established and identify real healthcare needs, as opposed to mere desires. These guidelines would be termed "necessary care guidelines" and would give the indicators or types of patients for whom specified services would be considered necessary. Applied as standards of care, these guidelines would specify patient management strategies required for patients with certain medical problems; physician adherence to these guidelines would serve as a defense in a malpractice action.[17] Ideally, these policies or guidelines would be developed by bodies or panels drawing on outcome data, public testimony, and expert consensus. In measuring treatment, *net benefit* would be defined in terms of longevity plus quality of life.[18]

Ethics of Rationing Healthcare

Former governor of Colorado Richard Lamm, in suggesting a working ethical principle for distributing healthcare resources for the elderly, created quite a furor among the elderly when he urged healthcare resources be distributed along a utilitarian principle so as to maximize the long-run general happiness of the entire community and not only the debilitated, chronically ill, or very elderly as individual members of it. In other words, he argued that the greatest health resources should go to the greatest number of individuals capable of using them effectively. The reality of this harsh statement meant that, in Lamm's view, the elderly had "a moral duty to forgo further healthcare and to accept their death."[19] Children, he maintained, had more opportunities to flourish and achieve happiness; therefore, it was only logical that they should deserve a greater share of health resources than the elderly. This, of course, once again raises the issue of intergenerational equity or justice.

A society surely cannot consider itself a noble one if it does not respect the individuality of its members—even when to do so creates the appearance of running counter to the general happiness of the community at large. Any society runs the risk of dividing itself if it seeks to withhold healthcare from the elderly based on the argument that the "return" of such an investment can never be realized economically because of the limited lifespans of the recipients. The Lamm thesis challenges society to reallocate its healthcare resources in a way that does not abandon the elderly yet achieves a balance in providing long-term health protection and happiness for its members as a whole. Sadly, current evidence discloses that this challenge is going unmet.[20]

MODERN RATIONING

Renal dialysis and heart transplantation are perhaps the two most relevant examples of contemporary rationing. When dialysis was in its infancy, it was a scarce and costly intervention with only a few dialysis machines in existence. In efforts to develop a scheme for the use of this new, scarce life-saving technology, different localities adopted varying policies for determining who should have access to the technology. In Seattle, Washington, social worth was used as a criteria in the decision-making process to decide ultimately on the relative value of the lives of those individuals competing for use of the process itself. When Congress was presented with this problem, it simply expanded Medicaid coverage to provide kidney dialysis for all patients in need—with average costs now running in excess of $1.5 billion per year.[21]

The rationing of heart transplantations was not congressional in origin but born from a complex regulatory scheme. Because of the experience with dialysis and the astronomical costs associated with its operations, Medicare held off allowing an extension of reimbursements for heart transplantation until 1987. Then, after a national study showed that heart transplant programs were no longer experimental and actually were having a high rate of success, and special advisory committees made recommendations supporting their use, Medicare relented. But in so acting, however, Medicare placed limits on patient eligibility and acted to discourage, and oftentimes deny, access to this procedure.

Before patients can qualify for heart transplant coverage, they must show not only that they have been receiving, for 24 months, disability benefits under Social Security criteria (which is not a requirement for kidney dialysis) but that they are not otherwise disqualified because of "seriously adverse factors" (e.g., old age). Indeed, for patients to be considered within coverage, they must show as such, if they are more than 50 years old, that not only do they have an "adequately young physiologic age," but that they have neither coexisting diseases nor a history of behavior or psychiatric illnesses that could interfere with rigorous postsurgical recovery regimens. Additional restrictions on reimbursement for these procedures were imposed on hospitals that mandated that programs of this nature be in existence since 1985, show a strong performance and survival rate, have substantial economic program support, and finally, use an adequate patient selection procedure.[22]

Although recognizing de facto rationing as a current feature of contemporary healthcare delivery systems, any further expansions of it should be delayed, it has been suggested, until the irrationalities of the current national system are resolved.[23] This suggestion is impractical simply because rationing is seen as inextricable given in the present system and its "irrationalities" are beyond correction within any reasonable period of time.[24] Others might suggest that this effort to distribute scarce resources in an equitable manner, that is, rationing, is not irrational at all.[25]

Because healthcare services, providers of healthcare, and the means to pay for their services are all scarce, procedures must be established and followed to allow for a fair distribution of them. As observed, physicians regularly engage in rationing by their regulation of the extent of participation in Medicare as well as in health maintenance organizations (HMOs).[26] Historically, during times of military engagement, field physicians decided routinely whom they would treat because they were "salvageable" and those from whom treatment would be withheld until the others were treated. Some were even denied treatment because of the futility of such actions. And, even today, emergency medicine—as practiced in emergency wards of major hospitals and in times of local or state disaster—utilizes the principle of triage.[27] A strong argument could be advanced that, indeed, the very bedrock of modern rationing is to be found, to one degree or other, within the principle of triage; surely an analogy can be seen between a military battlefield and the crisis in healthcare management[28] because in both, efforts must be made to balance the costs with the benefits of all actions taken.[29]

THE VALUE OF LIFE

Economists seek to place an actual monetary value for people's lives by employing two models. The first, called the human capital model, calculates the value of life only in terms of productivity: the present discounted values of one's future earnings. The second model is described as willingness to pay. Here, the monetary value of life is directly a function of one's willingness to use resources to increase one's chances of survival. Thus, in a hypothetical situation in which an individual annually demands an extra $500 in order to perform work that runs an additional 1-in-1,000 risk of dying, $500,000 is the monetary value of that person's life. No more than $500,000 need be spent under this hypothetical model to save a particular life.[30]

MEASURING QUALITY OF LIFE

A controversial, albeit growing, view in health economics is that the goal of all service should be to create as many years of healthy life as possible for as many as possible. The underlying basis for this view is, quite simply, the "assumption that for all alike a year of healthy life is equally valuable."[31] The productivity of healthcare, then, is measured in terms of years of healthy life or quality-adjusted life years (QALYs). Thus, when consideration of the cost of receptive treatments is combined with the length of lives extended and the quality of life they enhance, interesting examples can be posited that force striking conclusions. For example, because hip replacements produce QALYs at approximately one-twentieth the cost of renal hemodialysis, the conclusion is obvious: more replacements should be done. Using the same principle, there should also probably be more coronary bypass surgeries for individuals with severe angina and left main vessel disease and more screening and follow-up treatment for mild hypertension because of the qualitative results that follow these procedures.[32]

Instead of trying to structure a model that seeks to incorporate a defensible method of pricing life and health, QALYs are thought to be a more feasible means of prioritizing healthcare services. The goal of trying to obtain the most QALYs from a healthcare system does not force a search for an answer to the central question: namely, what amount of money should be spent per QALY. Thus, quality-adjusted life years will be of considerable use in those contexts in which the question of the amount of resources to spend on healthcare has presumably been answered, that is, when there is a health budget to stay within such as in the British National Health Service, an American prepaid plan, or in a rational Medicare plan operating in the 21st century.[33]

Although from one standpoint, QALYs disadvantage people with low quality of life; from another, they may not at all. There can be no question that incorporating quality adjustment, for example, in trying to obtain healthcare dollars devoted to dialysis, weakens the competitive position of one suffering renal failure. Accordingly, if a patient's self-determined quality of life is 0.6, that patient would gain only 6.0 QALYs for 10 years on $30,000-per-year life saving dialysis. The resulting $50,000-per-QALY cost would unquestionably give a patient with this profile a rather low priority in most healthcare efficiency judgments. In this case the patient would more likely lose out to hip replacements than if the benefit in unadjusted life years were measured and the patient then counted for 10.[34]

From another standpoint, however, the patient in this hypothetical situation would gain from this quality adjustment. For, if a kidney transplant would raise the quality of life from 0.6 to 0.8 for some 10 years, the transplant would then produce 2.0 additional QALYs above and beyond the benefit derived from dialysis. When a lower long-run cost of approximately $20,000 for the transplant and $50,000 for follow-up treatment of cyclosporin (i.e., $5,000 per year for 10 years) is calculated, the patient's claim for a transplant is seen in a much more favorable light for consideration than if the jump in quality of life had been ignored. Also, because of quality adjustment, hip replacements gain. Even though no saving of life is at issue here, 15 years at 0.99 instead of 0.9 constitutes, roughly, a 1.5 QALY gain from an $8,000 surgery. So "quality adjustments cut both ways for patients with low enough quality of life to affect allocations: it benefits them in competing for quality-enhancing services, though it disadvantages them in competing for treatment that only save their existing lives."[35]

Quality-adjustment ratings derive from the individual judgments of patients and citizens about relative health needs and thereby constitute QALYs. These ratings can be done in two ways: first, by questioning people to elicit their judgments concerning the relative quality of their own particular health conditions compared to being cured or dying. The second is an indirect process that would elicit a variety of individual judgments relating to the quality of a wide spectrum of health states and then extrapolate from that data a numerical quality-adjustment factor or index for each health status on the map. Assume, for example, that normal good health is 1.0 and death is 0.0. Once a particular intervention is presented (e.g., kidney dialysis), a sample of patients with kidney disease would be asked various descriptive questions, and their responses would be used to locate life with their condition and treatment on the previous map. Because earlier responses would have allowed a specific index of that location to be set, the quality-adjustment factor for that particular condition could be determined similarly. Some speculate that by the next century, QALYs will be totally accepted and used in planning and organizing health services.[36]

An Ethical Dilemma and the Americans with Disabilities Act

Rationing on the basis of quality of life—as opposed to cost, effectiveness, or cost-effectiveness—has a strong civil rights advantage; it measures the value of life to the individual patient as opposed to his or her usefulness to society. Yet rationing at this level forces an ethical dilemma: specifically, quantifying the value of life for individuals in varying states of disability and health. Because quality of life decisional standards are subject to being colored or influenced by prejudices toward disability, it could be argued that this standard of rationing might well be considered discriminatory and, furthermore, violate the purpose of the Americans with Disabilities Act (ADA), which was designed to eliminate differential treatment based on disability.[37]

Although yet to be tested in the courts, the ADA's definition of discrimination appears to proscribe implementation of any theory (or healthcare measure) that advances the notion that the quality of life associated with a treatment should in part determine the priority given to funding the treatment itself. In order to avoid further confusion on this issue, Congress should act decisively to amend the ADA, thereby allowing the states to deal directly with the issue of scarce healthcare resources and make whatever rational choices are necessary and base them on the most reliable and available measure of qualitative life.[38]

Risk-Benefit or Cost-Benefit Analysis

Perhaps the fairest idea for limiting or rationing care is to be found in risk-benefit analysis, which would show the risk and potential benefit of a medical procedure. In developing risk-benefit uses, although age might always be expected to weigh against an older person likely to have fewer years of vigorous life left, it would not necessarily be conclusive.

If, for example, a very elderly man with an aneurysm, failing kidneys, and other complications were presented for surgical evaluation, under a cost-benefit analysis, a decision regarding the merits of surgery would be simply tied to cost. Under risk-benefit analysis, if the likelihood the patient's surviving surgery were practically zero, whereas the likelihood of his living very long even if he did survive the surgery was very low, then surgery to repair the aneurysm probably would not be found cost-effective.[39]

Voluntary Limitations on Life

Some have advanced an argument for a societal rethinking that would promote a communitarian sense of justice and underscore the Christian doctrine of stewardship prohibiting the extension of one's own life at great economic cost to one's neighbor. The practical components for implementing this idea are still absent.[40]

In a similar theoretical, yet impractical vein, another proposal advances establishing a prudential life span account that would promote a basic theory of prudential resource allocation or life span approach to one's healthcare. Under this theory, a societal or moral obligation to foster whatever conditions are necessary to allow members of society to pursue their own conceptions of the good would be recognized. Consequently, individuals considering the whole course of their lives with complete impartiality between the various states of life itself—childhood, youth, middle age, early old age and advanced old age— would be required to develop rational plans for budgeting their resources. Under this theory, longevity could—if so desired—be extended indefinitely.[41] The central impediment to realizing this theory in practice would be the basic lack of education, sophistication, and imagination that the vast majority of Americans face that would prevent them from constructing a rational life-plan healthcare budget.[42]

RATIONAL CONSTRUCT FOR HEALTHCARE DECISION MAKING

By developing six levels of necessary healthcare, priorities can be established that for the most part would avoid rationing.[43] The first level would include caring in its most basic forms for the relief of pain; hospice, or comparable care for the dying; nursing or home care for the elderly or frail; simple mental health programs for the mildly disturbed; and basic care for those chronically ill, demented, disabled, retarded, or severely mentally ill.

Level two would incorporate nutrition, sanitation, programs of occupational health, a tolerably clean environment, preventive medicine, and health promotion, including accident prevention and prenatal care. Level three would encompass immunizations and protection against disease, antibiotics, and antimicrobials for the control of infection. At level four, emergency medicine and primary care would be targeted—but both would be limited to routine and relatively inexpensive forms of diagnosis and therapy (e.g., life-saving and emergency care, palliation of pain, and simple forms of surgery and rehabilitation). The fifth level of healthcare would include general, advanced forms of medical cure or restoration (e.g., advanced surgery, cancer, chemotherapy, extensive rehabilitation). Finally, level six would encompass highly advanced technological therapy (for example, dialysis, open-heart surgery, organ transplants, and total parenteral nutrition).

In devising a healthcare system tied to necessary interventions, as opposed to desirous ones, at levels one through four, the burden of proof for *not* providing them would lie with the government; for at these levels, almost everyone in society is challenged by these threats to personal integrity and health. Capital investments in these areas would obviously have the greatest impact on mortality and morbidity and reach, from a utilitarian standpoint, the greatest level of individual need. Funding the first four levels would achieve a core value structure. In other words, through the guaranteed delivery of healthcare services at that level, public interest as a whole is humanized. At levels five and six of this proposed construct, individualized, as opposed to communitarian, threats come into focus. Accordingly, to gain public access to this level of healthcare support, the burden should shift toward the benefiting individuals, requiring them to show that a claim for cure should be honored by society.[44]

Under this proposed construct, no clear or universal priorities need to be set and applied in all cases. Circumstances or situations could determine priorities. Particular communities within a city or state would thus develop their own acceptable sets of priorities and flesh out the construct itself through the political process, essentially following what the state of Oregon has done with its plan for prioritizing state-funded medical treatments.[45]

Absent some type of verifiable mechanism for allocating healthcare resources to the elderly, rationing may be effected over succeeding years by an insidious allocation process removed from the public view altogether and termed a "responsible system of allocation implemented inconspicuously" by private healthcare providers and practitioners without any standard of accountability. This sort of rationing, which would be most difficult to prove or prevent, would not only react to reimbursement formulae and market reward as well as implied regulatory messages from Medicare and Medicaid, but furthermore, would mask levels of personal and institutional prejudice in the vague imprecision of medical language and quasi-scientific criteria. Such a hidden and pervasive system of rationing must not be countenanced. In a free society, equity and justice demand that difficult decisions such as allocating healthcare be made openly so that assumptions about aging and the value of life for the aged can be presented, debated, and resolved within the political process.[46]

Chapter 5

Autonomy, Competency, and Guardianship Paternalism

As a goal, autonomy is perhaps important; but, as a working principle in long-term care cases, it is becoming less and less relevant. In order to make this concept more applicable to long-term care, it has been suggested that it be reconceptualized and conjoined with paternalism—thus formulating a principle of "autonomy respecting paternalism," and implemented through mechanisms of negotiated consent.[1]

Enhancing or safeguarding autonomy within the nursing home environment, where real-world (as opposed to theoretical) transactions occur, presents untold difficulties for the patients in long-term care facilities and their physicians. Among those difficulties are

> [s]uch factors as professional interventions being more social than medical, the need for a certain degree of regimentation in institutional living, the high prevalence of mental impairment that diminish as residents' decision-making capacity change even within the course of a single day.[2]

These objective conditions inhibit free choice for the nursing or extended care residents and thus restrict their powers of autonomy or self-determination.

Autonomy is either compromised or neglected every day in nursing homes. The reasons for this are not accidental, but socially structured; within the institutional life of nursing homes are embedded impersonal ways of daily operation, with staff members being socialized according to various professional norms that are barriers to even a semblance of autonomy. Often infantalized and cast in passive roles, nursing home residents are afforded few opportunities to enter into meaningful decisions in their period of heroic helplessness.[3]

Yet, if pursued in a simplistic manner, the principle of autonomy can easily serve as mere pretext for abandoning patients and giving up on their possibilities for rehabilitation. A patient's reluctance to go to rehabilitation, physical therapy, or even to eat—although autonomous in nature—may also be a symptom of depressive illness. Nurses have a choice: to go along with this patient action or, in the name of benevolent paternalism, countermand it through negotiated consent.[4]

GUARDIANSHIP PATERNALISM

The last decade has witnessed a serious debate over whether a physician's determination and implementation of a patient's best medical interests should be viewed as beneficent or as paternalistic and a direct interference with the patient's independent wishes. Positive acts of paternalism should result in a physicians using their skills to optimize the well-being of their patients.[5] One view holds that because mental as well as physical illnesses result in diminishing a patient's exercise of autonomy, physician paternalism should always be recognized as positive because it fills in the gaps that result from this receding patient autonomy.[6]

A more current view holds that losses of patient autonomy are not the result of illness but of the failure by the caregivers to allow patient participation in the health decision-making process. This perspective has been shaped by "the delivery of medical care in the last 25 years, which have made medicine less capable of addressing the full range of a patient's interests."[7] Regrettably, this "medical view" has become artificially fixed on objective scientific criteria, often manipulated by specialists who have not had sufficient communication with patients to establish a relationship. The end result of this view has promoted institutionalization of patients who could otherwise, with appropriate assistance, live in the community.[8]

Although beneficence has been, and generally should continue to be, the principle guiding proxy decision-making in health services, it should be remembered that beneficence—while guaranteeing positive benefits for the never-competent and the completely incapacitated person—de-emphasizes almost to the point of extinction the viewpoint and right of self-determination of any individual not in one of these two classes.[9]

Social work, as a discipline, plays an important role in deciding issues of competency for guardianship and providing intervention for protective services. Its primary concern is maintaining client autonomy and to that end works toward the goal of social independence, enabling the individual to achieve, under the least restrictive means of assistance, an acceptable standard of community living.[10]

When the law, through its processes, attempts to balance the values of beneficence and autonomy by an identification of the types and degrees of mental disabilities and those symptoms regarded as severe enough to warrant the appointment of a proxy, it provides a procedure for notifying all those who have an interest in the outcome and a forum for them to be heard. Such a process, by its very structure, provides the promise of an objective evaluation of various forms of information and a framework for objectively balancing the various competing interests with the ultimate goal of reaching dispassionate conclusions.[11]

DETERMINING COMPETENCY

Although competence is regarded generally as a sphere of legal judgment, clear legal standards are lacking for making determinations when a person is no longer competent to make medical decisions.[12] Adults are simply presumed competent unless found to be otherwise by a court of law. In clinical practice, it is rare to find either the courts or the guardians legally appointed by them to be involved in making medical care decisions. Rather, current procedures dictate an identification be made by healthcare professionals of those individuals whose competency to make a medical decision is in doubt. Physicians often go further and make de facto determinations of patient incompetence and then arrange for surrogate decision makers to become involved, usually asking family members to serve as surrogates. This clinical approach not only expedites the medical decision-making process but is considered both appropriate and fair because family members know the patient and can thus act in his or her best interests.[13]

In making these determinations about patient decision-making capacity, doctors are faced inherently with a dilemma: how to find the appropriate balance in their actions that protects patients from harm yet respects their autonomy. To advance the assurance of this balance, a sliding scale that holds ''the more probable or serious the risk posed by the patient's decision, the more stringent the standard of capacity that should be required'' has been suggested.[14] The problem with such a procedure, however, is that far too much latitude is given to the doctors who assess the harms as well as the benefits of medical treatment. Thus, determinations of incapacity could be made inconsistently among patients,[15] resulting in benevolent disregard for the value of patient autonomy.[16]

Presently, four decision-making models have emerged as constructs, all of which have been used with various degrees of approval in judicial determinations incorporated by statutes, the legal literature, and in actual clinical settings. And, although each of these models differ in terms of the degree of discretion left to the primary physician, all are designed to assess mental status by measuring, at one level or other, various mental functions such as level of consciousness; person, place, and time orientation; memory; etc.[17]

Under the first model, termed *manifesting a choice*, if a patient is capable of indicating a choice, that action in and of itself is considered sufficient to demonstrate decision-making capacity. This model focuses on patient autonomy, with the physician accorded little discretion. The second model or test measures the patient's *actual ability to understand* the information relevant to the decision to be made. Because objective measures of these skills are lacking here, the physician has substantial discretion to determine not only which information is relevant, but also what constitutes understanding of that information.

The third test model, *the nature of the decision-making process*, seeks to measure a patient's ability to manipulate information in a rational manner as well as the ability to appreciate the implications of the decisions. The central threat to autonomy with this model is that a physician may be given discretion to determine not only how rationality is measured, but what level of rationality is required.

The fourth model measures the *content of the actual decision* made by the patient. The test of the ability to grant informed consent is whether the patient makes the "right" choice. Obviously, because a doctor determines what the right choice is, this model assures the maximum level of discretion to the physician.[18]

Drawing upon, and thus seeking to complement, the fourth competency model, a structured format has been proposed for conducting the assessment of mental status that calls for, among other points, an independent examiner (preferably a physician) who should be not only conversant with medical illnesses but knowledgeable of the abilities associated with competence to grant informed consent. A greater degree of neutrality would surely be assured if an administrative law judge or master who has expertise in medical as well as legal matters were employed. The examiner not only should be aware of the patient's illness and proposed treatment, but, furthermore, should not assume that the patient has been provided all information necessary to make the decision.

Because decision-making capacities fluctuate, more than one patient examination should be conducted. Also, some patients may respond better to examiners with similar ethnic or cultural background and when family members are present to assist in explaining the concepts. When a finding of incompetence does result, this should be followed by a complete evaluation of the factors causing the incompetence with a realization that remediation of these factors could result in restoration of the patient's competence.[19]

ADULT PROTECTIVE SERVICES

In response to emerging trends in the living patterns of the elderly and the "deinstitutionalized" mentally incompetent, in the early 1980s, a new form of service termed "adult protective services" was initiated by many states.[20] This model was based on the previous decade of public policies supporting and promoting intervention by the government into the lives of the elderly. State laws tried to create a coordinated system of social and health services, based on the model of child protection services, that includes visiting nurses, home-delivered meals ("meals on wheels"), repairmen, homemakers, etc.—all coordinated by a caseworker who assesses the needs of each client and becomes responsible for delivering the appropriate level of services through other agencies. Federal funding for such programs was supported then and is supported now through Subchapter XX of the Social Security Act and Subchapter III of the Older Americans Act.[21]

Rarely are the protective services programs limited to clients who voluntarily accept their services. In fact, legislative provisions within particular states allow use of guardianships or conservatorships by the pertinent agency within the programs in order to ensure that the client accepts that level of assistance the caseworker determines to be necessary. Court orders for protective services may be obtained in some jurisdictions by emergency order if an imminent danger to a client's health or safety exists or entry must be obtained into the home of the uncooperative client. Some states even allow authorized state agencies to serve as "public guardians"—appointed as such by the courts when no private guardian may be found.[22] The development and expansion of these adult protective services programs derive from the state's police power, which allows for civil commitment proceedings for persons adjudged either dangerous to themselves because of mental illness or dangerous to others in the community.[23]

GUARDIANSHIP

A guardianship, or conservatorship as termed by some states, is for older adults an intervention of considerable magnitude and importance; because, all too often, ageist community attitudes associate incompetence and dependence with old age and thereby place older individuals at risk for loss of their autonomy. Indeed, those who have guardians are termed "wards" and normally include the disabled, incapacitated, or incompetent.[24] Depending upon the nature of the guardianship, the guardian may have very broad or very limited powers. A plenary guardianship, for example, confers a blanket grant of power upon a guardian for all necessary decisions affecting a ward's estate or person. Although used infrequently, most states provide for limited guardianships that restrict a ward's decision-making authority to certain areas. Temporary or emergency guardianships provide a third alternative and are time-limited and designed primarily to deal with a single issue (e.g., consent for medical treatment) or a set of limited issues.[25] All three types of guardianship provide challenges to patient autonomy; yet they may be justified under the principle of beneficent paternalism.[26]

The process for granting a guardianship consists generally of three steps with the first being recognized as preadjudication. At this stage the primary decision will be made either by family members, physicians, social workers, and/or attorneys to move forward with a guardianship proceeding. Based upon concerns for an at-risk individual's competency to make healthcare decisions or his or her ability to live cooperatively in a community without exhibiting eccentric and disturbing behaviors, and to ensure that the individual is able to carry on the daily functions of life, a guardianship may be pursued.[27]

The second, or adjudication phase, starts when a guardianship petition is filed in court. The court decides whether decision-making capacity exists—using one of the four models discussed earlier—and if so what level of protection will be granted. As might be expected, the medical report is central to a determination of incompetency. Most states, with the filing of the petition, provide for a statutorily prescribed procedure that includes notice of the hearing given to the proposed ward and affords sufficient time for the preparation of a defense.[28]

Although the proposed ward may be represented in all states by counsel, few require the appointment of counsel.[29] Most jurisdictions allow for the appointment of a guardian *ad litem* (who is not necessarily required to be an attorney) to represent the proposed ward's "best interests." The guardian's role is that of an independent evaluator and not that of an advocate for the proposed ward. More often than not, guardianship proceedings run the real possibility of being *ex parte* and nonadversarial—thus excluding the older person's presence altogether from the hearing.[30]

The third stage in a guardianship proceeding, postadjudication, has an open-ended character and encompasses a wide variety of activities that form a part of every case disposition and subsequent appointment of a guardian. Because courts rarely grant restorations to competency in plenary guardianships, namely because they are sought infrequently, a guardian serves until the ward dies. Throughout this time span, a variety of decisions must be made, including those regarding the ward's place of residence, daily activities, medical treatment, etc., that are dependent ultimately upon the changes in the health status of the ward.[31] Because the imposition of a guardianship normally presupposes an inability on the ward's part to make choices, particularly as to institutional and medical regimens, the extent of the ward's participation in decision making—and thus autonomy—is usually curtailed significantly.[32]

In many cases, a guardian's duties and sphere of decision making far exceed the confines of the law, extending to determining a ward's place of residence, medical care, personal care, nutrition, social contacts, recreation, and transportation. Although law-related, other decisions will include application/appeals for federal-state benefits, payment for healthcare, and long-term care (Medicare/Medicaid, supplemental health insurance, and long-term care insurance), home care (agreements with home care agencies, hiring home care directly), institutional care (facility admission agreements, residents' rights), and home equity conversion.[33]

A FUTURE AGENDA

To ensure autonomy and self-determination for all elderly individuals subject to guardianship proceedings, the states must act uniformly to guarantee the appointment of counsel for *all* proceedings for guardianship and to make such a provision particularly for those who are unable to afford private counsel. This goal could no doubt be best realized by the enactment of federal legislation requiring the mandatory appointment of counsel to elderly individuals who are subject to guardianship proceedings. A second step to strengthen the process would require each counsel appointed in guardianship proceedings to serve as a zealous advocate on behalf of the client.[34]

Additional reforms could be seen by mandating standards and procedures that ensure guardians file plans that include a statement of the ward's views and preferences and consider restoration (where possible) or maximization of the ward's mental and physical capacities as well. Annual reports by the guardian should be filed on not only the personal status of the ward but also of the estate. Outside individuals should be designated to investigate the actual circumstances of the ward, including a personal observation, and to report how the guardianship plan is working. If significant deviation from the actual guardianship plan is found, the appropriate court should review the guardianship itself, and make corrections where needed and impose sanctions.[35]

The American Bar Association's Commission on the Mentally Disabled has concluded that by the year 2035 almost one quarter of the population of the United States (nearly 71 million persons) will be classified as elderly. Estimates of individuals with developmental disabilities made in 1989 by the Federal Administration on Developmental Disabilities set the figure at 3.9 million, a figure that will surely increase because of improved rates of survival for infants born with disabilities and increases in overall life expectancy. Approximately 344,000 persons are admitted to state mental hospitals in any given year, in addition to the 130,000 individuals currently resident in state mental hospitals; these figures combine to provide a staggering picture of the potential need for guardians.[36]

Also to be considered in these statistics is the unknown, although greater, number of individuals who suffer from chronic mental illnesses but live in the outside world—deinstitutionalized in many cases—on the streets or in boarding homes that are free of institutional restraints or protections, as the case may be. These individuals will surely need surrogate decision makers for assistance with their personal or financial affairs or both. Finally, there are 1.5 million HIV-infected persons who will develop AIDS over the coming years; many in the later stages of this disease will experience significant mental impairments and will require temporary or indefinite surrogate decision makers.[37] When all of these human conditions combine, a tremendous strain on the judicial system will result as it seeks to provide guardianships and supervise protective services to these unfortunate members of society.[38]

In addition to the durable power of attorney discussed in Chapters 7 and 8, and case management discussed in Chapter 9, other alternatives such as money management programs (where, for one, the Social Security Administration appoints an individual, not necessarily a relative, to receive and manage the federal monetary benefits of the recipient received under Social Security) and home health and homemaker services, independent of or in association with adult protective services programs, need to be used more extensively as alternatives to guardianships. Additionally, more comprehensive use of living wills, trusts, and even civil commitment remain as other options.[39]

The goal should be, in all such cases, to divert inappropriate cases from the guardianship system and thereby shape the particular guardianship to address the actual limitations of the ward. Limiting continued guardianships to those actually in need will enhance the autonomy of all elderly and disabled populations and safeguard their independent lifestyles. This will reduce the number of those subjected to guardianships and impose the fewest possible restrictions on those who are subjected to them.[40]

Chapter 6

Informed or Negotiated Consent

John Stuart Mill asserted that "the only purpose for which power can be right-fully exercised over any member of a civilized community, against his will, is to prevent harm to others. His own good, either physical or moral, is not a sufficient warrant."[1] These words frame the principle of self-determination that undergirds the doctrine of informed consent, and from which important legal and ethical issues emerge in the evolving world of contemporary bioethics.[2] The informed consent doctrine is highly complex, and, perhaps more so than any other medico-legal doctrine, reflects the fundamental legal, moral, and ethical responsibilities of healthcare professionals in respecting the personal autonomy of their patients.[3]

The doctrine of informed consent is a standard designed to uphold the supreme values of personal autonomy and individual dignity.[4] Furthermore, it is a standard that symbolizes human freedom, honored in ethics and enshrined in law, and that demands protection from professionals who fall short of the ideal.[5]

Although the exercise of informed consent is an interactive process that primarily involves the caregiver and patient, the doctrine has generated consid-erable controversy in the courts, among legal scholars and within the healthcare professions.[6] As with any controversial issue, the competing philosophies assume polar ends of a hypothetical spectrum: those who support patients' absolute right to make medical decisions that involve their own bodies vie against physicians who are reluctant to share or relinquish their control over medical decision making, resulting primarily from concern that the grant of an absolute right may empower a patient to make detrimental medical decisions.[7] Regardless of which side is deemed to be correct, the informed consent process nevertheless requires a patient to exhibit skill, wisdom, personal force, and courage, while expecting the caregiver to provide acceptance, support, and respect in return.[8]

CREATION OF THE CONSENT DOCTRINE

In *Slater v. Baker*,[9] perhaps the earliest reported case involving a patient's consent, the court held a surgeon and apothecary liable for disuniting a substantially healed fracture without having obtained consent.[10] The court held it to be fully reasonable that a patient should be told what is about to be done to him or her.[11] By so ruling, the court had established the foundation for what would eventually evolve into the present-day informed consent doctrine.

Similarly, the general rule in the United States during the latter part of the 19th and the early part of the 20th century required a physician to procure a patient's consent before administering treatment.[12] The courts developed an extensive body of law through which they specified what sort of behavior on the part of a patient would amount to consent, hoping to provide congruity within the law during this evolutional era.[13] Nonetheless, the courts were generally unwilling to hold physicians liable,[14] and in those cases in which liability was found, its basis rested on the intentional torts of assault and battery or trespass to the person.[15] Although some patients did attempt to establish liability on the basis of inadequate disclosure of the risks involved in the treatment undertaken,[16] the emerging informed consent doctrine instead predicated the physician's liability primarily upon failure to disclose what the treatment would consist of and what its normal consequences would be.[17] Perhaps the most accurate depiction of the relationship between a physician and patient during this period may be presented as follows:

> In substance the physician said to the patient, "You need thus-and-so to get better," and the patient responded with . . . "O.K. Doc., whatever you say;" [or] "Go ahead and do thus-and-so;" [or] "Go ahead and do 'thus,' but I don't want you to do any 'so;' [or] "If that's what I need, then I'd rather be sick, and don't do anything at all. . . ."[18]

It was not until the 1940s that noticeable changes began to occur. The Nuremberg Code, promulgating requirements for ethical medical experimentation, emerged as a result of the atrocities committed in German concentration camps by Nazi doctors.[19] Despite the progressive changes in medical research codes requiring informed consent, reforms in patient consent requirements surrounding routine medical care were being implemented at a slower pace.[20]

Following World War II, significant advances in both medicine and technology allowed for the development of a number of new medical treatments, many of which were accompanied by greater risks than had previously existed.[21] Physicians now had the ability to keep patients alive for longer periods of time, and in turn, patients began to expect and oftentimes demand miraculous cures.[22] Doctors began specializing in specific practice areas and as more patients found themselves going to the hospital, they were increasingly being faced with a "bewildering spectrum" of nameless specialists and consultants.[23]

The technological advances of medical procedures were also paralleled by judicial reaction, signified primarily by a more common tendency for courts to hold the physician liable.[24] Eventually, "[a]s litigation over the contours of a legally valid consent proceeded, the concept of consent, like that of negligence, began to be viewed as being quite malleable, if not infinitely expandable."[25]

The doctrine of informed consent is the means by which individuals are informed of and may assert their preferences for alternative forms of available medical treatment.[26] This notion of providing the patient with pertinent medical information stems from a societal shift in attitude with respect to the physician-patient relationship.[27] A heightened awareness of the imperfections, injustices, dangers, and afflictions perceived to exist in society changed the traditional view that a patient was merely a passive entity within a paternalistic and hierarchical medical system.[28] Instead, the view shifted toward according the patient the right to direct personal medical treatment, and to base any treatment decisions on accurate and truthful information supplied by the physician.[29] In response to this evolution, the legal system developed the concept of informed consent.[30]

The doctrine of informed consent first appeared in American case law during the late 1950s. In *Salgo v. Leland Stanford Jr., University Board of Trustees*,[31] a California court emphasized that a physician had an affirmative duty to make "full disclosure of facts necessary to an *informed consent*."[32] Furthermore, the court asserted that withholding information essential to the patient's ability to make a rational, well-informed decision about medical care was a violation of this duty. *Bang v. Charles T. Miller Hospital*[33] represented another seminal case of informed consent and involved a prostate operation that resulted in the severance of spermatic cords.[34] In its decision, the Minnesota Supreme Court held the physician liable for having failed to provide the patient with information regarding alternative treatments.[35]

The *Salgo* and *Bang* cases in no way represented a consensus of American courts during the period. Although the United States Court of Appeals for the Fifth Circuit,[36] and the Missouri Supreme Court[37] did agree, in *dicta*, that the physician should have an affirmative duty to disclose information regarding diagnosis and treatment,[38] the Supreme Court of Washington[39] and a Louisiana district court[40] rejected the idea that an affirmative duty to disclose such information rested with a physician.

According to many commentators, a shift to the contemporary period of autonomy-directed informed consent did not occur until 1960,[41] led primarily by rulings of the Supreme Courts of Kansas[42] and Missouri.[43] In *Nathanson v. Kline*,[44] the Supreme Court of Kansas held that the physician was obligated to disclose the probable dangers and consequences of the suggested treatment, and to explain to the patient in simple language the nature of the ailment.[45] The Supreme Court of Missouri issued its ruling on informed consent in *Mitchell v. Robinson*.[46] The court held that physicians were obligated to inform patients generally of the possible hazards involved with specific medical treatments.[47]

By establishing a clear duty to disclose the risks of medical treatment, the impact of the Nathanson and Mitchell decisions manifested itself in a rash of informed consent claims.[48] Thus, in the years that followed, the courts were repeatedly called upon to decide issues involving physician disclosure to patients.[49] As a result, the courts developed a number of different standards for disclosure, along with exceptions to the doctrine.[50]

Two recognized exceptions exist to the general rule requiring informed consent: when disclosure would be so harmful to the patient as to be medically contraindicated and where the person is unconscious or otherwise incapable of consenting, and the harm from not providing treatment is imminent and outweighs any harm that might result from the proposed treatment.[51] No civil recovery can be obtained for failure to obtain an informed consent unless the patient establishes that the healthcare professional's failure to inform resulted in the direct cause of the injury suffered. Stated otherwise, if a patient would have allowed the medical procedure or surgical intervention without benefit of an informed consent, the patient cannot complain subsequently about a risk heretofore considered insignificant.[52]

CRITERIA NECESSARY FOR A VALID INFORMED CONSENT

There is broad agreement that three general criteria are necessary for a valid informed consent to exist: [53] 1) the consent must be *voluntary*, 2) the information provided to the patient must be *material*, and 3) the patient must be *competent*.[54]

Consent Must Be Voluntary

The fundamental issue with respect to the voluntary nature of a patient's consent is that the circumstances surrounding the consent process allow for the maximum freedom of choice on the part of the patient.[55] Patients should never feel as though their consent is being induced by medical staff pressure.[56] This component is a limited factor, however, in that it only affects certain groups that, by and large, have been identified as being particularly vulnerable to being pressured into consenting.[57]

Information Must Be "Material"

In deciding whether to undergo or forego treatment, patients must be provided with all information "material" to making that decision.[58] The application of this criterion is analyzed from two distinct facets. The initial inquiry is to the sufficiency of the information regarding a particular treatment method.[59] It requires that the information conveyed to the patient include some threshold level of data regarding the medical procedure being considered.[60] Beyond the sufficiency of the information is the standard of disclosure.[61] The basic test holds that a physician is obligated to disclose information that a similarly situated physician would do in like circumstances, although the test has also been construed to require disclosure of information that would "materially affect" a patient's decision.[62] Regardless of which test is applied, the information must be provided by the physician unless the task has been delegated to someone else.[63] Even with such delegation, however, the physician does not absolve himself or herself from the responsibility of seeing to it that the disclosure of information is properly undertaken.[64]

Although there are no published substantive estimates of the costs or benefits of informed consent,[65] there is a correlation between poor physician communication to patients and malpractice claims together with the incidence of malpractice.[66] Perhaps the major impediment to obtaining a truly informed consent is the inability of many patients to understand the risk information provided by a physician and to recall even less of the data as their condition worsens.[67] Indeed, it has been found that comprehension varied inversely with age and directly with education,[68] with elderly individuals showing a significantly less comprehension of consent information leading to a state of impaired competence.[69] In order to combat this deficiency, physicians need to consider changing the manner in which they describe risk to their patients and thereby assign a specific statistical probability to the possible medical or surgical outcome in question.[70] Frank patient discussion of the comparative risks involved with one procedure over another is both wise and practical.[71]

The Patient Must Be Competent

The final component of informed consent is the competency issue that, over the years, has received considerably less attention than the other two components.[72] The competency criteria deals with a patient's capacity to make a rational or intelligent judgment regarding medical information being presented to him or her.[73] It is generally undisputed that even the most educated laypersons may have serious difficulties in understanding the medical considerations being disclosed by a physician.[74] This problem of comprehension becomes even more compounded when, as observed previously, the patient suffers from medical disabilities or is aging.[75] The dilemma is then further augmented because no established criterion exists for determining the level of competency that meets the requirements of informed consent,[76] and there have yet to be developed objective, valid, and reliable methods for assessing a patient's decisional capacity.[77] Nevertheless, there is the often used phrase that a patient should be "informed of the risks, benefits, and alternatives to treatment," implying, however, the patient be capable of understanding these components before being judged to be competent.[78]

NEGOTIATED CONSENT

Although it is seen that the foundation of informed consent is now well embedded in both the legal and medical arenas, negotiated consent is far from being as widely accepted. In fact, the ideal of negotiated consent is only beginning to emerge as a viable alternative to the traditional informed consent standard, particularly with application to healthcare for the elderly.

The informed consent standard, which is based upon autonomy, emerged from the acute care environment and from a narrowly conceived view of the relationship between professional caregivers (physicians) and those dependent upon them (patients).[79] Similarly, the concept of negotiated consent recognizes the ideal of autonomy as well, yet in a more limited fashion.[80] Negotiated consent is a clash and balance of competing interests, and recharacterizes the relationship between autonomy and paternalism—commonly understood to be opposites— proposing that they, in fact, need not be inapposite.[81] Rather, the negotiated consent ideal recognizes the need for some version of "autonomy respecting paternalism" in the environment of long-term care, particularly involving elderly patients.[82] Fundamentally, paternalistic interventions that serve to enhance autonomy and allow the patients to decide and act in keeping with their own values compose the underpinnings of negotiated consent.[83]

Principles of Negotiated Consent

In light of the unique issues and moral dilemmas involved in long-term care for the elderly, the interactions between patients and practitioners are primarily acute transactions.[84] As such, enhancing the autonomy among patients of long-term care facilities is an extraordinarily difficult task.[85] The conditions at hand are very different from those encountered outside of residential care facilities, where informed consent is the prevalent model.[86] Recognizing these differences, negotiated consent attempts to address the various concerns involved and balance the involved parties' competing interests.[87] Under the negotiated consent standard, many legitimate views must be considered involving the patient, family, and institution.[88] The result is a shared or dispersed authority for decision making in which no single party has the exclusive power of decision[89] and a nonalgorithmic process whereby negotiation is not governed by strict deductive rules.[90] Instead, negotiation is more "heuristic in its cognitive style, implying less reliance on codes of ethics and more attention to opportunities for discussion."[91]

Even in those instances in which the ideal outcome is not attainable, a common situation among the frail elderly, negotiation serves to "make the best of a bad situation."[92] For example, gastrostomy (enteral) tubes are often inserted into the stomachs of patients in order to sustain them. Yet data shows this type of feeding does not prolong life significantly. A recent study revealed, however, no differential increases in anxiety among those elderly individuals with whom explicit discussions were held regarding the risks and benefits of the intervention; thus the conclusion is drawn that the elderly can make freewill decisions that have fatal consequences.[93] Through the process of negotiated consent comes the assurance that those decisions reached are not acts of arbitrary authority but rather the result of a process producing reasons for the outcome.

Necessary Elements

In order to effectively implement negotiated consent, there must be active participation by the patient or the patient's surrogate and consultation with all parties holding an interest in the decision.[94] Furthermore, the patient must have at least a cursory knowledge of legal and ethical rights and the opportunity for scrutiny and enforcement of those rights by an outside higher authority.[95] In addition, the element of power in the deliberative process plays an integral part of the negotiated consent formula. Obviously, little chance for negotiation exists if one party has such superior power as to leave the other party with no chance for deliberation.[96] By the same token, negotiated consent does not insist on absolute equality between the parties, either.[97] Instead, the doctrine essentially supports the concept of "shared decision making" between the physician and patient in those situations in which it is possible.[98]

Although the ideals of virtue and compassion called for in negotiated consent may be sophistic, they are by no means quixotical. The introduction of negotiated consent in healthcare for the elderly is designed primarily to urge a different set of ideals and emphasize that practitioners must demonstrate virtues alongside the purported rights a patient is supposed to possess.[99]

THE FUTURE: INFORMED OR NEGOTIATED CONSENT FOR THE ELDERLY?

In American society, individuals who reach the age of majority are permitted a broad range of choice.[100] They may choose their jobs, their relationships, and the patterns by which they live.[101] Generally speaking, individual choice is largely unregulated and unsupervised. These rights of choice, however, are often denied elderly persons because they are unable to effectuate preference without assistance.[102] In the United States today, as noted previously, nearly one out of every eight Americans is 65 years of age or older[103] and the need for medical care on the part of older Americans is disproportional to the rest of society.[104] Persons who are 65 years of age or older are hospitalized at 3.5 times the rate of those under age 65, and typically, the older the patient is, the longer the patient ends up staying in the hospital.[105]

As the population of aging citizens grows, so does the need for them to make pivotal decisions regarding their medical treatment.[106] Reality dictates that the capacity of elderly patients to make such decisions is often impaired by a higher incidence and prevalence of chronic brain disease,[107] coupled with the burden of coping with numerous other medical afflictions. Moreover, the risk for elderly patients may be compounded because they are more likely to be excluded from the medical decision-making process as a result of reduced physician contact, ageism, and paternalism.[108]

Even for the elderly patient, informed consent for medical decision making has been the standard consent practice in the medical community for a number of years.[109] Particularly for the elderly, however, this process has failed in a number of areas, one of which is the issue of a patient's competence to consent to treatment.[110] Thus, with the doctrine of negotiated consent as an alternative to the traditional model of informed consent, the needs and desires of elderly patients ideally have a greater chance of being addressed adequately and equitably.

Dependent elderly persons pose a special problem for healthcare professionals in that their decisions often require the involvement of helpers and facilitators.[111] Such involvement may result in differing standards of judgment and measures of worth being applied to an elder's individual choice.[112] The results are conflicting value systems that often reflect the competing concerns of institutional and individual self-protection and convenience.[113] In the end, the elderly person is at a great risk of losing the right to decide about the course and conduct of his or her life.[114]

In such a scenario, the model of negotiated consent provides a realistic and viable means by which the interests of all parties involved may be represented. Negotiated consent allows for the interaction of all affected parties, including the patient, family, clergy, and physicians.[115] This process assures the presentation of a multitude of differing views while, ideally, preserving the values of the patient.

The process of negotiated consent also combats another ill of the traditional informed consent doctrine. Commonly, informed consent can provoke anxiety and evoke previous experiences, fantasies, and associations for a patient, triggering an occasional primitive defense response.[116] With negotiated consent, the interaction of the parties and the commitment to shared dialogue should reduce the likelihood of such a response, if not completely eliminate it.

A further deficiency of the informed consent model, as applied to older patients, is their inability to comprehend the specific elements of informed consent information.[117] Thus, as a group, geriatric patients may have some impairment in providing their informed consent with regard to medical procedures.[118] Because the process of negotiated consent involves, among other things, the friends and family of the patient, it is likely that there is a greater sense of trust among the parties, particularly if the patient needs assistance to comprehend fully the intricacies of the specific consent.

The doctrine of negotiated consent is certainly not without its shortcomings. First of all, self-determination for long-term care residents is a valid ideal;

however, it requires opportunity, capacity, and motivation on their part.[119] Although the opportunity and capacity factors receive a majority of the attention within the medical community, the motivational factor must be addressed seriously, particularly with elderly persons.[120] If elderly patients are not sufficiently motivated to exercise the rights being secured for them, the doctrine of negotiated consent serves no additional benefit for the patients. Moreover, entertaining the multitude of opinions necessary for negotiated consent may require an overly burdensome and time-consuming recording process, and could even result in an invitation to litigation should the parties to the negotiation decide later that they are dissatisfied with the outcome.[121] Although perhaps a valid criticism, nevertheless, recording the outcome of the negotiation is obligatory for the process of negotiated consent to remain valid.[122] Finally, the lack of substantiality within the negotiated consent process is recognized.[123] Regardless, simply following the procedural standard for conduct will keep open the lines of communication and will serve to perpetuate negotiations, while perhaps even establishing boundaries for future negotiations to follow.

Ethics Committees as a Component

When communicative ethics for geriatric care collapse, the business of nursing homes becomes little more than a place for "bed and body work."[124] All too frequently, life in a nursing home has been likened to a rite of passage: a passage to nowhere![125]

If nursing homes were to institutionalize ethics committees, there would be great potential for using them as an important construct for assisting parties in negotiating agreements on complex ethical issues. One way to view the role of ethics committees is to consider them as mechanisms for protecting and advancing informal negotiation. Negotiated consent, then, remains an ideal worth striving for not because there is agreement, but because there is likely to be disagreement or uncertainty in healthcare management for the elderly. If the process of negotiation is protected and supported through the work of ethics committees, then it can only be hoped that they will be able to make a valuable contribution to the maintenance of some level of quality in long-term care in the future.[126]

Medical Information Privacy

From the concept or principle of informed consent to medical treatment has come a parallel theory of informed consent to release of medical information. Based as such on the voluntariness of consent and the adequacy of disclosure of information to the patient about what is to be done, this new theory rests upon an inherently false premise: namely, that patients are familiar with the data contained in their medical records and, further, that they understand what they are consenting to disclose. Because many patients, in fact, are neither granted access to their medical records, nor apprised of those portions made accessible to others, most of them are simply ill equipped to make choices regarding authorized disclosures.[127]

Even though the actual information found within patients' records are characterized as their personal property, traditionally, patients have not been allowed anywhere near total freedom of access to inspect their own records simply because the laws governing patient access are neither universal nor uniform and because of medical paternalism. The second point is crucial, for it is understood (by physicians) that when they assume responsibility for a patient's health, they must be accorded a broad base of discretion in order to withhold that medical information viewed as harmful to the patient.[128]

Some 27 states have enacted legislation requiring healthcare providers to grant patients a legal right not only to see but to copy their medical records.[129] And, the Federal Privacy Act, protects nonconsensual government disclosure of confidential information contained in a system of records to any person or agency without the written consent of the individual to whom the records pertain.[130]

The American Health Information Management Association recognizes limitations of access: 1) for patients adjudicated incompetent; 2) in cases in which the healthcare provider has determined information would be injurious to the patient or other person; and 3) for minors who are governed by legal constraints.[131] The clear argument advanced by the average patient is simply that access to medical records is but part of an effort to make an informed decision for consent to medical treatment.[132]

In contemporary medical practice, the concept of informed consent is viewed largely as a mechanism without force. Because healthcare reimbursers commonly require patient medical information in order to process claims, individuals are simply not in a strong position to forego such benefits and therefore have no choice whether to consent to disclose their medical information.[133]

Because medical records reveal healthcare information that may very well impact on decisions about one's access to credit, admission to educational institutions, and employment and insurance opportunities, improper disclosures or even worse, inaccuracies in the information, can form the basis for denial of individual access to these basic necessities of life and can even threaten one's personal and financial well-being.[134]

Increasingly, information from medical records is being reported by health insurance companies to national data banks such as the Massachusetts-based Medical Information Bureau (MIB)—the largest data bank in the country holding information on more than 12 million Americans and Canadians. MIB releases its information upon request from one of its 750 members (mostly life insurance companies). Individuals may contact the bureau in order to determine whether they have a file.[135]

The American Health Information Management Association, an organization of medical record specialists, assists individuals in obtaining copies of their medical records and assuring the information contained therein is accurate.[136] The association recommends six steps be taken in order to limit the release of personal medical information:

1. Always authorize release of medical records in writing and indicate name, address, and date of birth. Since Social Security numbers are so closely tied to financial information, they should be revealed with care and not indiscriminately.

2. A blanket authorization should *never* be signed because such an authorization could authorize release of *all* medical records.

3. Authorization should be limited as much as possible by indicating exactly how much information is to be released. For example, this could be written: "A summary of my treatment for a broken leg on December 30, 1994."

4. A stipulation should be made in writing why the information is being released (e.g., insurance reimbursement, or a second opinion) for such helps to limit future use of the information.

5. State to whom the information should be released and establish a time limit for authorization. Thus, "Release of information to Prudential Insurance, valid only until November 1, 1994."

6. Revoke authorization if it is believed the medical information may be misused. Although some states prohibit revocation in order to avoid payment of healthcare, they otherwise allow a right of revocation at any time.[137]

CONCLUSIONS

Ultimately, the fundamental element of negotiated consent is the recognition and appreciation of the contextual basis of human relationships.[138] The real world political model of multiple interested parties, competing interpretations, conflicting values, and uncertain outcomes must replace the prevailing juridical model of informed consent.[139]

Reality prevents the effective operation of informed consent in that the reciprocally necessary resources and attitudes so vital for informed consent to operate effectively are often absent from both the patient and provider.[140] Caregivers have little in the form of modeling, socialization, scientific training, or paternalistic outlook that would encourage them to assist patients in exercising their rights.[141] Furthermore, the fundamental structural support in the initial and ongoing training and education of medical professionals who must implement the standard of informed consent has not yet been fully provided.[142] Quality of consent is tied to manner of presentation and in the final analysis should be considered of equal, if not greater, importance than initial comprehension.[143]

In projecting the future of healthcare for the elderly, the standard of negotiated consent is undoubtedly a more desirable standard to implement for all parties involved. Despite the assault on its viability, the imperative of negotiated consent focuses ultimately on the concept of "keep listening" as opposed to "keep talking."[144] This goal, even though it is oftentimes difficult to achieve, may provide the elderly patient with a stronger sense of participation in the direction of his or her medical treatment and, hopefully, with a greater sense of trust and confidence and allow the "ethics of intimacy rather than the ethics of strangers [to] take root and flourish."[145]

Chapter 7

Advance Directives

Various estimates show, alternatively, that 9% of Americans have executed advanced health directives (i.e., living wills and durable powers of attorney), whereas less than 4%, or as many as 24% have executed living wills.[1] Other statistics show 70% die without a will.[2] Yet, interestingly, a 1991 Gallup Poll found 74% of Americans actually approved the use of living wills.[3]

Lack of available and verifiable statistics on people who have living wills make it very difficult, indeed, to prove an effect on mortality statistics. Stated otherwise, it is impossible to know if such wills are contributing to an increase in deaths among those age 75 and older. Yet, in Missouri, it has been suggested that living wills have been the cause of a 16% increase in death for citizens in this age group.[4] Perhaps the major reasons why living wills have little impact on the way people are treated at the end of their lives is because living wills often fail to reach physicians, or that, because of lack of education by doctors regarding what the law allows, the wills are disregarded or their directions considered too general and medically unreasonable to be enforced.[5]

According to current opinion polls, most Americans do not wish to be kept alive if their medical conditions offer no hope of any real recovery.[6] A survey of physicians by the American Medical Association found 78% of them agreed that in cases in which a patient is hopelessly ill or irreversibly comatose, life-support mechanisms should be withdrawn if requested by the patient or his or her family.[7]

Do not resuscitate (DNR) orders are one mechanism used to effectuate the wishes of individuals in this regard. The results of two studies of their current use is most revealing as to their effectiveness. In a study of cardiopulmonary arrests that occurred in a hospital, it was discovered that 75% of all patients were allowed to die in those cases where a DNR order had been given. In another study, 39% of all deaths in intensive care units were found to be to have been preceded by DNR orders.[8]

In addition to DNR orders, right-to-die statutes have been enacted. These, together with living wills, medical durable powers of attorney, and advance medical directives, have all been designed to carry out the will of Americans to die with dignity. As will be seen, there remains little, if any, uniformity among the states regarding the standards and procedures for achieving the goal of a dignified death.[9]

A 1994 study of the effectiveness of advance directives as a tool for enhanced physician-patient communication reveals a quite disquieting lack of implementation and a significant lack of discussion dealing with specific medical treatments. The study attributed the stagnant state of affairs to two attitudes: physician discomfort with broaching the topic of end-of-life treatment decisions, which engenders anxiety among patients, and a feeling among the patients that physicians instinctively know what kind of treatment to provide in the event decision-making capacity is lost.[10]

As to the first point, little concrete evidence supports the point that patients feel uncomfortable in discussing such medical matters. This study showed, to the contrary, patient concern about discussions of end-of-life medical treatments and a disappointment when they did not occur.[11] Because the most frequently cited reason given by both patients and physicians for not broaching the topic was simply that "the subject never came up," it may be concluded that physicians are shirking their responsibilities for not initiating discussion of this nature.[12] And, sadly, as to the second reason—medical intuition—empirical studies have provided little support for the patient's confidence that a physician's knowledge of the treatment wishes of their patients will guarantee the "right" decision being carried out at the end.[13] Studies show that, although anywhere from 16 to 55% of patients have discussed among friends or family their preferences for life-sustaining treatment, the discussions are vague and provide little specific information on actual end-of-life treatment preferences.[14]

RIGHT TO REFUSE TREATMENT

In 1990, the United States Supreme Court for the first time tackled the issue of right to die in the case of *Cruzan v. Director, Missouri Department of Health, et. al.*[15] Although the holding here recognized the due process clause of the Constitution's Fourteenth Amendment as the basis for conferring upon incompetent individuals a constitutionally protected liberty interest in refusing unwanted medical treatment (that included nutrition and hydration), the extent to which this liberty interest is exercised consistent with principles of autonomy or self-determination must be balanced against relevant state interests—here, the protection and preservation of human life and the need to guard against potential abuses by surrogate decision makers who may not act in the best interests of protecting the patient.

In those cases of patient incompetency, a refusal of medical treatment must be exercised by a surrogate decision maker. Here, the state is empowered by the equal protection clause of the Fourteenth Amendment to establish rigorous procedures that set a standard of evidentiary proof requiring clear and convincing evidence of whether the incompetent individual wishes a cessation of life-sustaining treatment. The state is not required to grant authority to make this type of decision to any close family members of such patients under a principle of "substituted judgment." The reason for this position is simple and straightforward: namely, no type of real assurance can be given in cases of this nature that the view taken by the family members would be consistent with that taken by the patient if he or she were confronted with a medical situation when competent.[16]

PATIENT SELF-DETERMINATION ACT

As a consequence of the Cruzan case, under the chief sponsorship of Senator John Danforth of Missouri, the Federal Patient Self-Determination Act of 1990 was passed by the Congress.[17] This legislation mandated that every hospital, nursing home, hospice, home health agency and health maintenance organization receiving Medicare and Medicaid funds must provide adult patient/enrollees with a statement of rights under state statutory and decisional law to make healthcare choices, including the right to refuse treatment and to execute an advance directive. The information provided must also outline the healthcare providers' own policies respecting the implementation of patients' wishes. The role of the institutions involved is that of disseminators of information and not of advocates. In this passive role, the opportunity to persuade the patient is limited significantly. This law, then, defers to state powers and, as such, has been considered a "mere procedural prophylactic" providing no substantive patient rights.[18]

Although healthcare providers are not allowed to discriminate against a patient in any way based on either an absence or presence of an advance directive,[19] the fear still persists that this law could be used by physicians to persuade or intimidate "undesirable" patients (e.g., financially disadvantaged, uninsured, old, or mentally disadvantaged) to forego life supports by signing a directive against their will.[20] Some healthcare professionals continue to assert that their ethics require them to oppose the termination of treatment and to do everything to save life. Others realize this simple ethical principle must be qualified because it conflicts with "a very strong and older ethical duty: the duty to relieve pain and accept death. . . ."[21]

In addition to the act's weaknesses, which have been related, three other particular failures must be stated. First, the legislation provides that in those states that have not enacted advance directive legislation, no patient protection is provided. Second, the act fails to address those cases in which patients have not executed advance directives yet find themselves in true emergencies (e.g., automobile accidents, strokes, or heart attacks). Finally, consistent with the deference to state action here, patients that do not qualify as terminally ill under their state statutes are not assured that their advance directives will be honored under this federal legislation.[22]

LIVING WILLS

A so-called "living will" is an instrument that indicates its maker's preference not to be started or maintained on a course of extraordinary treatment (sometimes specific modalities are designated) in the event of accidental or debilitating illness.[23] The biggest uncertainty surrounding living wills and their subsequent administration is whether healthcare providers are required, under pain of civil or criminal sanction, to execute the terms of the will. An interlinking concern is whether those participants charged with fulfilling the terms of the will are assured of immunity from civil or criminal prosecution.[24] Whether a refusal of life-sustaining therapies would constitute a suicide remains largely another vexatious and unresolved issue as yet.[25] Regardless of these points of great uncertainty, some 47 states and the District of Columbia have passed living will legislation.[26]

Those jurisdictions recognizing living wills are faced with addressing the issue of the nature of the medical techniques they will determine to be "extraordinary" and the type of circumstances that will "demonstrate that the person's previously expressed desire to forego treatment continued up to the time immediately prior to his or her disability."[27] Without legislative decisions that address these issues clearly and forthrightly, the courts will be faced to make case-by-case determinations of the parameters of life.[28]

In an effort to correct some of the weaknesses and uncertainties of living will legislation, more and more states are enacting natural death acts.[29] Spurred by California's bold and innovative Natural Death Act, which in 1976 formally established the requirements for a "directive to physicians," other states have begun to follow suit and authorize validly executed instruments relieving a physician, staff, and hospital from civil and criminal liability for removing or withholding life-sustaining treatments.[30] Considerable difference exists among the various legislative programs regarding the assessment of penalties for either disobeying the directive of a properly executed instrument or preventing the transfer of a patient seeking to come within the provisions of the law to another physician who will respect and follow the patient's wishes.[31] The triggering mechanisms of the legislation are often cumbersome and self-defeating. For example, before a patient may seek to benefit from the provisions of California's Natural Death Act, the patient must first receive a diagnosis as being in a terminal condition, which is construed as meaning "an incurable condition with death being imminent regardless of life-sustaining procedures."[32]

In actual practice, evidence suggests that patients' ability to have their wishes regarding the prohibition of life-sustaining treatment honored may be impeded in states where natural death legislation exists.[33] For, if such legislation is viewed by attending physicians and healthcare providers as the sole means for both initiating and implementing a decision to forego treatment and if they maintain that a decision of this nature cannot be made by a surrogate on behalf of another but only in strict accordance with an advance directive that has been executed properly by a patient, dying patients may in fact be subject to treatment the nature of which is neither requested nor beneficial.[34] There is additional fear that an improper inference may be drawn that if a patient has not executed a directive that is in compliance with natural death legislation, he or she does not wish methods of life-sustaining treatment to be ended under any and all circumstances.[35] In truth, examination of most cases would reveal that a directive was not executed because of either ignorance of its existence, an unawareness of its importance, or uncertainty as to how to execute it.[36]

Generally, right to die or natural death acts apply only to "competent adults,"[37] with children and those mentally incompetent being excluded. Yet some jurisdictions have made provision for proxy consent. In North Carolina, the controlling statute allows proxy consent for an irreversibly comatose patient who has not previously executed a living will—with consent being given by a spouse, legal guardian, or a majority of the relatives of the first degree.[38] No reference is made in the statute to any other type of incompetent patient. Virginia legislation does not expressly allude to the rights of patients with inadequate decision-making capacity and refers only to competent patients.[39] In New Mexico, provision is made for proxy consent for minors although not for incompetent adults.[40] Arkansas legislation, however, covers both minors and incompetent adults alike.[41]

DURABLE POWER OF ATTORNEY

As a consequence of the numerous weaknesses encountered with living will legislation and natural death acts, it has been suggested that additional safeguards should be used for implementing advance directions on life-sustaining modalities of treatment. Specifically, adoption of proxy directives through durable powers of attorney statutes would go far toward assuring an individual's desires regarding treatment (or, as the case may be, nontreatment) would be effected.[42] Forty-two states have enacted laws authorizing durable powers of attorney that enable the appointment of a proxy to act after a person becomes incompetent.[43] The language of these statutes is usually broad enough to accommodate the appointment of a surrogate to facilitate problems that involve healthcare for the incompetent, although the statutes were not enacted for remedying these specific problems of incompetence, however.[44]

Because the usual power of attorney, which may be either of general or limited nature, ceases when the principal becomes incapacitated, some states have created specific durable powers of attorney whereby an agent's authority to act is specifically mandated to continue after a debilitating event happens to the principal.[45] In this way, the power may be used as an ''advance proxy directive'' whereby an individual can nominate another whose express duty it will be to make all decisions regarding healthcare in the event the principal becomes incapacitated or otherwise unable to make decisions of that nature.[46] As can be seen, this promotes greatly the efficiency and fairness of the whole decision-making process for incapacitated persons.

As durable power of attorney statutes begin to be adapted and are applied to areas that they were not originally designed to accommodate, care and study must be undertaken to make certain these original procedures—initially enacted to ''avoid the expense of full guardianship or conservatorship proceedings when dealing with small property interests''—are not abused in cases of application to incapacitated patients.[47] At some point in time, procedural safeguards may well have to be designed in order to assure necessary and functional application of the durable powers of attorney. This does not negate their great potential and their already proven success in easing the heavy and emotional burdens of decision making and their added value in allowing the courts to respect individual and familial privacy by not forcing an intrusion into it.[48]

What occurs when the designated agent, in a durable power of attorney, becomes ill, incapacitated, dies, or wishes to resign? Although two states, Alaska and Missouri, allow, legislatively, the agent himself to delegate authority to another individual to succeed the first, two other states, Florida and Georgia, specify the agent's authority cannot be delegated.[49] In order to avoid such difficulties altogether, the principal should name at least one successor agent in the event the primary designee is unable to fulfill the appointment.[50]

GUARDIANSHIPS AND DURABLE POWERS OF APPOINTMENT

Crafted carefully, a durable power of attorney can be an important planning tool to either circumvent or even delay a guardianship. Yet there are reasons, such as unsatisfactory issues of subdelegation as just mentioned, that could easily result in a petition for appointment of a guardian for the principal. Still other reasons prompting a guardianship could include situations in which the agent does not have authority to make certain necessary decisions or take particular actions, the agent abuses authority and must be removed, or other interested parties become dissatisfied with past decisions of the agent and seek removal by appointment of a guardian.[51]

In the overwhelming number of states (43), a durable power of attorney is not terminated automatically by appointment of a guardian; rather, the agent becomes accountable to the guardian. But a few state statutes merely terminate the agency relationship in the power of attorney when a guardianship is created. Because of the possibility of failure with a power of attorney, it may be considered prudent to designate another individual to act as a guardian within the basic durable power of attorney itself.[52]

STATUTORY CLARIFICATION?

In August 1985, the National Conference of Commissioners on Uniform State Laws approved and recommended for enactment in all the states a Uniform Rights of the Terminally Ill Act.[53] This act authorizes adults to execute declarations to their physicians and healthcare facilities directing the withholding or withdrawing of life-sustaining treatment in the event they are in a terminal condition of health and thereby unable to participate in decisions concerning medical treatment. The scope of the act is quite narrow in that it but provides one way for the wishes of a terminally ill person regarding the use of life-sustaining procedures to be fulfilled.

This act is not intended to affect any existing rights and responsibilities of persons to make medical treatment decisions. Furthermore, its provisions are limited to treatment that is merely life prolonging and to those patients whose terminal condition is incurable or irreversible, whose death will soon occur, and who are unable to participate in medical treatment decisions. It does not address issues of the treatment of persons who have not executed a statutory declaration of this nature nor does it pertain to treatment issues for minors nor treatment decisions made by proxy. Although drawing upon the basic structure and substance of similar existing living will legislation, it simplifies procedures, improves the drafting of these wills, and clarifies language such as the terms "life-sustaining treatment" and "terminal condition."[54,55] Legislation of this type that endeavors to clarify terms and concepts in this critical area of concern must be applauded as a positive action. It of course remains to be seen whether the states will view the model as a clarification or an obfuscation.[56]

INCREMENTAL STEPS TOWARD PASSIVE EUTHANASIA

In 1973, the National Conference on Standards for Cardiopulmonary Resuscitation and Emergency Cardiac Care sought to establish a procedure that would allow physicians to indicate further medical treatment was not advantageous to particular patients in their care. Accordingly, the conference suggested that a simple "order not to resuscitate" (ONTR) could be indicated in the progress notes or chart for the distressed patient and, in turn, communicated to the hospital staff.[57] To be distinguished from other forms of medical care that terminate preexisting patient support systems, such as the discontinuance of respirators, ONTR includes instructions not only not to use inotropic or vasopressor drugs that increase cardiac contractility and maintain blood pressure, but to not initiate cardiopulmonary resuscitation.[58] Orders not to resuscitate are often referred to as "no codes" because they normally stipulate no emergency care is to be given when cardiac or respiratory failure occurs.[59]

The inherent problems associated with the 1973 Cardiopulmonary Resuscitation and Emergency Care Conference Report on ONTRs are today as real and complex as they were then. The central issues are determining with reasonable accuracy when an illness is terminal and when continued medical treatment contravenes the best interest of a terminally ill patient and whether using principles of triage, or the efficient and maximum allocation of scarce medical resources—together with quality of life factors—should be evaluated in the deliberative process.[60]

The result of what has been termed, "the growing medicalization of death," is quite simply that human acts of intervention have nearly totally replaced natural processes.[61] Indeed, what with almost daily discoveries of "miracle drugs," the perfection of new surgical routines, and the development of new sophisticated mechanical mechanisms designed to assist or relieve normal bodily processes, illness as such can no longer be thought of as having a natural course of progressive development.[62] Thus, sadly, although heretofore pneumonia had to be regarded as the friend of the elderly ill patients and cardiopulmonary seizure was an almost certain guarantee of death, now frenzied actions of a "code blue trauma team" can be witnessed almost daily in any metropolitan hospital as the team races to, as the case merits, jump-start hearts with electric paddles and drugs and reinflate lungs with artificial pumps.[63] Today, death is no longer a domestic family occurrence; rather it has been moved to a hospital or some type of healthcare institution.[64]

The patient's autonomy or right of self-determination in healthcare issues must always be balanced against the same professional autonomy of a physician. Thus, no force or coercion can be exerted to compel a physician to proceed with treatment for a patient who has rejected resuscitation if that physician considers a provision for patient resuscitation to be an ethical, moral, or professional obligation.[65] An important recognition of this professional autonomy for the physician must be allowed through maintenance of an option to transfer care of the terminal or at-risk patient.[66]

When courts are presented with a typical DNR case, they will normally use a test that balances the patient's qualified right to refuse treatment against two other factors: the prognosis for the patient and the degree to which the DNR order will be invasive to body integrity, with state interest weakening and the individual privacy right strengthening as the prognosis for recovery lessens and the degree of invasiveness increases.[67] Accordingly, in those cases in which invasive treatment such as surgery or dialysis is dictated, the pervasive judicial attitude has been to uphold the patient's right to refuse treatment—even though that might prevent a favorable patient prognosis.[68] The small number of courts that have considered ONTRs have approved them, realizing the highly invasive nature of cardiopulmonary resuscitation.[69]

1976 MASSACHUSETTS GENERAL HOSPITAL
PROTOCOL

In 1976, the Massachusetts General Hospital announced formally—although it had been in effect for 6 months—its protocol "Optimum Care for Hopelessly Ill Patients," which was the first step in the process of determining the level of care given to the critically ill (namely, the classification of their probability of survivability or, salvageability).[70] Consistent with the time-honored principle of triage,[71] four classifications were listed: Class A, in which "maximal therapeutic effort without reservation" will be given; Class B, in which the same level of effort is given, but "with daily evaluation because probability of survival is questionable"; Class C, where "selective limitation of therapeutic measures" is followed (orders not to resuscitate or to withhold antibiotics that would otherwise arrest or cure pneumonia); and Class D, "where all therapy can be discontinued," which would normally apply only to patients suffering brain death or having no chance of regaining "cognitive and sapient" functioning.[72]

A permanent hospital committee on the optimal treatment of the hopelessly ill is in place when professional medical differences of opinion arise regarding treatment of a terminal patient. Thus, although the primary or "responsible physician" has full authority over the treatment of the patient (including the right not to seek the committee's advice at all or to reject it once given), the final authority would appear mitigated by further provisions within the guidelines allowing the director of intensive care to go directly to the chief of service and impanel the committee—regardless of whether the primary physician wishes to pursue this course.[73] It is thought that a physician would have to be particularly foolhardy or, alternatively, courageous, to act against the institutional judgment of his peers—regardless of the decision to treat, withdraw treatment, or withhold treatment.

Institutional efforts of this nature present a model for effective and principled decision making. They also structure a verifiable process for evaluating the costs and benefits of treatment and nontreatment and thereby aid not only the healthcare providers in their decision making, but also the family members or surrogate decision makers who are advised, consulted, or approve the ultimate decision.

THE NEW YORK STUDY: A MODEL FOR THE
OTHER STATES

In April, 1986, the New York State Task Force on Life and the Law issued its study of orders not to resuscitate,[74] and proposed a model legislative scheme— from which in fact grew subsequent legislation—that will not only provide clear and comprehensive guidelines for decision making, but will establish a strong mechanism for arbitration of challenges to decisions of this nature.[75] This legislation embodies a number of major policies that are germane to this issue and that help clarify the medico-legal use of an order not to resuscitate. Thus, an analysis of the legislation, itself, is necessary.

Although affirming the present presumption under existing law that all patients admitted to a hospital consent to cardiopulmonary resuscitation (CPR) in the event of an incident of cardiac or respiratory arrest, the legislation makes provision for consent for the withholding of CPR or the issuance of an order not to resuscitate in all hospitals and residential healthcare facilities in the State of New York.[76] An attending physician must, subject to a narrow therapeutic exception, obtain the consent of a patient with decisional authority before issuing a DNR order.[77] This decision by the patient in a hospital may be either expressed orally or, before or during hospitalization, in writing.[78]

Before the issuance of a DNR order, the attending physician must first obtain the contemporaneous consent of a patient with decisional capacity.[79] If, at the time of the issuance of such an order, the at-risk patient lacks the capacity to forego CPR but had previously stated this wish in writing, the writing will constitute consent to the issuance of the order.[80] Interestingly, and wisely, the legislation recognizes a narrow therapeutic exception that permits a physician to obtain consent to a DNR order from another person on behalf of the patient. This exception is premised on the fact that isolated circumstances may occur in which a patient's capacity might be jeopardized and immediate injury might occur due to an actual discussion about resuscitation.[81] Although injury is not defined, the task force cited two examples of situations in which discussion would be inadvisable: a patient who has an arrhythmia and for whom such a discussion could trigger cardiac arrest and a patient who is in a severe state of paranoid depression or has suicidal tendencies.[82]

Unless it is determined that an adult patient lacks capacity, not competence, to make a decision about resuscitation, the presumption is maintained that every adult is entitled to make a decision about resuscitation.[83] The "competence standard" relates usually to an individual's ability to make all decisions, although the "capacity standard" is tied to an assessment of one's ability to make a specific decision about resuscitation.[84] In those cases where a patient lacks capacity to make a decision of this type or order, the attending physician is required to obtain the necessary consent from a surrogate or substitute decision maker in those cases in which such an individual is willing and competent to speak for the patient.[85] Provision is made for patients with capacity to designate an individual to act on their behalf if they are expected to lack capacity at the time the decision must be made.[86]

One of four medical conditions must be in existence and a written determination made thereof by a physician before a surrogate decision maker may consent to the issuance of a DNR order for a patient lacking capacity.[87] The four conditions are: 1) the patient is terminally ill, 2) the patient is irreversibly comatose or permanently unconscious, 3) resuscitation would be medically futile, and 4) resuscitation would impose an extraordinary burden on the patient in light of the patient's medical condition or the expected outcome of resuscitation.[88] The basis of the surrogate's decision is tied to a determination of the patient's known wishes or religious and moral beliefs. If these wishes or beliefs are either unknown or not ascertainable, then the basis will be the patient's best interests.[89]

In those cases where a patient lacks the capacity to make a DNR decision and a proper surrogate is unavailable, an order not to resuscitate can still be given if one of two conditions are met: 1) a determination is made by two physicians that it would be medically futile to undertake the act, or 2) based on clear and convincing evidence of either the patient's known wishes or in the absence thereof, a finding of the patient's best interests directs the issuance of a court order for a DNR.[90]

The consent to the issuance of a DNR order is narrow and confined only to cardiopulmonary resuscitation; it does not authorize an extension of consent to withhold or withdraw medical treatment.[91] The legislation also sets out a procedure for revoking a DNR order and directs, simply, that the patient make a written or oral declaration ''or by any other act evidencing a specific intent to revoke such consent or assent'' to a physician or to a nurse at the treating hospital.[92] For the surrogate, parent, or legal guardian, a similar procedure for revocation is provided.[93] Once the revocation of consent is obtained, it is to be entered immediately in the patient's chart, and notification should be given to the hospital staff of the revocation and cancellation.[94]

Section 13 of this legislation mandates all hospitals and residential healthcare facilities to establish a dispute mediation system whereby all disagreements arising among the decision makers (i.e., patients, physicians, family members, etc.) participating in the resuscitation decision may be aired. The mediation system allows any party to the controversy to come before it and, at the same time, reserves to all parties the right to seek judicial relief in the event the matter is not resolved. Once a dispute is brought before the mediation service, the issuance of a DNR is stayed automatically for either 72 hours or until the conclusion of the mediation process, whichever occurs first.[95]

Judicial review of actions allowed under the legislation may be sought essentially by either the patient; attending physician; hospital; facility director if the patient was transferred; any personal surrogate; or the parents, noncustodial parent, or legal guardian of a minor patient.[96] Even though provision is made for a required grace period of 72 hours once mediation has begun over a dispute regarding a DNR, the actual patient is not required to observe this period but ''may commence action for relief with respect to any dispute under this article at any time.''[97]

For the physicians and other healthcare providers who comply in good faith with a DNR order or, contrariwise, resuscitate a patient for whom an order has been issued because of their unawareness of the order or because they, in good faith, believed the order has been revoked, provision is made for a grant of civil and criminal immunity.[98] Equal protection from liability is also extended to persons designated to act for the patient who consent or decline to consent in good faith to the issuance of a DNR order.[99] Finally, it is stipulated in the legislation that no life insurance policy will be impaired or invalidated as a consequence of a DNR order nor can any person require or prohibit the issuance of a DNR order as either a condition for being insured or receiving healthcare services.[100]

To date, this proposal is the most balanced and comprehensive effort to both define, strengthen, and stabilize the rights, authority, and protections afforded not only the patient, but the family, surrogate decision makers, and healthcare providers who all participate at one level or other in the issuance of orders not to resuscitate. As such, it provides a vital structure for principle decision making, a blueprint for subsequent state response, and a framework for achieving a national construct for response to this most critical area of contemporary medico-legal concern.

A 1992 study proved the need for a comprehensive approach to resolving ambiguities in policy regarding use of DNRs. The study found that the medical standards used to determine the cut-off points for quantitative and qualitative futility were erratic. One third of the physicians wrote DNR orders for patients who they thought had a 5% or greater chance of survival; others issued orders for patients with a 20% or better chance of resuscitation.[101] Some authorities argue that when no clear medical benefits would result to a patient, issuance of a DNR order does not require a physician to consult with either the patient or the family.[102]

Another serious problem is physicians' uncertainty of their patients' CPR wishes. One report studying the practices of five hospitals with 2,600 patients hospitalized found this misunderstanding not only resulted in the higher use of hospital beds, ventilators, and CPR, but even prolonged dying for those patients preferring not to be given "extraordinary" lifesaving measures but who had failed to specify the medical conditions under which their wishes would be followed.[103] In those cases in which the patient's preference for not being resuscitated was accepted by a physician, estimated hospital costs were $20,527.00 per case, with life-expectancy averaging less than 6 months. Contrariwise, where physician misunderstanding regarding patient wishes not to commence CPR was found or a basic uncertainty about it existed, costs accelerated to more than $26,500.00 per case.[104]

UNRESOLVED QUESTIONS

A number of unresolved questions may be posited regarding the continued development and application of DNRs in healthcare decision making:

    1.   Will new and more effective procedures be developed that will involve patients directly in do not resuscitate orders before they become moribund?

2.   Will medical prognosis advance to such a degree that (at-risk) patients for resuscitation can be indentified with certainty rather than relying on a broad categorical designation of groups of such patients as is done presently?

3.   Because current studies show cancer, not cardiac disease or old age, is the most likely predictor of DNR status, does this represent a danger-point in subsequent efforts that might bias or predispose the issuance of a DNR order?

4.   What should be done to meet the demands of families who insist that all measure of life-sustaining treatment be done for moribund patients, who have never expressed themselves on the issue, when such actions would be futile?

5.   As a consequence of anticipated greater specificity and detail for DNR policies at hospitals, might broader categories of nontreatment decisions become acceptable?

6.   How far should needs to contain the level of health costs through rationing of expensive and scarce interventions be considered in issuing DNR orders?[105]

Chapter 8

Complexities in Treatment and Nontreatment Decisions

The complicated and often competing vectors in nontreatment decisions must be understood and dealt with, and this is surely no simple task in a pluralistic society where a high level of consciousness exists regarding healthcare.[1] The courts can only go as far as the medical profession is willing to go to provide it with an information base for its decision making. Of course, ideally, the judiciary should not even intrude into the doctor-patient or familial sphere of decision making. Perhaps this is too much to expect, given the vast amount of confusion regarding the "science" of orders not to resuscitate. The medical profession has everything to gain from efforts to control itself and define the parameters of its actions here. Its input into legislative proposals, such as the Orders Not to Resuscitate Study of the New York State Task Force on Life and The Law in 1986, are a laudable effort to bring clarity and structure to this area of concern and thereby prevent judicial intrusiveness.

AMERICAN MEDICAL ASSOCIATION GUIDELINES

In 1950, the majority of Americans died at home with their families and local physicians in attendance.[2] Now, as observed earlier, death has become "medicalized" with the result that human interventions replace natural processes and thereby prolong life in one form or other.[3] With a growing array of high-powered life-support techniques and so-called "miracle" drugs, death is but another matter of human choice and one laden with ethical complexities.[4] Of the approximately 5,500 Americans who die each day, 8% do so "wired and incubated, in an institution where the expensive technology is arrayed and controlled by specialists who likely know little about the patient beyond the medical problem."[5] Perhaps in recognition of this phenomena, an early 1985 Louis Harris poll of 1,254 adults disclosed the fact that 85% of them were of the opinion that a terminally ill patient "ought to be able to tell his doctor to let him die"; and 82% supported the notion of withdrawing nasogastric (feeding) tubes if the patient directs such action.[6]

Coincident with the New York state DNR legislation, a national poll sponsored by the American Medical Association (AMA), the results of which were released November 28, 1986, showed that nearly three of four Americans or 73% of the 1,510 respondents in this survey, favor "withdrawing life support systems, including food and water, from hopelessly ill or irreversibly comatose patients if they or their family request it."[7] Fifteen percent of the respondents opposed this option and 12% expressed uncertainty.[8] Interestingly, 70% of those younger than age 65 favored the proposal, as did 64% of those 65 years old or older. Of the older group, 15% said they were unsure compared with 10% of the younger group. The withdrawal of life support systems was more likely to be favored by individual respondents having at least a high school education as well as by those whose annual income was more than $10,000.[9]

On March 15, 1986, the Council on Ethical and Judicial Affairs of the AMA issued Guidelines for Withholding or Withdrawing Life Prolonging Medical Treatment for Terminally Ill or Irreversibly Comatose Patients,[10] which in essence recognizes that ethically a physician may withdraw "all means of life-prolonging medical treatment," including food and water, from patients who are terminally ill or who are in irreversible comas.[11] This policy statement is totally consistent with the conclusion of the President's Commission for the Study of Ethical Problems in Medicine and Biomedical and Behavioral Research that artificial feeding should be regarded as a treatment decision, and not mandated except where the benefits to be gained therefrom outweigh the burdens.[12]

Many individuals choose to make an emotional distinction between respirators and feeding tubes even though both are means of life support for comatose patients.[13] Somehow, an intravenous line is not only more familiar but less intrusive to a number of people than is an artificial respirator.[14] Interestingly, in what no doubt has become the most well-known case involving the withholding of medical treatment, *In re Quinlan*,[15] Karen Ann Quinlan's family maintained a successful legal action to have her artificial respirator disconnected; but they declined to seek judicial approval of a withdrawal of nutritional support from her,[16] and Karen "lived" in a coma for 10 years.

Although it has been suggested that the withdrawal of nutritional support from a terminally ill or irreversibly comatose patient is dangerously close to murder,[17] and that soon guidelines might include the exclusion of "severely senile, the very old and decrepit, and maybe even young, profoundly retarded children,''[18] the AMA statement declares specifically that "the physicians should not intentionally cause death.''[19] Because the Council position is no way binding, physicians who disagree with it are free to follow the dictates of their own conscience.[20]

Dr. Russel H. Patterson, Jr., a past president of the American Association of Neurological Surgeons, suggested that there is "a rather large jump between letting someone die and killing someone.''[21] He continued by stating that withdrawing extraordinary life supports from those who have no hope of ever regaining consciousness is often the most humane treatment available.[22]

> After a while—maybe weeks or months of seeing the patient with no concept of the present, no memory of the past and no hope for the future—a lot of families say, "Why does this have to go on? What's the purpose?"[23]

The AMA policy acknowledges that although the physicians' social commitment is to both sustain life and relieve suffering, these duties may conflict with each other from time to time. When an at-risk patient's informed choice is lacking, or an authorized proxy unavailable, the patient's best interest will be the controlling standard for physician action or inaction.[24] Acting humanely and with informed consent, a physician undertakes what is necessary, from a medical standpoint, to either control severe pain, or cease or limit treatment to the terminally ill who face imminent death; yet the physician should not follow a course of action that intentionally causes death.[25]

In making a decision whether the administration of potentially life-prolonging medical treatment (i.e., "medication and artificially or technologically supplied respiration, nutrition, or hydration") comports with the incompetent patient's best interests, the physician is required to make a determination of what possibility exists for extending life under both humane and comfortable conditions. The physician is, furthermore, required to ascertain the patient's previously expressed wishes and the familial attitudes of others who have custodial responsibility for the patient.[26]

> Even if death is not imminent but a patient's coma is beyond doubt irreversible and there are adequate safeguards to confirm the accuracy of the diagnosis and with the concurrence of those who have responsibility for the care of the patient, it is not unethical to discontinue all means of life prolonging medical treatment. . . . In treating a terminally ill or irreversibly comatose patient, the physician should determine whether the benefits of treatment outweigh its burdens. At all times, the dignity of the patient should be maintained.[27]

PAST PRACTICES

At a Yale–New Haven Hospital symposium entitled "Ethical Issues in Health Care" held in June, 1982, Dr. Paul B. Besson, the editor of the *Journal of the*

American Geriatrics Society, cautioned that there was a growing tendency in hospitals through the country to place a "no-code" order on the hospital charts of a growing number of elderly patients.[28] Several years before Dr. Besson revealed his findings, a study of the records of nine convalescent centers (i.e., nursing and retirement homes) approved by the federal Medicare program in Seattle, Washington, and of the 1,256 persons admitted to these facilities in 1973 for a 2-year period, revealed some rather startling statistics.[29]

Over the period of the study, 190 patients developed a high or continuing fever at some time or had an impairment of their central nervous system (e.g., stroke, aphasia, paralysis, senility, dementia, chronic or organic brain syndrome, or cerebral atheroarteriosclerosis). Active treatment, i.e., the use of antibiotics or hospitalization or both, was ordered for only 109 patients. No such treatment was ordered or administered for 81 patients, or more than 40%. Of those treated, 9% died; and of those untreated, 59% died. The authors of the study conclude that this obvious pattern of nontreatment suggests strongly that the physicians and nurses at these medical facilities studied did not intend to treat their patients actively when high mortality was expected.[30] It was determined that the lives of the untreated patients could have been prolonged for a short time if antibiotics had been administered or hospitalization followed.[31] The general conclusions of this study regarding the selective nontreatment of terminally ill complements other surveys of health professionals favorably disposed toward withdrawing or withholding life-prolonging treatment—with as many as 30% favoring euthanasia under certain prescribed conditions.[32]

In 1979, the Veterans Administration, which administers the largest hospital system in the nation with 1.2 million annual patient admissions, prohibited no-code or do not resuscitate orders being entered in a patient's medical chart.[33] In late August, 1983, the Administration promulgated a new policy that, by recognizing a patient's right to die, allows no-code decisions to be written in a patient's chart.[34] Decisions of this nature must be made by a senior physician with the permission of the patient. When the patient is not adjudged legally competent to make the decision, the consent of the family is necessary before it may be entered on the hospital records.[35] Although the policy prohibits the use of no-code order in those cases where a patient requests "voluntary euthanasia," and forbids physicians to "take any affirmative steps to 'hasten the patient on his/her way,'" in actuality this is a validation of a policy of passive euthanasia or letting the patient die.[36] Application of the 1979 Veterans Administration Policy meant, simply, that if a physician had decided to respect the request or right of a patient to forego futile life-saving therapy, this decision could not be entered formally in the patient's hospital chart. Accordingly, in cases where such a patient suffered cardiac arrest and his or her understanding physician was not on duty, resuscitation would normally be undertaken against the patient's wishes.

The new AMA policy incorporates an obvious quality of life standard of evaluation and it does so by utilizing the best interests of the patient test and mandating a cost-benefit analysis that in turn admixes principles of salvageability or triage.[37] Basic social justice demands each individual be given an opportunity to maximize individual potential. Yet a point is often reached where maintenance of an individual defies all concepts not only of social justice, but of basic humanitarianism. When an individual's medical condition is such that it represents a negation of any "truly human" qualities or "relational potential," then the best and most equitable form of treatment should be arguably no treatment at all.[38] In the final analysis, common sense and common decency should be the touchstones for decision making.

These policies of the American Medical Association[39] and the Veterans Administration[40] regarding the prolongation of medical treatment or what could be recognized as the right to die humanely and with dignity, coupled with the public medical record of actual occurrences of selective nontreatment of terminally ill,[41] bear witness to the fact that intelligent healthcare providers are exercising common sense, common decency, love, and compassion in their actions.[42] They are not bridled by complicated and obtuse distinctions between ordinary and extraordinary treatment standards, acts of commission and omission, and a plethora of philosophical concerns over slippery slopes. Rather, they act courageously and forthrightly and are motivated by the age-old command to do no harm and thereby serve the best interests of their patients.[43]

OTHER PROFESSIONAL POSTURES

In 1983, the President's Commission for the Study of Ethical Problems in Medicine and Biomedical and Behavioral Research concluded that artificial feeding should be regarded as a treatment decision and not mandated except when the benefits of its use outweigh the burdens.[44] And, as mentioned previously, the AMA's Council on Ethical and Judicial Affairs announced its conclusion in 1986 that all means of life-prolonging treatment, including food as well as water, could be withdrawn from a patient who is in either an irreversible state or a terminal condition.[45]

The position of the Roman Catholic Church on the use of nutrition and fluids and the operative standard it follows where this issue is raised is that under some exceptional circumstances the means of providing nourishment may be such that it should not be regarded as obligatory owing to the ineffective or burdensome nature of the act itself.[46] Thus, the withholding of nutrition and hydration does not have as its purpose the hastening of death but rather the cessation of a life from which the patient can derive no benefit because of a futile or terminal condition.[47] With one exception, prominent Catholic theologians are of one mind: nutrition and fluids need not always "be provided to all patients, including the terminally ill."[48]

Even though a judicially determined order to withdraw life-sustaining treatment would, as a consequence of these three major policy clarifications, contain no affront in any form whatsoever to the integrity of the corporate hospital wherein the terminal patient might be or to the particular medical community providing treatment, it may nonetheless be viewed by some health providers as an intolerable compromise or invasion of their own personal professional rights as physicians and nurses to use their skills in an actual effort to promote death.[49] For medical professionals who have that belief, the only option should be for the dying patient to be transferred to another hospital willing to cease all artificial life supports and coordinate as dignified a death as possible.[50] When transfers are not feasible because of costs or unavailable beds in other hospitals just for "dying," the issue becomes whether the care of a dying patient can be undertaken at home. Because of an unmistakable perception of pain, due to the marked change of appearance of a patient who is being withdrawn from fluids and nutrition, coping with at-home care can be difficult to manage or even sustain.[51] Thus, an apparently simple decision to withdraw treatment, which deserves to be respected, is in reality very complex, difficult to implement, and affects more than just the dying patient.

An artful act of self-deception has been used in the past to deal with this issue and continues being used today.[52] Namely, intravenous feeding of a critically ill patient is continued but at a diminished rate that, over time, will result in dehydration. Thus, both the gesture, and the equally important symbol of feeding is maintained, but at a rate that will not really sustain the patient's life for any period of time. Considered a "compromise" by those who wish desperately to hold to symbolic acts yet show some modicum of respect for the patient's direct wishes or perceived needs under a substituted judgment test or best interests to cease such treatment, this procedure is but a blatant act of self deception,

> . . . because an agent can carry it out only by failing to acknowledge that the patient will become malnourished and dehydrated while the IV line maintains the fiction and expresses the symbol of feeding. Otherwise the agent would have to take responsibility for the outcome. . . .[53]

The central question confronting the courts in regard to this issue is whether corporate hospitals should be mandated to provide a level of service for their patients that is both ethical from a professional standpoint and lawful.[54] The modern hospital must be recognized, institutionally, as a center where whatever standard of care and treatment can be provided and relief of pain can be sought in the last rite of passage.[55] Ideally, health laws should support both medical and nursing care that complements the patients' wishes and advances their best interests.

> The coincidence of autonomy and appropriate health care is very clearly present when a competent judgment or substitute judgment is made allowing a patient to spend his or her final brief moments of life in the health care setting that has been humanely treating and caring for the patient.[56]

When conscious awareness is lost and not capable of being reestablished and all aspects of comfortable existence are removed as well, actions that omit nourishment by tubes are not subterfuges for euthanasia, but merely good medicine.[57]

The Hastings Center Guidelines

In issuing its guidelines entitled *The Termination of Life Sustaining Treatment and the Care of the Dying*, in 1987, the prestigious Hastings Center of New York sought to set a new tone of acceptance and understanding of this area of concern. Consistent with the then newly enacted do not resuscitate order legislation in New York state,[58] the guidelines structure an ethical framework for analyzing problem cases involving long-term life-supporting technology, ventilators and dialysis,[59] emergency interventions (e.g., cardiopulmonary resuscitation),[60] nutrition and hydration of terminal patients,[61] antibiotics and other life-sustaining medication,[62] and palliative care and pain relief.[63]

Central to any efforts of problem-solving is an understanding, and thus an application, of four central values: 1) that the goal of medicine is always to promote the patient's well being or welfare, 2) a recognition of patient autonomy or self-determination that demands recognition of the right of the patient to determine the nature of his or her own medical care, 3) a realization that the integrity of healthcare professionals must be guaranteed by thus recognizing the stringent ethical obligations that physicians, nurses, and other healthcare providers have to their patients, 4) and a need to realize the importance of the value of justice or equity in critical decisions of termination of treatment; in other words, the individual patient has a right to an adequate level of healthcare as well as to the distribution of available healthcare resources.[64]

Cost-Worthy Treatment Decisions

Equally important in decision making was the issue of costworthiness. It was determined quite directly that treatment that is wasteful, useless, or harmful is simply not costworthy.[65] More specifically, it was found that

> [a]n ethics that aims to provide cost worthy care cannot assume that any medical intervention that offers some benefit, no matter how marginal, should be provided regardless of its cost to others. Such an ethic must ask whether treatment that is marginally beneficial is cost worthy in light of some satisfactory balance between benefit to the individual patient and alternative uses of these resources.[66]

These policy statements will be of indispensable value to healthcare professionals and other decision makers who are called upon to make the ultimate treatment decisions. These policies should also be of considerable value to legislatures who must act responsibly in designing frameworks, hopefully along the lines of the New York do not resuscitate model, and to the courts when they are called upon to interpret legislation of this design.

Handicapped Newborns and Incompetent Adults

The Final Rule of the Department of Health and Human Services promulgated on April 15, 1985, entitled "Child Abuse and Neglect Prevention and Treatment Program," is an effort to formulate a specific set of regulations regarding the medical treatment of severely handicapped newborns in state hospitals that receive federal grant assistance.[67] In order to ensure little latitude for medical judgement, the withholding of medically indicated treatment (including "appropriate nutrition, hydration, and medication") is only allowed under three circumstances: when the infant is either chronically and irreversibly comatose, and "the treatment would merely prolong dying" and "not be effective in ameliorating or correcting all of the infant's life-threatening conditions, or otherwise be futile in terms of the survival of the infant and the treatment itself under such circumstances would be inhumane."[68]

Even though severely handicapped infants are unable to express preferences regarding a continuation or discontinuation of their lives, their incapacity should not mandate a course of medical therapy designed toward some degree of salvageability even though these actions prolong "life" (or, at least a semblance of it) at the cost of significant suffering.[69] "Where treatment has a high probability of causing significant pain and suffering and a low probability of preserving a life valuable to the patient, should we not permit a decision to withhold it?"[70]

The question to be raised in light of this government policy for handicapped newborns is whether a standard of aggressive treatment should in fact be implemented and thereby enforced for all incapacitated (e.g., incompetent) patients unless it is shown that death would occur in the near future or, alternatively, the patient is irreversibly comatose?[71] For elderly senile patients with advanced colon cancer, the issue is whether it is always in their best interest to receive chemotherapy or radiation therapy to the point that survival becomes unlikely.

> Should the severely debilitated (but not comatose) stroke victim be resuscitated an indefinite number of times until respiration cannot be restored by any means? There comes a point at which further prolongation of one's life simply does not make up for the burden of continued aggressive treatment, especially if the quality of life prolonged is diminished by suffering and incapacity. If it would be cruel to prolong the life of adult patients under these circumstances, then it must also be cruel to prolong the life of handicapped infants under comparable circumstances.[72]

Although inhumane or cruel treatment is a serious consideration, the need to find healthcare resources to fund the needs of those receiving life-prolonging treatments is the other very practical aim. Cost-benefit analysis becomes a valid consideration in rationing scarce medical resources.[73]

The distinction drawn between defective newborns and critically ill adults is most alarming. Somehow feelings run much higher and are made within a vortex of high emotionalism when they are concerned with infants as opposed to adults and the elderly. Perhaps this is, in part, because aspirations are higher for the young than the old. In any event, treatment decisions for both groups should be made when cost-benefit analysis reveals that costs of treatment outweigh the long-run benefits and best interests of the patient and are thus unreasonable.[74]

LEGAL PERSPECTIVE: IS THERE A RIGHT TO REFUSE TREATMENT?

The preservation (or sanctity) of life was, and still is, an important state interest; for common law has always held life is sacred and, thus, has prohibited a person from either committing suicide or permitting his or her own destruction.[75] This general prohibition was equally applicable to those who were hopelessly ill as to those in good health.[76] A number of early cases likened a patient's refusal of life-saving treatment to suicide and, accordingly, the state's interests in preserving the sanctity of life weighed against a patient's right to die with dignity.[77] More recent cases have tended to ignore the suicide analogy,[78] and some have failed to mention the state's interest in the sanctity of life at all.[79] The analogy to suicide is wholly inappropriate because suicide is an act that has normally signified in popular perception a person who regards his or her life as worthless, whereas the decision to decline life-saving medical measures is a choice involving death that does not express an opinion that life is worthless. Indeed, to decline treatment does not imply a rejection of life any more than other behavior that involves high risks to life and health. Similarly, the right to decline treatment does not imply a right to commit suicide.[80]

In addition to the state interest in the sanctity of life, the state also, as a corollary, has a basic interest in preserving life, preventing suicide, protecting incompetents and third-party defendants, and the preservation of the medical profession's integrity.[81] Thus, in validating or invalidating a right to die by refusing to sustain medical treatment, the courts will balance the individual rights of self-determination or autonomy against these state interests in forbidding a refusal of treatment. The nuances of this balancing test must be based on the facts of each case, for no unyielding *a priori* standard can be set and applied in an equally unyielding manner. Common sense and reasonable judgments are all that can be expected or actually made in tragic cases of this nature.[82]

The most significant state interest in this issue is the preservation of life and what is, indeed, determined to be life is crucial to the assertion or maintenance by the state of its interest. The state will always act to prevent "irrational self-destruction."[83] The central question becomes, then, are there appropriately structured guidelines available to test the very rationality of decision making? What may seem reasonable to legally competent but suffering patients may seem irrational to their attending physicians. Sadly, the determination of a patient's right to die is tied essentially to a judgment call and inextricably to the facts of each medical situation.

Case precedent does, however, recognize that if compelled treatment will be brief and painful or extend life only as a consequence of great bodily intrusion, the "rationality" of original decision making by the patient will be given greater presumptive validity and at the same time the state interest in preserving life will be minimized.[84] Contrariwise, it could be maintained that a right to life exists in cases in which medical treatment preserves life itself, rather than merely seeking to prolong it,[85] produces little pain and suffering, and constitutes no significant bodily intrusion.[86]

CONCLUSIONS

For the terminally ill patient, the qualitative value of sustained life should not be an issue of great moment; rather, it should be merely conceded that the dying processes should not be prolonged unduly.[87] For the nonterminal but chronically ill, retarded, debilitated, or comatose patient, the state interest in preserving life is maintained if for no other reason than to protect such individuals from being eliminated, either by themselves when suffering from depression or under the direction of physicians who need hospital bed space or families who can no longer bear the social and economic costs of maintaining their lives.[88]

Of course, such valid tests as "the best interest of the patient," and "the substituted judgment test" allow a court to inquire into the lengths to which state action should be allowed to force a continuation of life in a terminal state. The length of one's life expectancy before it becomes diagnosed affirmatively as terminal is a vexatious issue. Would an individual suffering from AIDS with an expected minimum of 6 years to live be recognized as nonterminal and, as such, be forced to live on by the state?[89] It has been suggested that the closer one's "life expectancy is to zero, the more the condition becomes 'terminal' and the patient's interests" more determinative.[90]

Although there is thought to be a well-structured right of all competent people to refuse medical treatment based on any reason of their choice, a coordinate right to avoid being declared incompetent as a consequence of that refusal is only now beginning to be recognized.[91] Indeed, the United States Supreme Court has not made a definitive ruling that guarantees a constitutional right of a competent individual to forego a modality of medical treatment calculated to save his or her life.[92] Thus, care must be taken to recognize and deal separately with the related issues of whether other individuals are empowered to determine when and if life supports are not necessary in order to maintain continued existence.[93] Several prominent state jurisdictions have litigated the issue of the right of competent individuals to refuse treatment and concluded such a qualified right does exist.[94]

The validation of a qualified right to die,[95] when made, is derived from several theories: from the common law "right to bodily integrity,"[96] from a so-called penumbra "right to privacy" found by some courts in the Constitution,[97] from the first amendment right of "free exercise of religion,"[98] and to an increasing extent, from state natural death legislation.[99] The right to refuse medical treatment and thus die has been recognized as a "newly created constitutional right of personal autonomy."[100] There seems to be a growing notion that a refusal of treatment decision should be as informed as the initiating consent to it[101]; set within the context of a critically ill person's decision-making background, the doctrine of informed refusal is, indeed, an inherent part of the doctrine of informed consent.[102]

Chapter 9

Nursing Home Industry

A nursing home is not only a place to convalesce after a hospital stay, but one where an aged friend or relative may be sent because home care is not a viable option and, alternatively, a place where either loving and efficient care is provided or where residents are abused as well as exploited.[1] Sadly, the nursing home has traditionally assumed the symbol of the "zero point" of common life where modern culture finds no shared meaning in the experience of advancing age and, instead, becomes but a place where "bed and body" work is done.[2]

In the past, three kinds of nursing home facilities provided various levels of medical care and general physical care: the skilled nursing facility (SNF), the intermediate care facility (ICF), and the board and care home.[3] An SNF provided the greatest degree of medical care for the elderly without hospitalization. It provided skilled nursing care and related medical services in addition to rehabilitation services. A physician and a nurse were required to be there 24 hours a day.[4] An ICF provided a lesser degree of medical care for individuals not needing hospitalization nor requiring the medical care of an SNF, yet needing to be institutionalized. A nurse was present 8 hours a day, 7 days a week.[5] The previous distinction between an SNF and an ICF was eliminated by the Omnibus Budget Reconciliation of 1987 with the result that today all nursing facilities have a registered nurse on duty 8 hours a day, 7 days a week, and a licensed nurse on duty at all times.[6] The third type of facility for the elderly, which still exists today, is the personal care or "board and care home" (also called custodial care or domiciliary care facility). These facilities provide only rudimentary medical care with room, board, and some assistance in personal hygiene.[7]

AN EXPANDING ENTERPRISE

The nursing home industry will experience significant expansion as it parallels the growth of America's aging population. As observed in the Introduction and Chapter 1, various estimates predict that as many as 40% of all elderly Americans will be admitted to a nursing home during their lives, at any given time, and that upwards of 6% will be forced to reside in such a facility.[8] Rather than caring for acutely ill patients, nursing homes typically provide care for patients with chronic illnesses,[9] with the average elderly American having 3.5 chronic diseases and confined, according to an early study by the Institute of Medicine, for a minimum of at least 18 months.[10]

An evolutional process characterizes the nursing home industry as it assumes a greater role in delivering healthcare services. In response to the significant increase in consumer demand, rapid expansion and development is taking place throughout the nursing home industry. Thus, the traditional role of nursing homes serving as boarding houses for the elderly, while providing little or no medical care, has evolved into a high-profit business.[11] Nearly three quarters of all nursing homes are operated for profit by private firms, with 20% owned by nonprofit voluntary organizations and only 5% owned by the government.[12]

The appeal of nursing homes as a positive investment source is multifaceted. In addition to the perpetually growing market, nursing homes involve relatively low start-up costs and reasonable staff education costs.[13] Unfortunately, operating nursing homes as a source for quick profits often occurs at the psychological, medical, and financial expense of the patient.[14]

TYPICAL STRUCTURE AND OPERATION OF A NURSING HOME

As is common in most corporate operations, the nursing home staff is often divided into several departments. Generally an administration department is responsible for bookkeeping and payroll matters, along with departments responsible for housekeeping, dietary services, nursing, social services and rehabilitation, and staff training.[15] Within each department is a department head who reports directly to the nursing home administrator.[16]

The most common issues of concern to nursing homes are nursing care, housekeeping, and administration. The role of the registered nurse in most nursing homes is that of a supervisor, as the actual patient care is usually rendered by nonprofessional nurses' aides. Typically, the turnover rate each year of those staff members providing direct patient care is 70%–100%.[17]

QUALITY OF CARE IN NURSING HOMES:
ROLE OF MARKET FORCES

Although there exists no precise definition of "quality care" in nursing homes, it is generally agreed that the quality of care should be defined in terms of caregiving procedures and their outcomes.[18] Thus, given that a majority of nursing homes are profit-motivated institutions, competition in the marketplace would theoretically assure a relatively high standard of care among nursing homes. Competition, however, does not seem to control the nursing home market. Although selection of a facility is based, in part, on location, affiliation, reputation, and cost, the selection process is in no way dominated by such market controlling factors.[19] Indeed, unlike many service-oriented, profit-motivated institutions, nursing homes seem to have a unique hold over their market and need not cater to the high consumer demands for quality.

Several reasons exist for the unique market power possessed by the nursing home industry. Nursing homes are usually filled to capacity. In fact, occupancy rates in most metropolitan areas are well over 90%, with some areas facing occupancy rates of nearly 100%. Thus, given such a high product demand, there is a tendency for nursing homes to operate in a monopolistic fashion. This monopoly-type power stems, in part, from a desire by patients and their families to locate nursing homes within close proximity to friends and relatives. Furthermore, the limited number of available institutions within any given area fosters a waitlisting process for admissions whereby a patient's choice is ultimately restricted to the institution that will most readily admit the patient.[20] Cost is rarely a factor in selecting a nursing home because over 50% of all nursing home bills are paid by Medicaid.[21] As such, an institution has neither an incentive to hold down costs, nor a demand to increase quality and make the institution cost effective.[22] Finally, selecting a nursing home must often be done in an emergency situation, thereby precluding the opportunity for patients and their families to comparison shop. Patients in dire need of nursing home care are often compelled to choose a facility rather than remove themselves from the market until a more favorable choice becomes available.

Even if the opportunity to shop comparatively is available to a patient, once the selection of a nursing home is made, a patient rarely moves to a different institution. Indeed, despite low-quality or inferior care, such a patient could be harmed further by a sudden change in environment.[23] Moreover, given the scarcity of available information on nursing homes, the process of comparison shopping within the nursing home industry is itself a difficult endeavor.[24]

Accordingly, the significant constraints on consumer choice limit the power of the market to effect quality. The actual patients have very few, if any, objective evaluations of an institution's quality of service. Further exacerbating this problem is the difficulty in agreeing upon a list of objective criteria by which to rank the quality of care provided in nursing homes.

CASE MANAGEMENT

Case management is an emerging healthcare system in which a nurse is made responsible for an individual patient's care across an episode of illness. As such, the case manager handles assessment and prescription, delegation to coworkers, and collaboration with attending physicians as well as other relevant healthcare professionals. The central interlinking concepts to the various models of case management are standardization, efficiency, continuity of care, and interdisciplinary collaboration.[25] If this system is to be successful, nurses must better understand—through improved communications—the preferences of individual nursing home residents or hospital patients, for all too often nurses are the pivotal link in conveying this important information to the physicians.[26]

Case managers may also follow a model that finds them working for social agencies—whose administrative rules may either enhance or limit seriously the manager's responsibility to respect patient autonomy, act beneficently, and be just.[27] Presently, case managers are responsible for making important decisions affecting the lives of the frail, elderly, and disabled within and without the nursing home environment. They must seek to balance beneficence and respect for autonomy with the often multiple and complex interests of their patient/clients and their families.[28] Yet, when a final decision must be made to transfer a nursing home patient to a hospital, for example, this decision—which itself should be made in the nursing home environment in a timely manner—must be reserved for a physician or mid-level practitioner who is familiar with the patient's clinical condition.[29] Obviously, the case manager can, and will, have an important advisory role in the decision-making process at that point.

Case management can be used, furthermore, as an effective tool to lessen, if not prevent, a growing legal crisis within the judicial system; for, as seen, the case manager works with primary care providers to develop a plan for providing vulnerable individuals with appropriate services and monitoring their delivery. Attendant care services can, for example, be used to avoid the need for institutionalization and more serious judicial interventions—determinations of incompetency and civil commitments based on dangerousness to self or grave disability. And, as important, home healthcare services can be used effectively to avoid placing the elderly in nursing homes, thus avoiding yet another judicial intervention, the guardianship petitions resulting as a consequence of nursing homes seeking appointment of a surrogate decision maker for the vulnerable resident.[30]

COST OF CARE INDEX

A mechanism for assessing the potential and actual consequences of caring for an elderly person by informal care providers called the cost of care index (CCI) has been developed. As a case management tool, it has been structured with 27 items to measure six dimensions related to the "costs" of providing care to dependent elderly persons: social disruptions, personal restrictions, economics costs, value for care provision, care recipient as provocateur, and psychosomatic consequences. The index has been found, as used limitedly, to be of value for professionals in their decision making, family screening, peer group interaction, and counseling endeavors.[31]

LONG-TERM CARE AND COSTS

Long-term care may be defined broadly as those services provided to chronically disabled persons, many of whom are elderly, that are considered necessary for their health and general well-being. These services not only include congregate living arrangements with supportive personal care and homemaking assistance (e.g., home healthcare, visiting companions, delivered meals, transportation, and shopping assistance) but a wide variety of other services necessary to help maintain a standard of qualitative life and ease the day-to-day burdens of family care providers as well as, finally, nursing home care. Either a duly licensed agency or other licensed healthcare provider or a network of close friends and neighbors—together with the family itself—are responsible for the delivery of these far-reaching services.[32]

Typically, in the past, one's life course followed a simple and stable cycle that included full or productive employment up to a period of time when acute illness occurred, followed by sudden decline and then death. Previously, families assumed the full responsibility for the care of their elders during their final illnesses. Currently, care for the very elderly may extend not only for a period of years, but even decades—thus exhausting the ability of adult children to provide for the care of their parents and meet their own responsibilities of raising their children and maintaining a livelihood.[33]

One recent study suggests that excessive high-technology care for the elderly person in the last year of life may be, in fact, much less of a problem than the overall long-term care needs of the disabled elderly person in need of chronic support care. The study found, more specifically, that when the calendar year before the year of death was counted for the older old (85 +) decedents they appear to be neither more or less costly than persons who die at younger ages. The conclusion to be drawn here is that the costs for older decedents in end-stage illnesses should be viewed more as a function of aging and related disabilities than of medical interventions associated with final illnesses before death.[34]

According to a 1990 survey conducted by the Daniel Yankelovic Group for the American Association of Retired Persons, it was found that Americans are willing to pay $50 a month in premiums per household over their lifetimes for a good long-term nursing home insurance policy. More concern was registered for nursing home insurance than about insurance for the costs of home care. Interestingly, although the survey respondents (1,490 in all) expressed their willingness to pay the $50 monthly premium, that willingness was based on policy coverage for everyone in society, if it protected an individual for life, and if it included nursing home protection for the entire first 2 years in a nursing home.[35]

NURSING HOME PLACEMENT

The decision to place an individual in a nursing home is, essentially, an irrevocable act because rehabilitation and discharge are unlikely. Thus, this one decision has considerable ethical consequences. Both with voluntary and involuntary placement comes a kind of stigma akin to recognizing a moral failure—drawn as such from analogous acts of removal from society for mental incompetents through a civil commitment proceeding and for convicts. Prison inmates and those confined to mental institutions are stigmatized on both moral and social grounds; historically they were viewed as threats to society, with their incarceration a legitimate defense to the maintenance of social order.[36]

Entering a nursing home not only signals a transition from one moral status to another, but often a catastrophic defeat for the admittee or, alternatively, as a welcome relief to the family. No public declaration is made here, however, as with mental incompetents or public offenders. Rather, "an invisible change of state" or status occurs.[37] Nursing homes are a common source of societal antipathy, then, not so much because of the residents themselves, but because of the residents' absence of a future; in truth, they are seen as "our future selves."[38]

An admission to a nursing home results from a physician's recommendation, usually because hospitalization has occurred immediately before the placement and left the patient with little frame of reference to make a choice. The placement decision about long-term care has likely been formulated over time through a complex process of family communications involving elements of consensus, conflict, and negotiation,[39] based on the inability of the family or friends to provide necessary care.[40]

Rejecting placement in a nursing home should not be taken as *prima facie* evidence of diminished mental capacity. As with medical treatment, however, it is a refusal—more than an acceptance—that triggers questions about mental capacity.[41] In either case, evidence should be presented that shows any individual considering admission has a general appreciation of the attendant losses, benefits and risks of the consequences of the decision, as well as the particular style and form of life available in the particular nursing home. Accordingly, an insistence might be made

> that the patient not be *permitted* to make the irrevocable decision to enter a nursing home unless evidence was presented the applicant had such an understanding. This is an example of paternalistic intervention aiming to maximize long-run autonomy and ensure that a specific decision reflects an individualized concept of the good, not simply "weakness of will" or acquiescing to pressures and stresses of the moment.[42]

This approach would incorporate a modified version of paternalism shaped by a concern for personal integrity and maximal autonomy.

TRANSFER AND DISCHARGE

The three permissible grounds for transfer or discharge of residents recognized by the federal regulations governing nursing homes are medical reasons, the welfare of the resident or other residents, and nonpayment of expenses.[43] All too frequently, admission contracts either omit totally any enumeration of the reasons for transfer or discharge or, when listed, are found to be in conflict with state or federal standards.[44]

Typically, improper discharge provisions will be placed within various clauses setting forth unacceptable conduct to the nursing home. For example, one such clause that not only exceeds permissible grounds, but restricts the resident's right to refuse treatment was found to state: "Failure of the patient to accept and to pay for special nursing care when deemed necessary and proper by the home shall be sufficient reason for immediate removal."[45]

Whereas in the past only "reasonable notice" of involuntary transfer of discharge was required, in most cases now, a 30-day notice is required and stringent due process safeguards guaranteed.[46] A specific notice period is required by many states. Proper admission contracts should conform to relevant federal and state rules, but these contracts frequently omit reference to an advance notice time period or state a notice provision of shorter duration than permitted by the governing regulations.[47]

If an attorney, in reviewing an admission contract, finds questionable provisions that abridge the rights of a potential resident, namely, the client, one of three courses of action may be followed. First, the attorney may accept the lack of real bargaining power in nursing home preadmissions and perhaps try to approach the administrator as to the particular issues of concern with a view toward conciliation or negotiation. Second, the attorney may go on record with the nursing home regarding the alleged illegalities that could conceivably cause them to defer enforcement of the challenged policies because of the fear of subsequent bad publicity and legal action. The third choice is to file a complaint with either the state long-term care ombudsman or the state agency responsible for licensing and certification of nursing homes (normally the state health department) or both. Because the responsibility for enforcing state and federal nursing home standards rests with the designated licensing and certification agency, that agency will take corrective actions if violations are established.[48]

HOSPICE CARE

Hospice care is, quite simply, a multidisciplinary approach or comprehensive program of management that affords an opportunity to render palliative care for terminally ill patients with malignant disease who are beyond the possibility of cure.[49] During the Middle Ages, hospices were inns located at crossroads where travelers could receive food and shelter during their pilgrimages, usually to the Holy Land. In the 17th century, Vincent de Paul and the Sisters of Charity, working in France, established hospices for the poor and the sick. In the late 1800s, the Sister of Charity in Dublin, Ireland, created a shelter for the specific care of the incurably ill; then, in 1906, they expanded their facilities in London, England.[50] In the modern era, the hospice program was led and developed by Cicely Saunders and her establishment in 1967 of St. Christopher's Hospice in Syndenham, England. Hospice care, as an actualized concept, spread rapidly throughout England where it was provided almost always in free-standing units separate from hospitals.[51]

In the United States today, regulation of standards, review of the quality of hospice care, and evaluation of new hospice programs is coordinated primarily by the National Hospice Organization and the Joint Commission on Accreditation of Healthcare Organization. A growing number of states legislatures have set specific licensure requirements for hospices as well.[52]

Throughout the United States, hospices take various forms of organization with the three most common being home care only, free-standing hospice units, usually with a provision for home care, and hospital-based programs, again, usually with a provision for home care. Under this third type may be found either a discrete unit within a hospital or an indiscrete one. In the second subcategory, "swing beds" centralized on one nursing unit are used for hospice patients or a "scatter bed" approach is used throughout the entire hospital itself, with interdisciplinary teams operating throughout. Another organizational variation is to be seen in free-standing hospice units that are affiliated with a hospital. Here, the physical facility for terminal care is outside the hospital, yet the program is to one degree or other coordinated with in-hospital care.[53]

Conceptually, all hospice systems direct their efforts toward not only the alleviation and control of physical pain, but to levels of psychological, social, and spiritual pain as well. Thus, interdisciplinary teams are used to coordinate not only patient response but family (real or extended) as well. Indeed, family members, together with the dying patient, are regarded as the unit of care in the hospice system. This coordination involves not only the planning of death but the care phases of the dying process including round-the-clock medical and nursing services.[54]

Yet another alternative growing in popularity is dying at home. Under this plan, the terminal patient is surrounded by a loving and concerned family assisted, to the degree desired, by professional home care services (e.g., visiting nurses). Home care, although certainly less expensive than conventional hospital or hospice care, has the primary role of uniting the family in its common grief and penetrating the fear of death itself; or, in other words, coping with it.[55]

Healthcare professionals should never use the hospice as a convenient dumping ground in order to avoid the plethora of legal, ethical, and clinical problems encountered normally in caring for the terminally ill in hospital or nursing home settings. Indeed, caregivers should be aware that there are several potential legal implications to hospice management. Specifically, in terms of issues of informed consent and acceptable standards of care, hospice professionals bear the very same sorts of potential legal liability as they would with any other system of healthcare delivery. Additionally, hospice organizations are being forced to encounter the same issues that other institutional healthcare providers have for years: namely, health planning requirements (and certificates of need), licensure, accreditation, and fiscal reimbursement.[56] The last point is particularly vexatious because there is a cap on Medicare-certified hospice payments of $6,500 and an equally burdensome Medicare certification regulation requiring a hospice not to discontinue or diminish care provided to an individual because of inability to pay.[57] Accordingly, when patients exhaust their Medicare hospice coverage, the hospice must nonetheless continue to provide the same intensity of service.[58] The hospice election periods are limited to two 90-day periods and one 30-day period and must be used in that order.[59] Once hospice care is elected, the Medicare beneficiary is deemed to have waived most other Medicare benefits.[60]

Although the hospice system is now recognized as a permanent part of the Medicare reimbursement system, growth in Medicare-certified hospice programs is expected to remain low. This conclusion results from the fact that the requirements for certification simply do not offer any real economic incentive for hospice programs to fulfill the burdensome responsibility associated with the paperwork necessary to receive payments that, of economic necessity, will invariably fall short of covering actual costs of services.[61]

COMPLEX ETHICAL ISSUES

No doubt the central most ethical issue confronted within the hospice construct is the right of an individual to refuse curative treatment and seek a noble, controlled death. This basic right will be explored more fully in later chapters. Suffice it to note that in its 1983 Report on Deciding to Forego Life-Sustaining Treatment, the President's Commission for the Study of Ethical Problems in Medicine and Biomedical and Behavioral Research acknowledged the competent, informed patient's right to decide about his or her healthcare encompasses the decision to forego treatment and to allow death to occur.

For the incompetent terminal patient or one with diminished decision-making capacity, those most knowledgeable of the patient's ideals, lifestyle, and attitudes, or previously designated surrogate decision makers must seek to determine what the patient would have chosen, if competent, or what would be in the best interests of the patient. Judicial case determinations and legislative enactments will present a framework for principled decision making in attempting to resolve these issues for both the competent and the incompetent.[62]

Two related ethical issues are raised within the administration of hospice care: drug addiction and euthanasia. Drug addiction is a rather whimsical concern for a terminal patient seeking relief from pain.[63] Because the principal worry in cases of drug addiction is the consequences of ending such therapeutic treatment, this surely cannot have any validity here simply because the hospice patient remains on the therapy until death (which normally occurs within a short period of time).[64]

The ethical distinction between hospice care and euthanasia may be seen clearly in the following analysis:

> To fail to provide for the dying is to fail in a basic duty. The self-evident requirements of a dying man are to have symptoms relieved and to be allowed to die with dignity and peace of mind. If we evade all the difficult problems he presents, and just kill him, we have failed. Whether euthanasia were voluntary or not is irrelevant. It is our duty so to care for these patients that they never ask for euthanasia. A patient who is longing to die is not being treated properly.[65]

Although it must be realized and appreciated that the very best hospice care will not make every death either beautiful or easy, it must also be understood that the atmosphere of dying is surely made more acceptable or at least tolerable with hospice care.[66]

The foremost question confronting hospice caregivers should always be: "How can I help this person live the most fully during the days he or she has remaining," not "How can this person live as long as possible in the lowest risk situation at any personal cost or burden?" Thus, the focus is kept on the patient's quality of life as perceived by the patient, not on the possible amount of days he or she has remaining.[67]

Chapter 10

Ethical and Legal Rights of Long-Term Care Residents

Market forces are not the only factors affecting the quality of care provided by nursing homes. The more important medical and social obligations to the patient in providing the highest possible quality of care should far outweigh any profit-seeking motive. Nursing home care is expected to emphasize without compromise the amelioration of pain, suffering, disease, illness, injury, and handicap, while providing satisfactory living conditions, fostering relationships with family and friends, creating a sense of community, and supporting patient autonomy.[1] The difficulty arises in that, unlike economic factors, moral and ethical obligations are neither objectively identifiable nor measurable.

A PATIENT'S BILL OF RIGHTS

Through the Omnibus Budget Reconciliation Act of 1987 (OBRA '87), enacted December 22, 1987, which became effective October 1, 1990,[2] Congress sought to enact major changes in the regulation of long-term healthcare in the United States with the goal being "to use every reasonable means possible, both in terms of physical . . . medical, mental and psychological environment . . . to maintain or improve the well-being of each resident [in long-term care facilities]."[3] To achieve this end, the Secretary of Health and Human Services is authorized under the law to enter into individual agreements with each state to ensure that facilities are meeting stated Federal requirements for operation and certification.[4]

A very significant change in OBRA '87 was a codification of the rights of residents of long-term care facilities into a so-called "Bill of Rights,"[5] which follows:

1. The right to free choice regarding medical treatment
2. The right to be free from restraints
3. The right to privacy
4. The right to confidentiality
5. The right to the accommodation of needs of residents
6. The right to voice grievances
7. The right to participate in residential and family groups
8. The right to participate in other activities
9. The right of residents to examine state survey results of facilities
10. The right to refuse certain transfers within facilities
11. Any other rights established by the Secretary of Health and Human Services.[6]

Under the requirements of this legislature, facilities must ensure that residents are aware of these rights upon admission to the facility. Essentially, then, the bill provides nursing home residents with authority to make decisions and choices concerning their own lives and requires the recognition on the part of caregivers of a resident's power of self-determination and independence.

As a consequence of the codification of these patients' rights, advocacy of them on behalf of long-term care patients has taken a new, positive direction. In fact, patient-rights advocates have come into their own and are defined as those individuals who, representing patients, act to ensure that their enumerated rights incorporated into state or institutional "Patient Bills of Rights," are exercised and protected. Their primary goal "is to enhance the patient's position in making decisions, not to encourage the patient to follow facility routine or to 'behave.' "[7]

OBRA '87 also contains many other important requirements. Under the amendments, facilities are required to prepare written plans of care for all residents in their charge.[8] Furthermore, the law requires them to prepare annual comprehensive assessments on each resident.[9] These assessments must be reviewed every 3 months in order to ensure that quality care is maintained over an extended period of time.[10] The law also requires each state to play a role in adopting uniform instruments to be used in preparing these assessments.[11] Other important changes include a new provision that addresses the use of nurses aides in the long-term care facilities.[12] Because of their cost efficiency, these aides are the predominant frontline healthcare providers. They give a wide variety of care and service to the residents and, most importantly, serve as facilitators of communication and as "first lieutenants" in recognizing life-threatening situations and responding to them efficiently.[13] It is significant that the OBRA '87 amendment requires the states to adopt training programs for nurses aides and requires all aides to complete the training program in order to be certified to work in long-term care facilities.[14] This again works toward maintaining a level of quality assurance in the delivery of healthcare service to the elderly in these facilities and is a positive step toward the national goal of improving the well-being of every individual in long-term facilities.

At the state level, concern over the denial of fundamental rights to nursing home residents was the impetus for state legislatures to enact statutes granting specific rights, including those that 1) support self-determination and autonomy in patients' day-to-day lives, 2) provide for proper medical treatment, and 3) support continued placement in the nursing home.[15] Regardless of the specific nature of rights enumerated by the various state statutes, most state residents' rights statutes emphasize that the rights set forth are not exhaustive and represent only minimum guidelines for nursing home compliance.[16]

Nearly all state statutes, as well as the federal statute, contain a provision granting nursing home residents the right to be free from mental and physician abuse and from chemical and physical restraints.[17] The important consideration, however, is the ineffectiveness of a mere grant of such rights. The granting to nursing home residents of such rights must be coupled with enforcement mechanisms. Moreover, such rights confer concurrent responsibility upon nursing home management and staff and residents.[18] Thus, both parties must recognize that the residents' bill imposes behavioral obligations upon them. Management and staff must acknowledge the obligations generated by resident bills (i.e., the regulation of management and staff action or inaction), rather than viewing resident bills as merely enumerating obligations for the nursing home resident.[19] In turn, residents must recognize the responsibilities bestowed upon them with such bills.[20] Only through such a cooperative relationship can the moral and ethical obligations of the nursing home industry be fostered, thereby regulating the negative impact of market forces within the nursing home industry.

DECREASED DISABILITY AND NURSING HOME ADMISSIONS

Statistics released by the Census Bureau in 1993 showed a slower than expected increase nationally in nursing home populations during the 1980s.[21] This has lessened the pervasive fear confronting many Americans that as a consequence of growing old they may lose their minds and be "put away in a nursing home."[22] Research studies have found that fewer elderly Americans are suffering from those kinds of disabilities that in the past usually consigned them to nursing homes. Healthier life styles and advancing medical technologies that promote recovery from strokes, broken hips, and other traumas associated with old age, all combine to limit nursing home admissions. Other expanded levels of service that allow older Americans to forestall, if not prevent totally, residence in a nursing home include home healthcare, graduated care facilities, and assisted-living apartments.[23] Improving levels of education allow people to become more aware and, thus, informed on healthcare issues, with the result that they seek out those services that allow them to prevent nursing home admittance altogether and to remain physically active as well.[24]

Even with the improved statistical profile for lowered rates of disability, the nation is ill-prepared for the impending shock wave that will be recorded when the baby boom generation reaches old age. The dean of the School of Gerontology at the University of Southern California put it very simply: "If we don't make them healthier, we're going to need millions more nursing home beds."[25]

IMPACT OF ABUSIVE CARE ON THE ELDERLY

Elder Abuse and Neglect: Historical and Sociological Background

The trend of abuse and neglect of elder citizens in western nations is considered a relatively recent phenomenon. Primarily responsible for this disheartening trend is the fading of the traditional family concept of "a harmonious multigenerational unit that relied on mutual generosity and sympathy and was characterized by veneration of elders."[26]

In the years before 1800, there was a significant tendency toward preserving the independence of elderly citizens. In England, for example, 80% of all persons 60 years of age or older headed their own households. Indeed, elders were quite capable of supporting themselves, and little reliance was placed upon the multigenerational household to care for the aging population.[27] The economic demands of industrialization also blurred traditional age roles within the family setting. Maintaining a family's economic vitality depended on the productive contribution of all family members, regardless of age. Thus, cooperation within the family obfuscated distinctions between life phases. It was not until the 20th century that distinct separations among generations became apparent, thereby weakening traditional family unity. Childhood and old age have become two distinct life periods. Factors such as mandatory retirement for workers when they reach a certain age and government entitlement programs that address age-related needs have contributed further to societal acceptance of distinct life stages.[28]

This marked delineation of life phases has also resulted in changed socio-psychological relations among the generations. Younger adults are more focused on concerns involving their own lives than with obligations to and relations with their older relatives. Elders requiring care thus foster a sense of ageism or unfavorable attitudes toward older persons. When coupled with the advancement of available medical technology that continues to increase life expectancy, this growing population of elders becomes increasingly susceptible to physical and psychological abuse.[29]

Incidence and Prevalence of Elder Abuse

Obtaining accurate incidence and prevalence figures for abuse of elders is difficult. Victims and perpetrators commonly deny the occurrence of abuse. The
victim of abuse is often overwhelmed by the abusive situation and may be too
embarrassed by the potential ignominy to acknowledge that abuse is taking place,
hesitant to report acts of aggression committed by caretakers on whom the elder
victim relies, or simply uninformed as to where to find assistance.[30] Furthermore,
complaints of abuse are often minimized by health professionals. Health professionals often lessen the significance of elder abuse complaints either because of
disbelief, fear of accusing the perpetrator, or because of a lack of awareness
regarding the extent of the abuse problem.

Although broad categories of elder abuse have been identified, namely,
physical abuse,[31] psychological abuse,[32] and financial or material abuse,[33] there
exists a lack of uniformity among the definitions for each category. As a result,
deficiencies plague the identification of abuse types and victims. Nevertheless,
estimates indicate that approximately 10% of Americans over 65 years of age
are exposed to some type of abuse. Of that figure, approximately 4% are suspected of being victims of moderate to severe abuse. Thus, one in every 25
elderly Americans may be the victim of such abuse, an increase of approximately
100,000 abuse cases annually since 1981.[34] Nationally, reports of elderly abuse
rose 62% between 1988 and 1991.[35]

Despite the failure to reveal the precise causes of elder abuse through systematic, scientific investigations,[36] hypotheses exist regarding the reasons for
elder abuse. A majority of experts believe family problems to be a major factor
in perpetrating elder abuse. Such factors as a lack of close family ties, family
violence, lack of financial resources, psychopathology in the abuser, and lack of
community support all contribute toward abuse in an institutional setting. The
complex health problems faced by elderly Americans also influence the occurrence of abuse. Physiological and metabolic changes, a higher incidence of
disease, an increased prevalence of chronic illnesses, severe functional disabilities, and a higher incidence of multiple health problems all serve as contributing
causes of elder abuse.[37]

Research has also indicated that elder abuse does not occur in isolation, but
rather, elder abuse is a recurring epidemic in up to 80% of cases.[38] Victims of
elder abuse typically have at least one physical or mental impairment requiring
care by others. Furthermore, elder abuse occurs irrespective of race, ethnic, or
socioeconomic background.[39]

CONCERNS ABOUT NURSING HOME CARE

Sanitation Concerns

Despite the moral and ethical obligations owed to patients that should heavily
influence the nursing home industry, the lack of a competitive market and the

availability of substantial profits ultimately prevail as predominant factors shaping some nursing home operations. Though it should not be said that occurrences of abuse pervade every nursing home, it should be acknowledged that this is a concern in some cases. A 93-volume report by the Health Care Financing Commission disclosed abominable conditions pervading the nursing home industry.[40] The report revealed, for instance, that 33% of skilled nursing homes in Michigan failed to serve patients' lavatory needs.[41] Sixty-two percent of Alabama nursing homes failed to handle food under sanitary conditions.[42] In 21% of all nursing homes, procedures for preventing the spread of infections were found inappropriate.[43] These deficiencies also lead to deaths. Fourteen residents of California nursing homes died in 1992 because of abusive treatment.[44]

Use of Physical and Chemical Restraints

The problems in some nursing homes extend beyond sanitation concerns. Routine use of chemical and physical restraints unrelated to diagnosis and treatment considerations has also been identified as a prevailing problem within the nursing home industry. Surveys of people taking care of nursing home residents in the Northeast reveal that 1 in 10 admitted to physically abusing a resident in the previous year. The abuse being alluded to ranged from excessive restraints on elders to striking them with objects. A third of those surveyed admitted to having witnessed physical abuse of nursing home residents.[45] On any given day, nearly 500,000 older Americans are physically restrained to their beds and chairs, resulting in an estimated 25 to 85% of all nursing home residents facing daily physical restraints.[46]

Restraints are ostensibly used as a means of protecting a patient with physical or mental disabilities from avoidable injury caused by falling or wandering away from a nursing care facility. Restraints may also be used to protect residents from injury by other violent patients.[47] Thus, the fear of liability on the part of nursing homes is offered as justification for the use of restraints on their elderly patients.[48] Although this may be valid in some cases, research has yet to provide any empirical data suggesting either a reduction in injury or an improvement in behavior as a result of using restraints on patients.[49] In fact, the risk of using restraints on elderly patients is significant. Restraints can lead to physical dangers such as strangulation and to medical ailments caused by immobility and increased agitation.[50] Furthermore, restraints can lead to misdiagnoses because of assumptions that restraints are causing symptomatic behaviors or because the restraints are masking of symptoms.[51]

Forced Psychotropic Medication:
The Current Dilemma

There are additional causes for concern beyond the practice of restraining patients. It is estimated that anywhere from 20 to 50% of nursing home patients are given drugs—ostensibly to control such behavior as aggression, verbal abusiveness, and wandering. In *Davis v. Hubbard*,[52] the United States District Court for the Northern District of Ohio set forth the issues and arguments relied upon by later courts in grappling with the issue of patient consent before administering medication in state mental hospitals. The *Davis* court ruled that the state did not have unlimited power to administer psychotropic medication to all persons confined in institutions for the mentally ill.[53] In *Davis*, the plaintiffs maintained that a state must obtain informed consent of the patient before administering psychotropic drugs.[54] In response, the state asserted that it is wholly within the realm of its power to medicate all persons who are mentally ill and confined to an institution.[55] In support of this contention, the state maintained that pursuant to its police power, a state may prevent patients from harming themselves or others within a hospital. In addition, the state argued that it is accorded the power for compulsory treatment under the state's *parens patriae* powers.[56]

The court concluded that as a constitutional minimum, the state must have probable cause to believe that the patient is presently violent and constitutes a danger to the patient or others, before the state may administer drugs over the patient's objections.[57] Furthermore, the court rejected the state's argument that its *parens patriae* power enables the state to drug all mentally ill persons confined to an institution. In fact, the court held that mental illness is no basis for compelled treatment.[58] Thus, according to the court, no legitimate state interest justified the state's administration of psychotropic drugs absent the informed consent of the competent patient unless the patient presents a danger to himself or others in the institution.[59]

Rennie v. Klein[60] represents a further clarification of the *Davis* opinion. Essentially, the court's ruling accorded patients a qualified right to refuse treatment, thereby requiring some level of procedural due process before being forcibly administered psychotropic drugs.[61] On subsequent appeal, the United States Court of Appeals for the Third Circuit agreed that a plaintiff does have a liberty interest that is infringed by compulsory medication.[62] The court asserted that "liberty interests may spring from the Constitution itself and can be recognized without regard to state law."[63] Furthermore, the court held that even in the case of involuntary civil commitment of a patient, a "patient retains a residuum of liberty that would be infringed by compulsory medication without complying with minimum requirements of due process."[64]

Rennie v. Klein returned to the United States Court of Appeals for the Third Circuit on remand from the Supreme Court[65] with instructions for a decision to be reached pursuant to a newly espoused "professional judgment" standard articulated by the Supreme Court in *Romeo v. Youngberg*.[66] Under this standard, a court's role is simply to make certain that professional judgment was exercised by the staff at an institution.[67] Nevertheless, even with the newly espoused Supreme Court standard, the Third Circuit reached the same result as it had in its initial disposition of the *Klein* case.[68] The Third Circuit held that psychotropic drugs may be constitutionally administered to involuntarily committed mentally ill patients whenever, in the exercise of professional judgment, such an action is deemed necessary to prevent patients from endangering themselves or others.[69]

A noticeable dichotomy exists between decisions based on state laws and constitutions, and cases yielding to due process protections found in the Fourteenth Amendment of the Constitution of United States. Generally, the former provide greater protection for a patient's interest to be free from forced medications as compared to the latter.[70] In *re Orr*[71] exemplifies the divergent approaches of state and federal authority. In *Orr*, the Appellate Court of Illinois held that an involuntarily admitted patient may refuse medication unless, under the *parens patriae* doctrine, he or she has been adjudicated incompetent in a separate proceeding.[72] The court relied on Illinois statutory law and noted that the *parens patriae* doctrine was inapplicable in this instance because the patient had not been adjudicated incompetent under the state probate act.[73] Furthermore, mere involuntary committal does not imply a lack of competency under Illinois law. The court looked to common law and constitutional theories to support its decision that the trial court exceeded its statutory authority in issuing an order authorizing the state to forcibly medicate the plaintiff.[74]

The problem of elder abuse inflicted through the forced administration of psychotropic drugs is perhaps best addressed in a report in the *Archives of Internal Medicine* that suggests that nursing homes *need not give* heavy doses of drugs to their residents.[75] The report suggests that alternatives to the use of antipsychotic drugs, such as behavioral techniques, should be implemented as a means for influencing resident conduct.[76] A study of 60 nursing homes in eight western states found that 50% of tranquilizers were not medically justified.[77] A separate study found that 60% of New Jersey nursing homes fail to follow properly prescribed drug dosage and use.[78]

Lifting Restraints

Before the passage in 1987 of the Federal Omnibus Budget Reconstruction Act, restraints were used on about 40% of all nursing home residents.[79] Since 1992, however, strict new regulations, a growing apprehension within the medical community of lawsuits for illegal restraints (e.g., assault, battery, and false imprisonment),and a reevaluation of the need to "protect" the residents from themselves and others have combined to reduce the use of restraint to about 22% at nursing homes nationally.[80] Although restraints were originally thought to provide a safer environment for all within the nursing home atmosphere, in most cases the opposite was true—with serious physical injuries and significant psychological trauma resulting from the restraints. Current OBRA guidelines allow use of restraints only when they are ordered by a physician "to ensure the physical safety of the resident, or other residents" and are specific in terms of circumstances and duration.[81]

Working toward a national goal of lowering the use of restraints to or under 5% of nursing home residents should parallel the effort being made to reduce pharmacological restraints. Defined as the regular use of a neurolytic, anxiolytic, or sedative-hypnotic agents to control behavior, these types of restraint were, according to 1992 statistics, used for anywhere from 11 to 58% of nursing home residents. The same reports state that chemical restraints were reported to have been used on about 32% of the 1.5 million residents of nursing homes in the United States.[82]

At one fourth of the 158 Veterans hospitals, patient wandering is a significant problem. Yet even with high-risk patients who include the physically impaired or mentally disoriented, it is suggested they be monitored closely through direct staff observations or electronic detection devices, or both, rather than by the imposition of restraints.[83]

Additional Abusive Factors

Reports also indicate that residents of nursing homes are often prohibited from leaving the nursing home grounds. Increasing nursing home staff could help this situation because more time could be given to the pursuit of a quality lifestyle for nursing home residents. Conversations within nursing homes are generally limited to topics involving aches and pains, death, and food. Furthermore, in some circumstances, many residents have very little to do during the day and simply try to pass the time.[84]

The prevalence of elder abuse within the nursing home industry is attributable in large part to economic factors. Low pay and poor working conditions, along with long hours and bureaucratic red tape, contribute to the prevalence of abuse within the institutional setting. In addition, in order to cut costs, institutions may provide residents food in lesser quantity and of poorer nutritional value. Finally, when these factors are coupled with the often pessimistic attitudes of formal caretakers that their patients will inevitably die despite their efforts to help them, there develops a certain callousness whereby denial becomes the primary psychological defense against a situation otherwise perceived as hopeless.[85]

Solutions to the Problem of Elder Abuse in Nursing Homes

Perhaps the most significant difficulty in addressing abuse and neglect of the elderly in the United States is the subconscious unwillingness to acknowledge even the existence of something so "alien to the American ideal."[86] As a result, a lack of understanding and limited available information represent barriers in resolving elder abuse. Nevertheless, viable proposals exist that can allow for substantial progress to be made in eradicating the prevalence of elder abuse.

ETHICS OF AUTONOMY IN LONG-TERM CARE

Perhaps the foremost ethical and moral question to be found with nursing home issues is what can and ought to be done to arrange care in these facilities that advances more respect for the personal autonomy of the residents.[87] As described in Chapter 5, competency is an inextricable given in determining autonomy; if a person is incapable of making an informed deliberation, that person cannot be recognized as one capable of acting autonomously. Yet competency, in itself, does not promote autonomy because in order for one to act autonomously, one must not only have an ability to think, deliberate, and choose but an opportunity to make choices.[88] For nursing home residents, autonomy may be recognized only to the degree to which healthcare providers at the home, as well as families and administrators, create and manage conditions that promote autonomous actions.[89]

Defects of vision, hearing, and speech, and cognitive impairment are quite common in nursing homes and effect, obviously, the degree to which communication can be maintained between resident and staff. This diminishes the extent to which autonomy may be recognized and granted even under the best of circumstances. One 1987 study found that 63% of nursing home residents suffered from dementia or memory impairments and 47% had either senile dementia or organic brain damage.[90]

Inherent conflicts within nursing home environments arise when the staff is committed to values that are different from those guiding the lives of residents. Yet, the core values of justice, fairness, and dignity rise to the level of ethical conflicts only in direct proportion to the degree to which autonomy is not shaped and enhanced within the nursing environment by the staff itself.[91] For the nursing home resident, practical autonomy means simply having sufficient information to exercise a choice of opportunities and ability to live with the results of such decisions.[92] Yet providing opportunities for more freedom of choice often brings more risks to safety. Thus, if more freedom to move about is provided, it can be expected that there will be more fractured hips and more residents who may wander off and become lost.[93]

Although the three enemies to autonomy for the elderly in long-term care in nursing homes are routine, regulation, and restricted opportunity,[94] in actuality, these are complemented by the most recurrent or dominant complaint of scarcity.[95] Indeed, problems of autonomy are essentially complaints of "not enough."[96] More specifically, complaints focus on the scarcity of single rooms, which promote privacy; a prized chair in the dayroom; displacement of some residents when other family events are scheduled in the residence; regimented mealtime, dressing, grooming and toileting schedules due to limited staff; unresponsive service (especially night calls not being answered promptly); lack of facilities for privacy where one may talk with a mate, friend, physcian, or attorney; and unfairness in allocating the most desirable spaces within the residence (e.g., most truculent residents obtaining preferred areas).[97]

In order to promote actions within nursing home environments that advance options for personal autonomy, absolute rules should be displaced by procedural mechanisms that advance procedural equity among all residents. Similarly, care should be taken not to restructure every incident within the nursing home as a healthcare decision—thus often depriving authoritatively, as such, participation by the resident in seeking a resolution to the difficulty. A fairer allocation of nursing home resources (e.g., rooms), together with a more participatory climate for routine decision making, would advance a positive climate for shared responsibility and thereby avoid the need for legislative, administrative, or judicial oversight.[98] The major challenge for long-term care settings within nursing home environments is to strive for and design a practical way of balancing the altruistic goals of autonomy or self-determination (together with all the personal vagaries associated therewith) for the residents with the very pragmatic needs of the nursing facilities to be protected legally within the confines of their staffing and resources and, at the same time, the public desire for an efficient and coherent system of regulating the facilities themselves.[99]

LONG-TERM CARE OMBUDSMAN

Older Americans Act of 1965

Passage of the Social Security Act in 1935 marked the onset of major national legislative action designed to address the status and conditions of America's older citizens. Since this first legislative act, Congress has enacted in piecemeal fashion over 50 programs designed to assist elderly citizens.

In order to combat the effects of their piecemeal approach of legislating elderly issues and to better organize and deliver social services to older citizens, Congress, in 1965, approved the Older Americans Act.[100] The objectives of the act were to improve the lives of the elderly in all areas, ranging from income, housing, and health, to long-term care and transportation.[101] Title II of the act established the Administration on Aging, a U.S. Department of Health and Human Services agency responsible for elder advocacy and coordinating federal agencies that have programs benefiting the elderly. In addition, the Administration on Aging serves as the government's chief advocate for the elderly and as the fund allocation and granting agency for programs authorized under the Older Americans Act.[102]

Under the act, each state has a unit on aging. The state is then divided into a number of smaller planning and service areas, each coordinated by an area agency on aging. Upon these area agencies falls the responsibility for planning services and coordinating the delivery of services for older persons. Generally, the provision of such social services, including transportation, nutrition, employment, case management, counseling, and legal services, is contracted out to local providers.[103]

The state units or agencies receive the act's federal funds from the Administration on Aging. In turn, the state agencies pass along the funds to area agencies on aging. The money is then allocated according to annually developed area plans. Supervision of the state and area agencies is performed by individual advisory councils, typically composed of elderly members.[104]

Relevant Amendments

In an effort to address public concerns over abuse and substandard conditions in nursing homes and to improve the quality of care for residents of long-term care facilities, Congress amended the Older Americans Act in 1978, 1987, and 1991. The 1978 Congressional amendments mandated the establishment of a long-term care ombudsman program in every state. The amendments directed each state to "establish and operate, either directly, or by contract or other arrangement with any public agency or other appropriate private non-profit organization" an ombudsman program.[105] The programs are funded by formula grants to the individual states.[106]

The 1987 amendments contained no significant changes to the law. Congress did, however, expand certain service provisions to address the new and emerging needs of the older population. In particular, the 1987 amendments sought to provide for persons at risk of abuse, neglect, or exploitation. The amendments required states to address a variety of activities, including providing public education on elder abuse, procedures for reporting such cases, and the coordination of the state agency on aging program with state and local adult protective service activities.[107] Along with the requirements of the amendments was a special funding trigger, which precluded the allocation of funds under the program until total appropriations for programs funded in fiscal year 1987 exceeded the previous year's level by a minimum of 5%. As such, although the program did bring the issue of elder abuse to the forefront, the program was not funded until 1991.[108]

The 1991 Older Americans Act Reauthorization Amendments (OAARA) were a further attempt at addressing the issue of elder abuse. In short, the OAARA reauthorized and amended the act through fiscal year 1995. The amendments eliminated the funding trigger put in place by the 1987 amendments and appropriated the largest amount of funds to date for the purpose of assisting states in combating elder abuse.[109] The bill provides for minimum allotments to states and United States territories that have small populations aged 60 and older and also ensures that states that received funding through the 1991 appropriation will receive funds at least equal to their 1991 allotments over the course of the succeeding 4 years.

Role of the Ombudsman

In its most rudimentary definition, an ombudsman can be defined as a patient advocate: someone who works to make the lives of long-term care facility residents better.[110] More specifically, an ombudsman is a "government official appointed to receive and investigate complaints made by individuals against abuses or capricious acts of public officials'' and ''one who investigates reported complaints from consumers and helps to achieve equitable settlements.''[111] Although the typical ombudsman remains impartial in his or her investigations, the nursing home ombudsman serves as an active advocate for the elderly. As such, an ombudsman is charged with the protection of both the rights and the welfare of nursing home residents. Thus, the ombudsman must resolve the tension between the ''legal'' and the ''social'' welfare perspectives of elderly Americans in nursing homes.[112]

An additional role of the ombudsman is to attempt to resolve problems of long-term care facility patients by recommending to the proper agencies, committees and boards changes in the system to benefit institutionalized residents. The amendments to the Older Americans Act mandate that the ombudsman have access to the residents of long-term care facilities and to the residents' records. Furthermore, the ombudsman must protect confidentiality, in order to limit retaliatory acts by a facility against whom the ombudsman received information.[113]

Because the federal mandate requiring a long-term care ombudsman program is not highly specific, noticeable diversity exists among the various state ombudsman programs. Each state has designed its own program, which vary based on the amount of funding, the statutory role, and political factors. Disproportional federal funding seems to be a major roadblock to program consistency. The equation currently implemented by the federal government requires a distribution of funds in accordance with the number of persons in a state that have reached the age of 60, rather than the number of persons actually provided with nursing home care.[114] The formula leads to severely underfunded programs in some states, whereas other states have overfunded programs because the number of elderly citizens does not proportionally correlate to nursing home care needs.[115] Thus, based on the amount of funding a state receives, substate programs may be limited and the state programs may be compelled to seek volunteers rather than highly qualified professionals. In essence, states receiving greater funding per nursing home bed are able to provide additional services, and ensure a higher quality of services provided, in comparison to states lacking adequate funding.

There are also advantages to the individual state programs. A great deal of flexibility is created by a lack of homogeneity among state programs. Individual state programs are better able to address concerns unique to their elderly populations. Furthermore, successful programs adopted by one state are readily shared with other states, saving costly studies or experimentation. Each state has the freedom to expand or contract a given program in response to changes in demand among the elderly.

New Jersey Paradigm

The ombudsman program implemented in New Jersey perhaps best demonstrates the positive impact of establishing unique state programs. In 1957, New Jersey became the first state to establish an office devoted solely to the needs of the elderly—the New Jersey Division on Aging. In 1976, the New Jersey Legislature enacted an "Act concerning the responsibilities of nursing homes and the rights of nursing home residents" in an effort to ameliorate the harsh conditions faced by elderly nursing home residents. The act imposed certain minimal requirements on providers of nursing home care, such as limits on the number of residents a nursing home may accept, and delineated certain rights for residents, including the right to privacy and the right not to be deprived of any constitutional, civil, or legal right solely by reason of entering a nursing home.[116] In 1978, New Jersey established the New Jersey Office of the Ombudsman for the Institutionalized Elderly to further protect the state's elderly long-term care residents. Pursuant to further amendments, New Jersey established a reporting requirement obligating all persons, who as a result of information obtained in the course of their employment, reasonably suspect or believe that an institutionalized elderly person is being or has been abused or exploited to report such information to the office of the ombudsman. Furthermore, New Jersey enacted penalties for the failure to report such incidences. Under this amendment, the office of the ombudsman is officially charged with the responsibility of guarding against the abuse of elderly nursing home residents.[117]

The ombudsman becomes actively involved with the welfare of an abused elder upon receiving notice of possible abuse occurring at an institution. First, the ombudsman conducts a prompt and thorough investigation, which includes a "visit with an elderly person and consultation with others who have knowledge of the particular case."[118] Under the broad investigatory powers granted to the ombudsman, the ombudsman may make whatever inquiries thought necessary; hold public and private hearings; inspect premises, books, records, and files of the facilities and government agencies; subpoena witnesses; and compel the production of records and other evidence. Moreover, the ombudsman has the authority to hire any professionals necessary to assist in the investigation.[119] Once verified, a complaint is either passed along to the appropriate licensing entity, such as the state department of health, or referred to the legal staff for additional investigation and possible legal action. The ombudsman also has the authority to contact the county prosecutor later if criminal abuse is suspected and the ombudsman may institute actions for injunctive relief or civil damages.[120]

New Jersey is one of four states that has chosen to place its ombudsman office under the auspices of an independent state agency. The result has been beneficial in that the New Jersey ombudsman program has been strictly limited to investigations, unlike other state programs in which the ombudsman office is also responsible for licensing, inspecting, regulating, or enforcing regulations.[121]

Under the New Jersey program, the appointment power for an ombudsman has been granted to the governor, in contrast to most states where an administrative agency selects the ombudsman. Thus, the New Jersey approach results in the ombudsman being a political appointee, rather than an individual brought up through the ranks of an administrative agency. Although many states rely on volunteers and substate agencies to operate the ombudsman office, New Jersey relies solely on a centralized ombudsman office staffed by salaried employees. Although the New Jersey structure limits the function of the office, it also serves to maintain consistency within the state and prevent errors often resulting from large and inexperienced staffs.[122]

An ombudsman operating under a structured program as implemented in New Jersey plays a vital role as an advocate against the abuse of elderly nursing home residents. By monitoring the incidence of nursing home abuse, the ombudsman serves to protect the nursing home resident's rights. The ombudsman has the ability to act in a quasi-judicial fashion and as such, is armed with substantial power to eliminate abusive nursing home practices.

Reaction to the long-term care ombudsman solution has varied. Some have approved of the notion of an ombudsman authorized to initiate lawsuits and administrative actions on behalf of nursing home residents, whereas others have characterized the long-term care ombudsman as an overly burdensome, intrusive exercise of state power in an essentially private domain.[123] Nevertheless, relatively widespread approval of the ombudsman as an advocate for the rights of elderly nursing home patients remains.

A MORE ACTIVE CRIMINAL JUSTICE SYSTEM

Another prerequisite for preventing elder abuse in America's nursing homes is invoking maximum use of the criminal justice system. Criminalizing elder abuse and giving such crimes greater priority is an effective means of combating elder abuse.[124] As of 1986, only 17 laws had been enacted among the states that classified abusing an adult as either a misdemeanor or a felony. Four additional laws provided for injunctive relief or restraining orders. Penalties in the states with such laws ranged from fines of up to $10,000 to prison terms of up to 20 years.[125]

Prosecuting abusers of the elderly is a difficult process. Victims are often reluctant to press charges against their abusers because many experience enormous feelings of guilt that perhaps they have caused the attack. Further, victims may be frightened of the entire judicial process, especially the prospect of having to face their assailant in the courtroom.[126]

In recognition of nursing home abuse as a "callous disregard for human dignity," the attorney general's office of Massachusetts, for example, has taken an aggressive approach in recent months in prosecuting crimes against the elderly.[127] The office, along with other law enforcement officials and legislators, has proposed to heighten the criminal status of the abuse and neglect of nursing home residents from a misdemeanor to a felony, punishable by up to 10 years in prison. As a misdemeanor, nursing home abuse cases in Massachusetts are only punishable by up to 2 years in prison and must proceed through local district courts. This process is time consuming and provides the defendant with a chance to intimidate the witness, many of whom are incommunicative or senile. Furthermore, the current laws are extremely vague, making it necessary for prosecutors to piece together existing laws relating to assault and battery to secure charges.[128]

Responsibility for the arrest and prosecution of offenders must be placed upon professionals of the criminal justice system (i.e., police and prosecutors). These individuals must take every precaution to ensure the victim's safety and to respond to the problem of elder abuse by securing the maximum penalty possible for the abusive treatment of elderly. This action sends a message to society that indicates the severity of the crime. Furthermore, having prosecutors, rather than victims, file charges alerts offenders that threats and manipulation of the elderly are no longer viable means of avoiding criminal responsibility.[129]

Chapter 11

Death with Dignity

RIGHT TO A GOOD DEATH

Even though theology and ethics are logically independent,[1] traditional moral attitudes regarding euthanasia are affected profoundly by theological ideas—and three in particular: that God alone has total dominion and control over all human life, that death is a form of punishment, and that to kill innocent life places one's soul in jeopardy of eternal damnation.[2]

If a "right to die" is but merely a right to the inevitable,[3] the proper question is why the claim to the inevitable? The answer lies in a recognition of the vast technologies of medical science that make life almost endless.[4] Advanced medical techniques, such as artificial respiration, cardiac massage, uterine curettage, intravenous feeding, and a limitless availability of antibiotics not only forestall death but introduce untold confusion and lack of agreement in determining when in fact death occurs.[5]

Because a "good" death is now quite improbable for most, it is understandable that most people when asked the manner in which death would be preferable reply that a death without warning (as in an accident) is their choice. The most common fear remains that of dying under protracted circumstances in a hospital, being the victim of modern technological processes. Thus, according to present levels of conception, or misconception as the case may be, "the only way for a person to die in euthanasia is to be killed some how."[6]

For the bioethicist, the right to die with dignity is grounded in one basic principle: avoid human distress.[7] This right has three ethical parts: a right to have full information provided a patient by one's physician regarding one's medical problems in order that one may give an informed consent to treatment or nontreatment; a right to both "human company and care" that includes not only relief from pain, but the maintenance of a treating environment free of noxious stimuli; and, finally, a right to die unmolested by meddlesome procedures, including a right to refuse certain types of treatment.[8] This composite interest in a right to die continues to be obscured and generally frustrated by the present use of the term "euthanasia" in all its stated and more subtle definitional and practical applications.

Euthanasia, as a term, concept, or attitude has been used under various and confusing circumstances to denote "any good death," "any assistance in helping dying patients in their dying (including the cessation of treatments)," and "only acting directly to kill the dying patient."[9] The intriguing fact emerging from any study of euthanasia, then, will be that it can mean "any good death" as well as a "morally outrageous death."[10]

Active euthanasia involves killing whereas passive euthanasia does not; one is not acceptable, the other is being tolerated and accepted more and more. But how can letting die be in some way preferable—from a moral standpoint—than helping die? If all other morally relevant factors—intention, motivation, outcome—are the same, why should there be a difference? In truth, the difference between killing and letting die has no moral significance.

> In active euthanasia, the doctor initiates a course of events that lead to the patient's death. . . . In letting die, the agent stands back and lets nature take her sometimes cruel course. . . .[11]

The traditional argument against adoption or acceptance of euthanasia is that a rational patient simply does not and cannot choose euthanasia.[12] If this were so, it would have to be maintained further that no autonomous and rational decision could ever be made by a patient to refuse a modality of treatment that was life sustaining.[13] Yet this is not what the vast majority of active euthanasia opponents assert. Rather, they maintain that a patient can in fact make a rational choice to follow passive euthanasia—but not active euthanasia.[14] The inconsistency is obvious. The crucial question that begs answering is whether a patient "can rationally choose an earlier death over a later one."[15] Accordingly, it is submitted that if one can make a rational choice to follow passive euthanasia, then one must also be entitled to make a rational choice to follow active euthanasia[16] or, as termed in this chapter, "enlightened self-determination."[17]

BENEFICENT EUTHANASIA

"Beneficent euthanasia" is defined simply as the painless inducement of a quick death.[18] The most common paradigm of this would be an individual who suffers from an irreversible condition, such as disseminated carcinoma metastasis, has excruciating and incurable pain, is beyond reasonable medical doubt that death is imminent, and having been told of this condition requests some means of "easy death." Aside from a desire to help such an individual, no other relevant conditions exist.[19]

The crux of the argument for beneficent euthanasia is found in what is termed a societal obligation "to treat members kindly"[20] consistent with a principle of beneficence.[21] Suffering should at all times be minimized and kind treatment maximized.[22] This position should be able to be advocated without fear of it being viewed in reality as another Nazi-type plan for extermination.[23] The fear that the use of euthanasia, however qualified, runs the risk of destroying the social fabric of society is unfounded.[24] Beneficent euthanasia's utilization is consistent totally with the basic human need for dignity or self-respect. It should not be viewed as a punishment but simply as a matter of meeting this basic need and at the same time executing the societal obligation or collective responsibility of treating all members of society with compassion.[25]

Perhaps at the heart of any discussion of euthanasia is whether such life-ending acts are cruel in and of themselves[26] or whether they are morally justified. A consideration of whether in point of fact the act of euthanasia is administered to a *person* is as important.[27] For one to be recognized as a person, one must have rational awareness.[28] Is a "betubed, sedated, aerated, glucosed, mechanically manipulated" individual capable of being considered rationally aware?[29] Arguably, one simply is not a person under these conditions,[30] and the individual who acts deliberately and with set purpose to relieve such suffering, incurably ill, and extremely debilitated individuals should not be recognized as having committed an act of murder.[31] But, for this conclusion to have merit, some type of set criteria or characteristics for personhood must be acknowledged as either correct or acceptable,[32] or an incontrovertible definition of it agreed upon.[33] Sadly, it must be recognized that none of the criteria posited have achieved such a mark.[34] Yet there is wide agreement that when there is no "relational potential" or a capacity for love and engaging in interpersonal relations, owing to an absence of cerebral functioning, there can be no recognition of personhood.[35]

BLURRED DEFINITIONS AND A POSITED CLARIFICATION

A good number of physicians and moral theologians use "euthanasia" only in connection with active euthanasia, preferring as such to refer to "passive euthanasia" as "the right to death with dignity."[36] The reality of the present situation is that many of the old, chronically ill, debilitated, or mentally impaired are allowed to die by withholding the aggressive medical treatment provided young, mentally normal patients.[37]

Because little if any substance depends upon what label is attached to the actions under consideration, the debate about the distinctions becomes pointless.[38] Indeed, because of the blurring of distinctions between active and passive euthanasia, there is really no distinct difference between the two.[39]

> If death is intentionally caused by doing something or withholding something there is no morally significant distinction to be drawn between an active means to death and a passive means to death. Both are alike or intended means to death; and both the intention and the result are the same—the death of the patient. If one simply withholds treatment, it may take the patient longer to die, and he may suffer more than he would if more direct action were taken and a lethal injection given.[40]

To establish clarity of analysis, it has been suggested that euthanasia be redefined as either the putting to death or the failure to prevent death in cases of terminal illness or injury.[41] The motives behind such an act would be to either end comatoseness, permanent suffering, and anxiety, or perhaps the patient's perceived sense of burdensomeness.[42] Thus, as newly clarified, at least one other person is seen as causing or helping to cause the death of a competent individual who desires death; or, in the case of an incompetent, makes a substituted decision regarded as in the individual's best interests to either cause death directly or to withdraw some mechanism or process that sustains life.[43]

In its Declaration of Venice of October, 1983, the World Medical Assembly concluded that the best interests of the patient should be the operative standard under which healthcare matters are decided upon.[44] This appears to be a principle grounded in common sense and preeminently reasonable as well; however, the number of situations or cases in which the medical profession operates counter to the best interests of many of its patients is growing. Letting die, to be more specific, often involves a course of inaction that directly conflicts with the best interests of a patient, as illustrated by the following case.

> A woman is dying of terminal cancer of the throat. She is no longer able to take food and fluids by mouth and is suffering considerable distress. She would be able to live for a few more weeks if medical feeding by way of a nasogastric tube were continued. However, the woman does not want the extra two or three weeks of life because life has become a burden which she no longer wishes to bear. She asks the doctor to help her die. The doctor agrees to discontinue medical feeding, . . . and the woman dies a few days later.[45]

Death was obviously in the best interests of this woman. The method, however, for allowing its occurrence was not. If a lethal injection had been given, a quick and painless death would have resulted. Rather, after having the nasogastric tube removed, she lingered a few days, dying ultimately of dehydration and starvation.[46] Was it in this patient's "best interests" to be starved to death? Did society in some manner triumph because this individual was forced to suffer an undignified ending but avoided being "killed" mercifully?[47]

The sad, but very real, fact is that a swift and painless death is not always the result that follows from cessation of life-sustaining treatment[48]; for example, the patient whose kidneys have failed and dialysis or transplant surgery is not pursued, although generally remaining conscious, will experience normally one or all of the following: nausea and vomiting, an inability to concentrate and, eventually, convulsions.[49] What type of justification can be given for utilizing a method of treatment involving more suffering, instead of less, as being in an individual's best interests?

ACT OF TREATMENT VERSUS OMISSIONS OF TREATMENT

In classical Greece, medical practitioners were given three roles: alleviating the sufferings of the sick, lessening the violence of diseases that afflicted them, and "refusing to treat those who are overmastered by their diseases, realizing that in such cases medicine was powerless."[50] Indeed, the most common duty of all Greco-Roman physicians was "to help, or least to do no harm."[51] It was purely a matter of discretion when a hopeless case was taken by a physician.[52] This prevailing sentiment of physicians in this period of civilization found strong precedent in Egyptian and Assyro-Babylonian medicine.[53] As a medical point of view, in fact, it continued in vitality throughout the Middle Ages.[54] It is commonly thought that Francis Bacon writing in *De augmentis scientairium*, in the late 16th and early 17th centuries, advanced the conclusion that medicine should seek to prolong life and expand longevity and the notion has grown in an exaggerated and misdirected manner since that time.[55]

So it is seen, then, that whereas a physician's so-called duty to prolong life *qua* life has no classical roots, the idea of "respect for life" does have a rich tradition of observance.[56] But remember that even though physicians would not actively seek to terminate a life either by abortion or euthanasia, they were also not required to actively prolong life itself.[57] Even with the rise of Christianity, although abortion, suicide, and euthanasia became sins, the prolongation of life never "become either a virtue or a duty."[58]

MORALITY OF ACTIONS

Pope John Paul II approved the "Declaration of Euthanasia" adopted by the Sacred Congregation for the Doctrine of Faith on May 5, 1980, and in so doing advanced broad principles of humanistic care and treatment for the dying.[59] Acknowledging that one may seek to utilize advanced medical techniques of an experimental and high-risk nature in order to combat an illness, the declaration allows for the interruption of these processes when they render unsatisfactory results.[60] But before actions of this nature are allowed, the patient's "reasonable wishes" and those of the family, together with the advice of the attending physicians, must be considered.[61] Deferring to the physicians' expertise in matters of this nature, the declaration allows that they "may in particular judge that the investment in instruments and personnel is *disproportionate to the results foreseen.*"[62] Furthermore, they may conclude that "the techniques applied impose on the patient strain or suffering *out of proportion* with the benefits which he or she may gain from such techniques."[63] A clear and unequivocal example of a cost versus benefit analysis has been submitted as a proper standard of evaluation.

One may, of course, consistent with the declaration, "make do with the normal means that medicine can offer."[64] Thus, if such a course is followed, "one cannot impose on anyone the obligation to have recourse to a technique which is already in use but which *carries a risk or is burdensome.*"[65] A refusal of this type is not in any way to be regarded as an act equivalent to suicide, but rather an acceptance of a human condition or desire to avoid the use of a modality of treatment "disproportionate to the results" or a wish to prevent excessive financial drains on the patient's family "or the community."[66] Again, the element of economic feasibility of treatment is set forth as a proper vector of force in ultimate decision making. The need to ration scarce medical resources so that they may be expended on those who have a real possibility of recovery is also implicitly recognized in the declaration.[67]

The declaration concluded that, "When inevitable death is imminent in spite of the means used, it is permitted in conscience to take the decision to refuse forms of treatment that would only secure a precarious and burdensome prolongation of life, so long as the normal care due to the sick person in similar cases is not interrupted."[68]

ORDINARY VERSUS EXTRAORDINARY TREATMENT

The principles of ordinary versus extraordinary life-sustaining processes or treatments are relative, not only as to time and locale, but also in their application to specific cases. In essence, these concepts serve as basic value judgments that aid in reaching a determination whether a given modality of treatment presents an undue hardship on the at-risk patient or whether it provides hope for direct benefit. Thus, if too great a hardship would be imposed on the patient by following a particular medical or surgical course of treatment and no reasonable hope of benefit was to be derived therefrom, such actions would be viewed properly as extraordinary and not obligatory.[69] In practice, many physicians choose to equate "ordinary" with "usual," and "extraordinary" with "unusual" or "heroic" medical practice.[70] Once it has been decided to withhold heroics, no rational process has been developed that facilitates decision making regarding what treatment should be pursued and what withheld. Indeed, sometimes half-treatments are initiated thereby allowing, for example, intravenous feeding but at a rate that will result in dehydration over time.[71] Such a gesture maintains the vital symbol of feeding although it does not sustain the life of the patient over an extended period of time.[72] Although deceiving, this practice nonetheless serves as a type of artificial compromise for those wishing to respect the symbol yet at the same time act in accordance with patients' needs and, often, their present or previously expressed wishes.[73]

Determining whether medical or surgical treatment is either ordinary or extraordinary may be regarded as a quality of life statement. And, in reaching this statement, knowingly or unknowingly, the decision makers involved (legal, medical, and ethical) use a substituted judgment to conclude whether in similar circumstances to that of the patient they would or would not wish to survive in such a physical and mental state. Obviously, decisions of this sort are made within a varied and complex vortex of highly charged emotions.[74]

If love or humanness is to be recognized ultimately as the binding force of life, humankind should seek to maximize a full response to life in a loving or humane manner. If this course is followed, suffering is minimized, overall social good advanced, and value or utility in living achieved.[75] Thus, simply stated, if an act when undertaken would cause more harm than good for the individual in question and to those associated closely with that person, the act could be considered an unloving one. In cases of this nature, a basic cost-benefit analysis is almost always undertaken whether on a conscious or unconscious level.[76]

On a case-by-case basis with the standard of reasonableness as the linch-pin—as opposed to an unyielding *a priori* ethic—healthcare providers should balance the gravity of the harm caused against the utility of the good that will result from extraordinary care. As such, the decision makers should be ever mindful of the ethical imperative to minimize human suffering at all levels when making ultimate decisions.[77] In reality, this mandated balancing test validates a cost-benefit analysis.[78] Only after recognizing that all life is sanctified by creation and is not only qualitative to the individual in peril as well as to humankind in general may inquiry proceed into whether the medically handicapped individual possesses an ability to enjoy loving relationships with others, and whether the contemplated course of treatment maximizes that potential utility of life—assuming it exists—or, contrariwise, minimizes present suffering.[79]

Measures of an extraordinary nature undertaken for the specific purpose of prolonging a life of suffering should be recognized not only as unjust to the individual in distress but as an act of effrontery to the societal standard of decency and humanity.[80] The physician's primary responsibility is to relieve suffering when it occurs—not to seek the survival of a patient at all costs. Indeed, an overly aggressive modality of treatment for a terminally ill patient—regardless of age—should be recognized as a taint on the very doctrine of *primum non nocere*. If therapy would be futile and to no end other than mere survival, it should not be administered.[81] Thus, the artificial feeding of a terminally ill patient in irreversible coma should be regarded as a treatment decision and not mandated unless benefits clearly outweigh burdens.[82]

Moralists suggest that three commonly accepted principles are at the center of an individual's—and not the relatives' or the medical profession's—responsibility to preserve his or her life:

Per se he is obliged to use the ordinary means of preserving his life. *Per se* he is not obliged to use extraordinary means, though the use of such means is permissible and generally commendable. *Per accidens*, however, he is obliged to use even extraordinary means, if the preservation of his life is required for some greater good such as his own spiritual welfare or the common good.[83]

Application of the principle of double effect, although recognized as an exception to these three controlling principles, is not extended to those cases regarded as morally impossible; thus, the use of extraordinary means is not included within the principle, itself.[84]

The investment of economic and social resources in prolonging a life where such actions constitute an inordinate drain on familial and societal resources and achieve little more than extending the dying process are not mandated morally under the ordinary-extraordinary principle.[85] Indeed, the very concept of ordinary means for preserving life has been defined as "all medicine, treatments, and operations, which offer a reasonable hope of benefit for the patient and which can be obtained and used without excessive expense, pain, or other inconvenience."[86] Contrariwise, extraordinary or optional means of treatment are taken to be all those medicines, treatments, or surgeries that are incapable of being administered without excessive outlays of money or other inconveniences and, if in fact followed, would offer no reasonable hope of recovery or positive benefit.[87] The likelihood of success in undertaking the treatment is a valid consideration.[88] Accordingly, if for example a class of newborns for whom treatment would be so prohibitively costly and so unlikely of success could be identified, treatment would be excused.[89]

A number of relative factors must be weighed in deciding whether to excuse a modality of treatment. As noted, the successfulness of the proposed treatment is a major factor for consideration; and, of course, there are degrees of success. Although it is one matter to administer oxygen in order to alleviate a medical crisis for a patient, it is another matter to use that same oxygen to merely prolong a life for which hope of recovery is negligible. Degrees of hope are a second factor to be evaluated when it concerns complete recovery. Thus, while in one case oxygen is administered in order to end a patient's bout with pneumonia and may and usually does offer a very high hope of complete recovery, in other cases the patient's physical condition may be so fragile that there is but an equally fragile hope of recovery from the medical crisis. The degrees of difficulty in obtaining and using ordinary means comprise the third set of factors; some means are easy to obtain and use and are inexpensive and others are much more difficult to obtain and to use.[90]

Intravenous feeding problems present a unique paradigm for study of the ordinary-extraordinary conundrum. For example, when a cancer patient in extreme pain has established a systemic toleration of any drug (meaning that dosages provide only brief relief from ever-recurring pain), the attending physician realizes the incurable prognosis of the disease. If the patient has a good

heart, however, death will be drawn out for several weeks. The physician re-
members the one thing that will end the patient's suffering and cut off intravenous
feeding. This done, the patient dies the next day.

> The case involves the principle that an ordinary means of prolonging life and an
> extraordinary means are relative to the patient's physical condition. Intravenous
> feeding is an artificial means of prolonging life and therefore one may be more liberal
> in application of principle. Since this cancer patient is beyond all hope of recovery
> and suffering extreme pain, intravenous feeding should be considered an extraordi-
> nary means of prolonging life. The physician was justified in stopping the intravenous
> feeding. . .[91]

Further subtleties and ambiguities in the taxonomy of ordinary versus extraordinary care are seen dramatically in three landmark case opinions. In the
case of *In re Dinnerstein* a Massachusetts court observed that its task was to
discern the rather slight ''distinction between those situations in which the withholding of extraordinary measures may be viewed as allowing the disease to take
its natural course and those in which the same actions may be deemed to have
been the cause of death.''[92] In *Superintendent of Belchertown State School v.
Saikewicz* it was held that no extraordinary means of prolonging life should be
pursued when there is no hope that the patient will recover. ''Recovery should
not be defined simply as the ability to remain alive, it should mean life without
intolerable suffering.''[93] Finally, in *In re Quinlan*, the New Jersey Supreme
Court opined, ''One would have to think that the use of the same respirator or
life support could be considered 'ordinary' in the context of the possibly curable
patient but 'extraordinary' in the context of the forced sustaining by cardiorespiratory processes of an *irreversibly doomed patient*.''[94]

CIRCULAR TERMINOLOGY

It has been suggested that both the terms *ordinary* and *extraordinary medical
treatment* are ''incurably circular until filled with concrete or descriptive meaning,''[95] and that, furthermore, this language be abandoned in favor of a classification that merely recognizes ''treatment medically indicated'' for a nondying
or salvageable person that would thus be expected to be helpful and ''curative
treatment not indicated (for the dying).''[96] Of course, the central weakness of
this posture is that no objective criteria or concreteness is set forth with this
classification itself that would enable a decision maker to act unerringly. No
guiding or unyielding *a priori* standard is proffered, only a standard of situational
reasonableness tied to the facts of each case. Perhaps, however, within this
weakness is to be found the very strength of the suggestion: a straight recognition
that no definitive position can be taken.

Another suggestion has been to ban the artificial distinctions between ordi-
nary/extraordinary treatment and focus instead on whether, in a given case,

medical treatment is "morally imperative" or merely "elective."[97] A refusal of treatment would be accepted when a competent patient could present reasons relevant to declining physical or mental health or to familial, social, economic, or religious concerns, that were valid to that individual.[98] The incompetent patient is faced with the knowing reality that he or she is unable to make reasonable choices. Thus, the decision maker in this setting—spouse, parent, child, next of kin, guardian, or physician—may refuse treatment on morally acceptable grounds when such an action would seem "within the realm of reason to reasonable people."[99]

The question remains: What is the test of reasonableness?

> A reasonable person would find a refusal unreasonable (and thus treatment morally required) if the treatment is useful in treating a patient's condition (though not necessarily life-saving) and at the same time does not give rise to any significant patient-centered objections based on physical or mental burden; familial, social or economic concern; or religious belief.[100]

Both of these new classifications regarding ordinary/extraordinary treatment are inescapably tied to a standard of qualitative living perceived as such by the patient, family, or healthcare decision maker. Does this mean that all ultimate decisions regarding treatment or nontreatment are essentially cost-benefit ones? The feasibility of structuring a framework for principled decision making or, for that matter, a construct to aid in decision of this nature was explored in Chapters 2 and 4.

Ideally the concepts of ordinary and extraordinary means of treatment should be disregarded totally not only because of their imprecise terms of definition and application but also because they tend to support paternalism.[101] Whereas standards of customary medical practice determine what ought to be done, both the disease entity and the medical technologies needed to treat it displace the patient as the focus of concern. Indeed, the patient-person becomes subordinated totally to the patient–disease bearer.[102] A simple recognition that no form of treatment is either obligatory or optional is demanded. Rather, everything depends upon the condition of the patient.[103] Thus, the only reasonable standard of evaluation is the ratio of benefits and burdens of the treatment to the patient. Competent patients should always make this determination themselves. For an incompetent patient, however, a proxy must use the previously expressed wishes or values of that patient when they are known or may be determined.[104]

DOUBLE EFFECT

The principle of indirect or double effect, one of the basic principles of Catholic medical ethics[105] and one also intuited by many others not necessarily members of the Roman Church, is that the administration of a potentially lethal narcotic that would relieve the intractable pain of, for example, a cancer patient is in some way different, morally, from a knowing act that would murder that patient, justifying it on the grounds of acting mercifully.[106] Stated otherwise,

> The principle is intended to provide a halfway ground between a straightforward utilitarianism, which would simply consider the relative weights of the good and bad consequences of an action in order to make a moral judgment of it, and a variety of sterner moral positions, which would either deny the moral relevance of consequences to actions altogether or would judge immoral any action with bad consequences, no matter what other good consequences it had.[107]

The net result of recognizing and applying the principle of double effect is that certain actions indirectly producing certain evil consequences are justified so long as four conditions are met: the action undertaken, independent of its effect, must not itself be inherently held to be morally evil; the evil effect must not be utilized as a means to produce the good effect; the evil effect is merely tolerated and not sincerely intended; and, finally, regardless of its evil consequences, there is a proportionate reason for undertaking the action.[108] Utilization of this principle provides the justification, for example, of removing a cancerous fetus-bearing uterus and the administration of pain-relieving narcotics that may produce respiratory depression.[109] The principle's legitimacy has been attacked, alternatively, because it leads to discriminations that are wrongful by excusing acts it should not (thought to be killings, by some) and forbidding other such acts it should allow.[110]

A principle of such ambivalence is open, obviously, to these and other logical deficiencies. Some suggest that validation is recognized because of its "psychological validity."[111] A hypothetical example attempts to bring this point into focus. Confronted with a patient's intolerable pain and pleas for relief that cannot be mitigated by lesser doses of nonlethal drugs, a physician chooses to administer a dose of an analgesic that will likely cause death. A sharp contrast is seen between the attitude and the manner in one whose motive is relieving pain compared with one whose motive is premeditated killing.[112] If there were a purpose to kill, would it be seen in the way a syringe would be grasped, the words that might be either spoken or withheld, a look in the eyes?

> And would not the consequences of the difference be compounded almost geometrically at least for the physician as he killed one such patient after another? And what of the repercussions of the difference on the nurses and hospital attendants? How long would the quality and attitude of mercy survive death-intending conduct? The line between the civilized and savage in men is fine enough without jeopardizing it by euthanasia. History teaches the line is maintainable under the principle of double effect; it might well not be under a regime of direct intentional killing.[113]

Whether the lessons of history substantiate the alleged "psychological validity" of the principle and establish that it is efficacious and merits ready use and retention seem dubious, at best. Rather than continue to enshrine an awkward concept, it should be replaced by the relatively simple and enduring standard of what is, under a given set of facts, *reasonable*. Guided or supported by the principle of triage and a consideration of what actions are in the best interests of the patient, a cost-benefit analysis should be undertaken in order to decide whether one modality of treatment or nontreatment should be pursued.[114] Thus, reasonable, humane, and cost-effective actions should be both the procedure used and the goal sought.

The intensive care unit (ICU) found within the average hospital in the United States not only seeks to treat and to return patients suffering from serious injuries or acute disease to their original environments, but also to serve as a sophisticated, state-of-the-art hospice.[115] Even when there is no hope of recovery, studies have shown that approximately 19% of patients in ICUs are nonetheless admitted and stay.[116] It seems reasonable and sensible for patients to decide not to be treated in an intensive care unit, not because they wish to die sooner, but because in that setting access to family and friends will be more difficult and treatment more costly.[117]

Choices of this nature should not be confused or tied to the principle of double effect. Rather, when tragic choices are simply not between different chances of survival with different treatments but only between extending the process of suffering and death or shortening it, the principle has little pertinence or significance.[118]

> Patients may very well sensibly decide to forego treatment or ICU care so that they may in fact finally die and end their travail. They may directly will their deaths and thus within one strict interpretation of moral theory, passively commit suicide.[119]

Physicians in England are not allowed to initiate any actions that have, as their primary purpose, causing a patient's death.[120] Accordingly, under the Suicide Act of 1961, a physician who were to endeavor to facilitate the request of a terminally ill patient for assistance in terminating his or her life would be subjected to criminal prosecution.[121] A physician is also, under this legislation, not allowed to honor suggestions from the family of a gravely ill patient to end the life of such a patient.[122] Yet, because one of the basic commitments of the medical profession is to ease pain, if acting to ease suffering a physician must introduce and follow a modality of treatment that may in fact hasten death, these actions are legally permissible so long as the understanding is maintained that the course of treatment is only for the relief of pain or associated distress.[123] This is a preeminently reasonable modus operandi for dealing with the double-effect construct. Whether actions of this nature or constructions of the principle of double effect painlessly expedite death and thereby unwisely validate the traditional perception of passive euthanasia or passive suicide (more correctly termed "self-determination" in this chapter) and should accordingly be restricted or even forbidden socially and legally will be examined forthwith.

LEGAL DISTINCTIONS

The legal distinction between acts of commission and omission is to be found in the determination of a legal duty and the distinction between action and inaction. Within the law of negligence is a deeply rooted distinction between misfeasance and nonfeasance or, in other words, between a state of active misconduct that brings a positive injury to others and passive interaction that fails to take steps to protect them from harm. This distinction is validated by the fact that in misfeasance the defendant creates a new risk of harm to the plaintiff. Contrariwise, in nonfeasance, the defendant has not worsened the situation and has merely failed to benefit the plaintiff by interfering in his or her affairs.

> Liability for 'misfeasance' . . . may extend to any person to whom harm may reasonably be anticipated as a result of the defendant's conduct, or perhaps even beyond; while for 'nonfeasance' it is necessary to find some definite relation between the parties, of such a character that social duty justifies the imposition of a duty to act.[124]

It is argued, accordingly, that the distinction between assisting with the death of a patient and allowing the patient to die explicitly parallels within the American legal system the ways in which culpability is assigned to either ''causing'' or ''permitting'' harm to be inflicted upon others.[125] For, in those instances where an act can be found that caused a wrong or harm, once the agent who has brought about the harm is identified, liability is assessed.[126] Interestingly, with cases of omission, however, liability will not be imposed unless a ''relationship'' between the parties is established.[127]

The act of turning off an artificial respirator in use by a patient may be classified traditionally as either an act of commission or an act of omission.[128] Though a distinction may not be drawn easily here, because either action stems from the activity, the physician, if found to have committed an affirmative act of commission, may be held liable for murdering the patient.[129] Crucial to the determination of the nature of the action would be a characterization of whether the act, itself, caused life to be terminated or was more properly considered as an omission to render aid to sustain life—thus permitting it to end. The operative verbs here are ''caused'' and ''permitting.''[130] In ''acting'' or ''causing,'' an act of intercession is made to terminate life; whereas with acts of ''omitting'' or ''permitting,'' a simple failure to intercede in a course of action to preserve life is recognized with the end result that death is permitted to occur.[131] In determining legally whether the act of turning off a respirator is one of commission or omission, consideration must be given to the doctor-patient relationship (as opposed to a nonassociated one), patient reliance, and reasonable expectation, as well as to the physical act of turning off the respirator, itself, and the circumstances surrounding it.[132]

It could be argued that the most crucial of all elements—motive—is the testing rod in aiding a determination of whether acts were those of commission or omission.[133] Accordingly, a deliberate act of killing, but one not done with a particular motive or evil will, that is designed to allow the ending of life for a terminally ill patient and thus thereby relieve a life of suffering should not be classified as murder.[134] Inasmuch as no personal gain or good inures to the actor but rather to the recipient of the immediate action, this is another reason not to recognize the act as murder.[135] Noble intentions, however, are not always exculpatory. For example, if one subscribed to the belief of metempsychosis and decided to hasten another along toward the road to ultimate perfection before the other person became either tempted or corrupted with moral guilt, this act would surely be held to be murder.[136]

Under one line of philosophical reasoning, acquiescing to a request for murder made by one fully conscious, who for physical or psychological reasons finds life unbearable and finds no other act suitable to bring a resolution to the quandary, would not be an act of murder. But, for a murder to be committed, there must be an infringement of rights as opposed to simply a volitional release of the right to life.[137]

> . . . if something is a right at all, then it can be given up; just as a gift, if it is a gift, can be renounced. Therefore, in cases where the quality of life has reached a certain subjective minimum, the individual has a right to give up that life, to request euthanasia. Consequently, in such cases euthanasia would be morally acceptable.[138]

CRIMINAL LIABILITY

For criminal liability to be imposed for not executing a duty owed, the leading American case holds that this duty must be,

> . . . a legal duty, and not a mere moral obligation. It must be a duty imposed by law or by contract, and the omission to perform the duty must be the immediate and direct cause of death.[139]

Because the relationship between physicians and patient is basically contractual, that is, arising from the nature of an offer and acceptance, a physician has no obligation to treat all comers. Only when treatment is undertaken does the law impose a duty to continue the level of treatment, in the absence of a contrary understanding, as long as the individual case requires.[140]

For the terminal patient desiring a swift, painless death, discharging the attending physician, in theory, terminates not only the physician's duty but also eliminates the primary basis for the physician's criminal liability.[141] Therefore, the question of an imposition of criminal liability arises only in those cases where the physician has not been discharged or has failed to withdraw from a case with proper notice and thus, presumptively, the physician-patient relationship continues.[142] The physician may not seek a termination of this relationship by abandonment of the patient or the possibility of criminal liability may arise.[143]

The history of American case law of euthanasia presents an interesting record of a system that has prosecuted for the offense in a limited way.[144] In fact, as early as 1916, the predominate view was that even when life is taken, with consent, in order to relieve either suffering or an "other greater calamity," and the resulting death is thus of meritorious character, such action would normally form the basis of a criminal prosecution.[145] Yet, both judges and juries are reluctant to act affirmatively here.[146]

A survey of American case law reveals 12 cases involving active euthanasia of which only one resulted in an actual conviction for murder; three others were maintained for convictions lesser than murder, seven received acquittals, and one failed because of no indictment.[147] In construing this same survey, one authority has noted that there were actually nine acquittals in all as seven were allowed on the grounds of temporary insanity.[148] Observing that the standards for finding insanity are "tightening," he concluded that future acquittals of cases similar to these 12 may be more difficult to obtain.[149]

INTERNATIONAL PERSPECTIVE

Dutch Action

Since the early 1970s in the Netherlands, voluntary euthanasia has been an inherent part of the practice of medicine and accepted more or less by Dutch law.[150] The goal of the Royal Dutch Medical Association has long been to control this area rather than seek to prohibit it simply because it realized if rigid prohibitions were established, they could not be enforced uniformly or verified.[151] Consequently, the association promulgated guidelines to assist those physicians participating in euthanasia that tested the voluntariness of the patient's decision to undertake the act itself, whether the request was well considered and the result of a durable death wish, and made because of an unacceptable level of suffering.[152] The primary physician on the case is also required to consult with colleagues in order to test the need and validity of the patient's request for euthanasia.[153] The guidelines have been criticized as too loose [154] and questions have been raised as to whether the criteria state necessary, as opposed to merely sufficient, conditions for lawful euthanasia.[155]

Largely in an effort to test the effectiveness of these guidelines for euthanasia and at the same time conduct its first truly national survey regarding the prevailing practice of voluntary and involuntary euthanasia, in 1990 the Dutch government undertook a retrospective study of the practice of more than 400 physicians in this field.[156] The results were startling in many ways: the first being an official admission that active involuntary euthanasia is practiced regularly and at rates higher than expected.[157] The reasons given by physicians for routinely disregarding the guidelines (or rules of careful conduct) were listed as the patient's quality of life and lack of prospects for improvement together with familial concerns of not being able to cope with the medical condition of their loved ones.[158]

The survey revealed that of approximately 130,000 deaths each year in the Netherlands, there were 25,306 cases of euthanasia[159]; of this number, 14,691 cases were determined to be involuntary in nature—11.3% of the total deaths in the country.[160] One thousand cases within this figure were listed as examples of active involuntary euthanasia. A further breakdown showed 8,100 cases where excessive morphine was given for the purposes of ending life, and of this figure, in 4,941 cases (61%) this was administered without patient consent.[161]

Involuntary euthanasia is defined in the Netherlands as a deliberate act undertaken to terminate life without a patient's consent.[162] It is practiced routinely as a justifiable part of medical practice and viewed as but a form of charitable assistance for those dying.[163] Some physicians will acknowledge their actions to be involuntary euthanasia. Others classify administering a lethal overdose of morphine without the patient's knowledge as merely a procedure designed to relieve pain and, thus, not an act of involuntary euthanasia.[164] The central, albeit imprecise, element that separates murder from euthanasia, then, is the intent of the actor; malice (or evil intent) to commit a fatal injury is necessary to establish a legal action for murder. As noted, where a proper medical reason directs action (e.g., alleviating pain), the physical consequence of which is to end life, the legal consequence will not normally subject a physician in the Netherlands to a charge of murder.

Final Resolution

In February 1993, the Dutch Parliament became the first European country to officially permit euthanasia. Yet the legislation stops short of legalizing the act, which remains punishable by up to 12 years in prison. This parliamentary action endorses the existing procedures followed by the medical community.[165] Thus, while technically breaking the law against euthanasia, physicians who assist in administering it will be immune from prosecution if they follow a detailed 28-point checklist (or "carefulness requirements") proving that the patient is terminally ill, suffers unbearable pain, is in a clear state of mind, repeatedly (at least three times) asks to die, and the physcian ascertains that the request comes from the patient and not from family or friends. Further, the request to die must not be based on impulse or temporary depression and instead must reflect "a lasting longing for death." The assisting physician must be convinced of the patient's suffering is nothing short of "perpetual, unbearable, and hopeless" and must obtain a second medical opinion confirming the prognosis.[166]

Other International Responses

The European Union's legislative branch, the European Parliament, has begun to explore a draft proposal that, if enacted ultimately into legislation, would compel every member state to legalize euthanasia.[167] It has been predicted that, even if a version of the proposal is eventually reported from the appropriate legislative committee, the full 518-member Parliament and the executive body would reject it.[168]

The prestigious British Institute of Medical Ethics, however, concluded in 1990 that when the need to relieve intense and unremitting pain or distress caused by an incurable illness cannot be relieved by pharmacological, surgical, psychological, or social means and the subsequent act to alleviate the condition outweighs greatly the patient benefit of a further prolongation of life, acting in good conscience to effect the patient's wishes, a physician is justified ethically in assisting death.[169]

LEGISLATIVE INITIATIVES IN THE UNITED STATES

On April 25, 1994, the Michigan Commission on Death and Dying (a citizen's commission) recommended by a 9 to 7 vote (with 4 abstentions) that the state legislature authorize physician-assisted suicide and structure a set of restrictions that would prevent abuse. The draft recommendations of the commission would authorize this type of suicide for those 18 or older who suffer from a "terminal condition" that would likely lead to death within 6 months or who suffer from an "irreversible suffering condition" involving "*subjectively* unbearable or unacceptable suffering from a *physical* condition." If these recommendations were to be acted upon subsequently by the state legislature, Michigan would become the first state in America to legalize physician-assisted suicide.[170]

The commission recommended punishment for those who assist in a suicide without following the mandated procedures of imprisonment up to 4 years and a fine of $2,000. It was recommended further that only the person wishing to die, not the attending physician, could seek to initiate the procedure itself. It has been suggested that these recommendations accommodate suicide rather than assist its completion.[171]

In late May 1994, the New York State Task Force on Life and the Law, appointed by Governor Mario Cuomo, concluded legalizing acts of assisted suicide would not only be "profoundly dangerous" but pose "extraordinary risks" for the elderly, the poor, and others without access to good medical care. Instead of validating acts of assisted suicide in cases where intractable pain and depression exist, the advisory panel urged the medical profession to act more aggressively in managing both.[172]

The California and Washington legislatures, together with Maine, New Hampshire, Iowa, and Michigan, have sought to enact legislation that in one form or other would permit "physician aid in dying" (instead of terming the act *euthanasia*), as it is referred to in the 1992 California initiative Death with Dignity Action. Under all of these proposals, which thus far have failed, it would have been made legal for terminally ill mentally competent individuals to execute a directive (revocable under the California plan), witnessed by two disinterested parties, requesting assistance in ending their lives. No civil, criminal, or administrative liability would be imposed upon any physician, nurse, or other healthcare professional who chose to participate.[173]

EMERGENCE OF A CLEAR JUDICIAL STAND

On May 3, 1994, in a case of first impression in the federal court system, a district court judge in the state of Washington held that a state statute imposing criminal sanctions for physician-assisted suicide violated the Fourteenth Amendment's due process clause as well as the equal protection clause.[174] This will have enormous significance in validating what will undoubtedly be recognized within a few years as a constitutionally protected liberty interest in dying for terminally ill adults.

This decision was based on two United States Supreme Court decisions[175]: one held that a competent individual has a constitutionally protected liberty interest found within the due process clause of the Constitution to refuse or withdraw unwanted medical treatment even if death results consequently[176] and the other re-affirmed the right of an individual to make personal choices concerning marriage, procreation (here, abortion), and family.[177] The Washington Court concluded that mentally competent, terminally ill adults with no chance of recovery could make no more profoundly personal decision than to end their lives under such circumstances. In this regard, the Court refused to draw a distinction between refusing life-sustaining medical treatment and physician-assisted suicide by an uncoerced, mentally competent, terminally ill patient.

Fortifying the constitutional merit of its position, the Court concluded that whereas the state had enacted a Natural Death Act,[178] which recognized a fundamental right of all citizens to control their own healthcare decision (including decisions to withhold or withdraw life-sustaining treatment in instances of terminal condition or permanent unconsciousness), to deny a comparable right to those similarly situated who do not need life support would be a denial of equal protection of the laws guaranteed by the Constitution.[179]

GROWING STATE CONSENSUS

At the state judicial level, there is a growing consensus that a legally protected right does exist for competent patients, or other surrogate decision makers acting on behalf of incompetent patients, to direct when life-sustaining treatment may be withheld or withdrawn together with an ethical commitment or recognition of a professional responsibility among healthcare providers to abide by and assist in whatever reasonable way to effect these medical directives.[180]

CLINICAL STANDARDS FOR ASSISTED SUICIDE

Although precise standards regarding the frequency of patients' requests of physicians for assisted suicide is unavailable, it is reported commonly that in the

United States approximately 6,000 deaths each day are thought to be in some way either planned or assisted indirectly. This second classification includes actions that have the double effect of hastening death yet primarily relieving pain also, as well as those that either discontinue or fail to initiate potentially life-prolonging treatments.[181] Interestingly, some physicians, in fact, regard suicide as the last act in a continuum of care they can assist in providing hopelessly ill patients.[182]

Whenever thought, analysis, and final action are given over to the issue of physician-assisted suicide, all three should be focused on the strengthening of autonomy or self-determination for the incurably ill patient, thereby giving the patient greater control over death. All final plans of action should be directed toward effecting the implementation of a standard of compassion that recognizes that an individual's ultimate fate should rest with the individual or, if allowed legally, by a previously designated surrogate decision maker.[183] In the final analysis, it is the physician's responsibility to create a medical environment that promotes a peaceful death.[184]

Assisted suicide, to be sure, is treatment of an extraordinary and irreversible nature. Before undertaken, certain clinical standards should be met. First, all types of palliative or comfort care should be discussed with the patient who is suffering with an incurable condition that is causing severe and unrelenting pain. When uncertainty exists regarding either the medical condition of the patient or the prognosis, a second opinion or opinions should be sought to dispel uncertainties.[185]

The second step toward verification of a decision for assisted suicide requires that the attending physician ascertain that this ultimate request for an act of controlled death is not simply the result of faulty administration of comfort care. Thus, full discussion must be had with the patient before a decision to utilize death assistance is accepted; it should be fully understood that such actions should never be used "to circumvent the struggle to provide comprehensive care or find acceptable alternatives."[186] The third step recognizes that the physician ascertain that the patient's declaration of death preference be not only clear, serious, and unequivocal, but be given freely and seen as a choice to die instead of continuing life in a state of pain and suffering.[187]

The patient's capacity to understand the significance of this request for assisted suicide should also be established to prove the soundness of his or her judgment. When it is suspected that depression is distorting rational decision making or a reversible mental disorder is clouding rationality, psychiatric evaluation should be sought—again, to establish beyond a doubt the patient's comprehension of his or her decision.[188]

The fifth clinical standard to be followed is met when an act of physician-assisted suicide is carried out within the context of a real doctor-patient relationship. In other words, ideally the physician has witnessed the progression of the patient's illness and his or her suffering as the primary physician. If no such preexisting relationship can be established, the physician must endeavor to know the patient personally so that a full understanding can be had of the reasons behind the request.[189] Obviously the physician should not be forced to assist the patient in suicide if the physician objects as a matter of conscience. Yet that physician should help the patient secure a transfer of care to a more receptive physician.[190]

In order to test not only the voluntariness and rationality of the patient's request, but the accuracy and the diagnosis and the prognosis as well as palliative care alternatives, as a sixth step, a consulting physician should be brought into the case. The consulting physician should review the supporting case materials and, furthermore, examine and interview the patient.[191]

Finally, all primary participants in the assisted suicide (i.e., patient, primary physician, and the consultant) must acknowledge, in writing, their consent to the procedure.

> A physician-assisted suicide must neither invalidate insurance policies nor lead to an investigation by the medical examiner or an unwanted autopsy. The primary physician, the medical consultant and the family must be assured that if the conditions agreed on are satisfied in good faith, they will be free from criminal prosecution for having assisted the patient to die.[192]

A CONSTRUCTIVE PROPOSAL: REDEFINITION AND RE-EDUCATION

What is needed desperately in order to bring a contemporary sophistication— legal, medical, philosophical, ethical, and moral—is a strong stance regarding the terms "euthanasia" and "suicide," or, quite simply, re-education. More precisely, a change in the essential definition of euthanasia as a word, concept, principle, attitude, or legal action is proposed. Therefore, those acts heretofore called euthanasia of one form or other would henceforth be known as acts of enlightened self-determination. Freed of the shackles of confusion and indecisiveness, actions undertaken within the context of an irreversible medical crisis or terminal illness[193] would be understood not as an act of autonomous rational suicide (or active euthanasia of oneself), or a refusal of treatment, but rather merely an act of enlightened self-determination. For the incapacitated or incompetent individuals, the action taken on their behalf by surrogate decision makers would be viewed similarly and the actions of these decision makers judged on their reasonableness and fairness to terminal patients and their immediate family or extended family.

This proposal would begin to foster a new attitude toward death; one that redefines one of the basic tenets of medicine, the recognition that old age is an honorable estate, into the agreement that it is unjust and inhumane to insist that old people suffering from a terminal illness or otherwise severely incapacitated be forced to live through a period of miserable decline and painful helplessness.[194] The competent decision maker, at whatever age, suffering from a severe debilitating (terminal) disease, as well as the incompetent patient who is similarly situated and further inconvenienced by infancy, mental incompetence, or unconsciousness, would also be accorded the privilege of holding first-class citizenship. And, with this would come an inherent recognition of the fact that because of debilitation, the elderly suffer more than the comatose or the vegetative simply because they are conscious, or at least semiconscious of their inescapable misery.[195] The result of this new attitude toward healthcare would be an unyielding recognition that a right of personal autonomy is possessed by all.

Rational assisted suicide and all the varieties of euthanasia would no longer be considered. The major focus of all inquiry into actions previously classified as suicide or euthanasia would be simply: did the individual in question, exercising his or her powers of rational thinking, exercise an act of enlightened self-determination or autonomy? For the incompetent suffering from a similar terminal illness, the question to be answered would be: did the surrogate decision maker, acting with rationality and humaneness, and thereby within the best interests of the terminal patient, or employing the principle of substituted judgment for that individual, exercise an act of enlightened self-determination? Obviously, the healthcare providers, and when brought into this matter, the courts, would themselves act under the presumption that an individual or his or her duly appointed surrogate decision maker acted properly. This position is a quantum leap not only in thinking and hoped-for action but it is an eminently fair and reasonable contemporary approach to an age-old problem.

Chapter 12

The Future

THE WHITE HOUSE CONFERENCE

The fourth White House Conference on Aging was held in May 1995, and brought together 2,200 delegates to study complex issues grouped under five headings: social security benefits, pensions and savings, healthcare and long-term care, research, and grandparenting.[1] Although hundreds of proposed policy needs were drafted before the conference began, the number one issue emerging at the conference itself was long-term care and healthcare needs.[2] With the delegates themselves fearing the loss of independence through the physical and financial consequence of illness or infirmity, support was strong to develop long-term care insurance policies that would cover not only nursing homes but also home care and include activities such as home-delivered meals, home health visits by professional caregivers and health personnel and other services—all designed to decrease admissions to nursing homes.[3] Great interest was shown by the delegates in advancing gerontological research by combatting crippling diseases such as Alzheimers and Parkinsons that force significant admissions to long-term care facilities.[4]

NEW DIRECTIONS IN SOCIAL SERVICES

The political agenda for the elderly remains uncertain and is indeed fraught with economic difficulties. Encouragingly, however, within the foreseeable future, a wider range of social services will be offered for the elderly—tied as such to the goal of helping them get the things they need in order to assist them in maintaining a semblance of independence and self-sufficiency in daily living. Among the services will be senior centers for socialization; talking books; homemaker assistance; meal programs (e.g., Meals on Wheels); telephone reassurance to give the isolated older person a sense of contact and support; and adult day care where not only meals but custodial care, physical therapy, rehabilitation, and psychotherapy are provided for families who are unable to leave their loved ones alone during the workday.[5] Use of these services to their greatest possible extent forestalls—if not prevents totally in many cases—subsequent reliance upon protective services through the appointment and administration of guardianships.[6] Home sharing will also become another viable alternative to the use of protective services and nursing home admission. Under this arrangement, specifically designed housing is built to be shared by six to eight independent older adults who will participate in the shared life experiences and obligations of residential living.[7]

There will always be more people trying to get into nursing homes than there are spaces to accommodate them. As businesses, nursing homes must seek to cover their costs and will consequently try to limit the number of Medicaid residents in their facilities. Because nursing homes receive from Medicaid a very large share of the long-term care bill for older people, one way for state governments to contain costs is by simply restricting the number of nursing homes built. Even with the wider development and use of home care programs, the reality of social demographics of aging point conclusively to one fact: namely, that not only the fast-growing older population but the aging of the older population, itself, will combine dramatically to increase the number of nursing home spaces needed.[8]

Every day in nursing homes, autonomy is routinely compromised or neglected. It could not be otherwise because the very social structure within the nursing homes is embedded in an institutional setting. On one side are the dependent elderly and on the other the professional caregivers. The professional norms that regulate the atmosphere within a nursing home act as barriers to autonomy in that the residents are unavoidably cast in a passive role (at times almost infantilized) and presented with few real opportunities to make meaningful life decisions.[9]

Generally, functional independence, freedom from chronic pain, positive prognosis, ability for self-care, mobility, degree of cognitive acuity, and perceived burden on family are all considered by those pondering the decisions of life-extending care. Indeed, the emotional well-being of older patients, themselves, is tied to their functional independence and the maintenance of their mental faculties.[10]

NEW NORM OF SOCIAL RESPONSIBILITY

A new social norm appears to be developing throughout parts of the country that acknowledges a limit to the government subsidization of the elderly poor and a familial responsibility to assist in their care.[11] Although little is known empirically about the deterrent efficacy of relative responsibility, the policy behind such legal recognition is designed at least in part to deter increasing welfare costs.[12] Before such a principle could be embraced nationally, however, there would have to be some marked degree of community consensus as to its fairness. Although some maintain consensus exists that financially responsible adults should support their aged parents, others question whether enforcement of this responsibility would be self-defeating in that family dissension and controversy over this issue would weaken family ties. Especially for adult children at the lower end of the income scale, enforcing a shift of subsistence funds from one generation to the other "distributes economic desolation in between the generations."[13]

Another troubling consideration is the recovery costs involved in implementing relative responsibility laws; for if it costs more not only to identify, but to find and then prosecute responsible relatives than could be actually collected from them, the maintenance of such programs would surely undermine the tax-saving purposes originally thought.[14]

GOALS

As the population ages, elder abuse in nursing homes will escalate as a widespread phenomenon that warrants heightened scrutiny. Both states and the federal government have recognized the existence of the problem and have taken steps toward controlling elder abuse in nursing homes. Nevertheless, society must examine its attitude regarding the intrinsic worth of the institutionalized elderly and strive to respect their rights, to treat them with full recognition of their dignity, and to preserve their individual autonomy. There must be better education regarding elder abuse and additional legislation enacted advocating stringent penalties for the violation of nursing home residents' rights. Providing an ombudsman with legal authority to enforce such laws is an important step toward eliminating instances of elder abuse in the nursing home setting.

If the choice were available, most elderly Americans would probably choose not to enter a nursing home. Our current collective psyche dictates that entering the regimented environment of a nursing home results in a negative experience. Thus, the nursing home of the future must present its residents with a broad spectrum of benefits and options within a setting that is more accurately characterized as an interactive living center rather than as an institution. Its goal must be to allow its residents to live out their remaining days fully and not suffer abuse by the very people who are charged with caring for them.[15] To effect this, however, society as a whole must direct itself to promoting this goal.

SEVEN QUESTIONS FOR THE FUTURE

The ethics of healthcare decision making is infused in almost every aspect of the delivery of healthcare services to the elderly. The future direction of national programs in America will be shaped by seven fundamental questions and by how a consensus can be reached to answer them.

> 1.   Because wide disagreement and a lack of hard scientific data about the types of treatment that are effective exists currently, how can healthcare services be prioritized?
> 2.   Is it fair to expect physicians, who fear not only malpractice suits but expressing professional concern for providing quality patient care, to know when a diagnostic test is necessary, when another type of treatment is warranted, and when care should be merely palliative because of the futility of prognosis?
> 3.   Should physicians continue to serve in dual, yet contradictory roles, as both primary caregivers and gatekeepers to the whole healthcare delivery system?
> 4.   How can patient autonomy be respected when patients demand levels of treatment that physicians judge professionally to be worthless?
> 5.   When equal treatment for all could mean only a basic level of care for everyone—even those able to pay for needed treatment—is it still possible to be just in administering such a system?
> 6.   Do physicians have, in addition to a duty to act beneficently toward their individual patients, a larger duty to act similarly toward society regarding the distribution of scarce medical resources and the need to reach a utilitarian basis of delivery?
> 7.   Will rising costs that can no longer be shifted mean ultimately that medical ethics will be viewed as secondary to the economics of the marketplace?[16]

Additional questions must be posited regarding the design and implementation of specific finance mechanisms if the public sector is to continue its substantial role in the financing of long-term care. First, should a public long-term financing program be open-ended and allow consumer choice among a comprehensive range of social and support services as well as facility-based and community-based health or should limits be placed on the scope and the duration of service coverage? Second, should a requirement be made that a specified amount of private funds be expended before public spending commences or, rather, should public funding be taken as the initial payer with a safety net of private financing being used as a secondary support mechanism? Third, what is the source of public dollars needed to finance long-term care programs and what group of individuals will benefit from those expenditures? What types of revenue tax (e.g., dedicated taxes or redirection of existing revenues) can be used to maintain the programs? Should an intergenerational basis be structured for participation in the revenue collection and the long-term care financing coverage or should it be limited to persons over a certain age? Finally, in order to qualify for eligibility in these programs, should individuals be admitted on the grounds of medical diagnosis or functional criteria?[17] Even if extensive healthcare reform legislation were to pass Congress, few hold to the opinion that an effective plan could be phased in and begin to affect costs in less than 3 to 5 years—with a total of 10 years needed in order to get all of the reforms working in a satisfactory manner.[18]

A number of ways have been suggested to curtail the present level of the nation's medical expenses and thereby chart a realistic level of health reform. The first simply requires those with health insurance to pay more. Second, the level of health benefits should be reduced by simply doing less for the sick. Thus, procedures should only be undertaken when they are determined to be medically beneficial; and in line with this, the very sick (and often aged) should not be kept longer than a reasonable period or "normal life span"—for surely a full and total life can be achieved by late 70s or early 80s.[19] Whereas in an average day, a third of all hospital beds are empty, some hospitals must simply be closed as inefficient businesses. New incentives for patient care among physicians must be established. Presently, doctors tend to order more of those procedures that pay them handsomely than they would otherwise do. Because they order 75% of all medical care, by cutting payments for these procedures and curtailing their actual use, physicians will be forced to halt the rise in medical costs. Finally, healthcare delivery can be made more efficient if fewer administrative personnel and less paperwork are used. Presently, it is estimated that a staggering 18 to 24% of United States health dollars are spent on administration, whereas those countries with government health systems spend around 10%.[20]

CONCLUSIONS

Among medical researchers, near unanimous agreement exists that if the two leading causes of morbidity and mortality—cardiovascular disease and cancer—were to be eliminated completely, overall life expectancy would increase by less than 7 years; for those over age 70, the expectation would be even less. The reason for this state of affairs is that the significant technological accomplishments in medicine and public health have only extended the average life expectancy by allowing more individuals to reach the traditional Biblical upper limit of approximately fourscore.[21]

Every major disease is age-dependent. Thus, after age 30, a steady and almost inexorable increase in the probability of morbidity and mortality from one disease or another occurs and that probability doubles, as one grows older, about every 8 years. It is at the cellular level, then, that the more fundamental disruptions occur during the whole phenomenon of aging and disease. And, it is becoming even more increasingly evident that the progressive cellular degeneration associated with aging is in reality a precursor to the development of an even more increasingly severe disorder. Accordingly, once a disorder becomes manifest, increased strain is placed upon the organism, which accelerates the total degenerative process.[22]

Over the last 60 years, the biomedical model of decision making for the elderly has dominated the healthcare system—placing as such a disproportionate emphasis on specialization and pathology management rather than primary care, prevention, and the attendant psychosocial, ethical, and moral issues of health-care delivery.[23] All too often, biomedical solutions have been tied to technological advances including prosthetic limbs, renal dialysis, and a nearly unending stream of services needing only money to execute them.[24]

The new emphasis on healthcare delivery for the elderly should not only stress the value of preventive medicine but recognize the exceedingly complex interplay among the physical, emotional, and social factors in a holistic setting, instead of coming to that all too frequent and familiar diagnosis of senility and a prognosis of either chronic or irreversible.[25] Finally, only by limiting ethically inappropriate and medically unnecessary care will medical costs ever begin to be brought under control;[26] in the final analysis, the most efficacious health policy for a nation or a community is its strategy for controlling the social issues of its medical knowledge and resources.[27]

Two rather simple "solutions" to old age should be pursued: namely, a continued pursuit of those ends that give meaning to existence (e.g., devotion to individuals, to groups and causes, or to creative work) and a reluctance to dwell on old age as a state, but rather as but a continuum in a justified life.[28] To pursue longevity in an obsessive manner distracts from the natural quest of the soul by confusing its mandate to master the fine art of living well and, thus, completely.[29]

Sample Attorney's Letter to Client Appointed as Guardian

Dear Guardian:

Now that you have been appointed Guardian of the Person and Estate of
_____ (the "Ward"), I would like to outline your
principal responsibilities.

Basically, as Guardian of the Person you must decide where the Ward will live and
how meals, personal care, transportation and recreation will be provided. As Guardian
of the Estate, you must take control of the Ward's property, establish a budget and pay
the Ward's debts when they become due, invest prudently the Ward's property and
periodically report to the Court about the assets, receipts and disbursements of the
Estate. All of this is discussed below in greater detail.

I. Responsibilities as Guardian of the Person
A. Place of Residence

As Guardian of the Person, you determine where in the State the Ward should live.
This power is not unlimited. [For example, you may not place the Ward in a mental
health treatment facility against his or her wishes.] You cannot make the Ward a
"prisoner" by denying the pleasures of visiting family and friends. You must notify the
Court whenever you change the residence of the Ward for anything other than a temporary period of time, and you cannot move the residence of the Ward to a place outside
of the State without prior Court approval.

The Ward should be allowed to remain in his or her usual residence as long as
there is proper and affordable help (both in terms of people and equipment) available at
the residence to make it safe and comfortable. To make the residence safe and comfort-

able, you may have to have the locks changed to insure that no unauthorized person gains access to the residence. You may also have to have the residence thoroughly cleaned to eliminate unsanitary or unsafe debris. You should contact the local gas, electricity, water, garbage and telephone companies to make sure these services to the residence continue on an uninterrupted basis. It may also be necessary to make repairs or modifications to the residence. You may want to consult with the local building department about repairs that may be necessary to bring the residence up to local building codes. Most local fire departments will conduct a safety inspection upon request. Also, the U.S. Consumer Product Safety Commission (call 800-638-2722) publishes a booklet, entitled ''Home Safety Checklist'' which describes various steps that can be taken to make a residence safer and more comfortable for the elderly and disabled.

If the Ward will be alone in the residence for anything other than brief periods of time, you may want to consider having the Ward subscribe to an emergency medical response system—one touch of the button will bring help to the Ward in minutes. Such systems are maintained by many local hospitals.

Most Wards require some assistance in connection with day-to-day living. This assistance can range from someone to do simple errands (such as buying groceries once a week) up to full 24-hour nursing care. Assistants can either be hired through agencies (listed in the Yellow Pages under '' _____ '') or directly by you. Assistants hired through agencies generally cost more than assistants hired directly by you. However, if you hire assistants directly, you will be responsible for verifying employment eligibility (through the completion of Immigration and Naturalization Form I-9), for preparing employment tax documents (such as Internal Revenue Service Forms W-2, 940 and 941 and their State counterparts) and for arranging workers' compensation coverage (beginning on the first day of employment). Regardless of whether the assistant is hired through an agency or directly by you, you are responsible for establishing guidelines for the assistants and insuring each assistant follows those guidelines.

At some point in time, it may no longer be feasible, for either physical or financial reasons, for the Ward to continue to reside in his or her own residence. If this occurs, you are responsible for finding a new residence and arranging for the move. Even if the Ward is placed in a care facility, you are still responsible for insuring that the Ward receives appropriate health care, nutrition, grooming, recreation and social stimulation. You should visit the facility periodically and regularly review the Ward's chart with the nursing shift supervisor to make sure that appropriate care is being given.

B. Nutrition

Proper nutrition is essential to the physical and mental well-being of the Ward. Ask the Ward about his or her likes and dislikes. Also, consult with the Ward's physician to determine what types of food and beverage should and should not be provided. Have the physician or a recommended nutritionist prepare a diet plan. Then arrange for the purchase and preparation of the appropriate food and beverages. Very often the Ward will not be able to prepare his or her own meals. There are several organizations in the County that will deliver prepared meals to a Ward's residence. There are also senior centers throughout the County which provide at least one hot meal as part of the daily program.

C. Health Care

You should make sure that the Ward has appropriate health insurance. This may include Medicare, a health maintenance organization, Medicare supplemental health insurance, long-term care insurance, and, if the Ward is eligible, Medicaid coverage. If the Ward suffers from a special medical problem (such as Alzheimer's Disease or Alcoholism), you should educate yourself about the problem, what is likely to happen over time and what can be done to minimize the adverse effects.

[Unless you were specifically given health care powers by the Court, the Ward retains the right to make health care decisions. However, you may consent to medical treatment for the Ward if the Ward does not object, and you may require the Ward to receive medical treatment in emergencies. Emergencies are situations where the Ward is unable to give consent for medical treatment and such treatment is required to alleviate severe pain or, a medical condition exists which, if not immediately diagnosed and treated, will lead to serious disability or death.]

[If you believe the Ward no longer has capacity to give informed consent for medical treatment, you should call me. You can petition the Court for a determination that the Ward lacks the capacity to give informed consent for medical treatment and request that the Court grant you, as Guardian, exclusive authority to make health care decisions. However, even if you are granted such authority, you may not place the Ward in a mental health treatment facility or consent to the administering of experimental drugs against his or her will. You may not subject the Ward to convulsive (e.g., electro shock or insulin coma) treatment. Nor may you consent to the sterilization of the Ward unless it is surgically necessary for the treatment of a life-endangering disease.]

Whether acting in emergency situations or under exclusive health care authority, you must act in good faith and base your decisions on sound medical advice. It is important to continue to use the health care providers the Ward has used in the past, as long as these persons are qualified to perform the required care.

Many Wards have executed a directive to physician (more commonly known as a "living will") [or a durable power of attorney for health care]. Usually, such documents specify what action is to be taken with regard to prolonging life through life support systems. If you believe that the Ward had the capacity to understand the nature of the document at the time that it was signed, we should respect his or her wishes. If you have doubts as to the capacity of the Ward at the time the document was signed, you should seek directions from the Court. [You cannot revoke a durable power of attorney for health care executed by the Ward prior to the establishment of the Guardianship. However, if you believe that the person designated in the power of attorney is not acting in the best interests of the Ward, you can ask the Court to revoke the power.]

D. Recreation

A Ward's disabilities may make it difficult to continue many of the activities that have been the source of happiness over the years. Lack of outside stimulus often results in accelerating the Ward's physical and mental decline.

You have a duty to ensure that appropriate stimulus is provided and that the Ward has the physical means of enjoying the stimulus. Talk to the Ward about what he or she would like to do. If the Ward likes to read, make sure that reading material is continually available and that the Ward has properly fitted glasses and a reading light. Large print books and books on audio tapes are available at most libraries and many book stores. If the Ward enjoys music, make sure that a radio or stereo is available. If the Ward has hearing problems, make sure he or she has a properly working hearing aid. If the Ward shares a room with someone, make sure he or she has earphones. Other sources of pleasure are favorite food and drink, lotions and powders, and, for some, television.

Encourage the Ward to call and write family and friends. Similarly, encourage them to visit or write back. Encourage local family and friends to take the Ward on periodic outings. Even extremely impaired people enjoy being taken to restaurants, to the park and out for drives. Several local organizations will make daily telephone calls to the Ward "just to chat." Many churches have volunteers who will visit the Ward on a regular basis.

If it is appropriate, you should encourage and arrange for the Ward to attend a local senior center that offers a variety of daily activities.

E. Control

If the Ward is a danger to others, you should take all reasonable steps necessary to reduce the danger. For example, the Ward should not be allowed to drive if the Ward has an alcohol, drug or other problem that might impair the Ward's ability to safely operate a motor vehicle. If the Ward has a violent temper, he or she should not be allowed access to guns or other lethal weapons. If you fail to control the Ward you may have to pay, with your own funds, any damages caused to others by the Ward. Because of this, you may want to get liability insurance to protect yourself.

II. Responsibilities as Guardian of the Estate
A. Take Control of Property

Your first duty as Guardian of the Estate is to take control of the Ward's property. This involves identifying what the Ward owns and arranging for the transfer of title or possession to the Guardianship. The property may include cash and uncashed checks, bank accounts, stocks, bonds, receivables, partnership interests, life insurance policies, real estate, furniture, jewelry and automobiles, as well as the right to receive payments from the government, insurance companies, employers and trusts. You should immediately open a checking account, a savings or money market account and, if appropriate, a safe deposit box, all in your name "as Guardian of the Estate of_____ ," to serve as a place to deposit funds, documents and property that you discover. You should use the Ward's social security number for the accounts, not your own. Use the checking account to deposit *all* receipts and pay *all* expenses. Separately record each receipt and each expense in the checkbook register so that you will later have the details necessary for the accounting you must submit to the Court. If the checking account balance is larger than immediate needs, you should write a check and deposit it in the savings account. If you later need money to pay bills, withdraw the money from the savings account and deposit it into the checking account and pay the bills with checks drawn on that account. The law requires you to keep the Ward's property separate from your own property at all times. Thus, you should never put the Ward's money in the same bank account in which you put your own funds. You, of course, may never use the Ward's property for your own benefit, unless the Court has given you prior approval to do so.

The best source of information of what the Ward owns is the Ward. You should review with the Ward his or her financial records, such as current bank and broker statements, income tax returns, account ledgers, deeds and insurance policies. You have a right to enter the Ward's safe deposit box and remove the contents, upon presenting a certified copy of your Letters of Guardianship (the document issued to you by the Court clerk) to the financial institution. If the box is rented with another person, that other person should be present when the box is opened.

You also have a right to interview other people who may have knowledge of the Ward's property, such as the Ward's accountant and stockbroker. You may want to send a letter to all banks and savings and loan associations in the area to find out what accounts the Ward owned as of the date of your appointment. The funds in each account should be transferred as soon as reasonably possible to the Guardianship accounts. Most financial institutions will waive early withdrawal penalties on time deposits made by the Ward before the Guardianship started. However, you should always check with the financial institution before you withdraw funds from an account. If the institution will not waive the penalty, you should defer transferring the funds to the Guardianship accounts until the deposit matures. Generally you should limit to $100,000 the total amount of deposits with any one financial institution. If the Ward is going to be receiving wages or a monthly Guardianship allowance, you may want to keep one small checking account open in the name of the Ward as a depository for these funds.

Although the Ward's stocks and bonds will ordinarily be in a safe deposit box or with a broker, it is not uncommon to find certificates in the Ward's residence. Therefore you should make a careful search of the residence. You should write to the transfer agent to have title re-registered in your name "as Guardian of the Estate of _____." Again, even though the certificates will be in your name, you should give the transfer agent the Ward's social security number. If you believe that the Ward owns a security but you are unable to locate the certificate, you should write to the company and obtain a replacement certificate.

Property which is co-owned with another person (such as a joint bank account), or co-controlled by another person acting under a power of attorney, creates special problems. [If the **only** other owner is the Ward's spouse, you (with my help) should determine whether the funds are community/marital property. The spouse, if legally capable, has the full right to control and manage the community/marital property and you have no right to assert control over it unless the spouse agrees in writing.] The other owner(s) should be contacted immediately to determine what portion of the property belongs to the Ward and what portion belongs to the other owner(s). Before dividing the property, you should call me to determine whether such a division would disrupt the Ward's estate plan. If no immediate agreement is reached as to what part belongs to the Ward, you should consider taking control of the entire property so as to prevent the other owner(s) from disposing the Ward's share. We will then seek instructions from the Court concerning the disposition of the property. We will normally want to ask the Court for authority to revoke any financial power of attorney that may exist.

You should deposit valuable jewelry, stamp and coin collections and other small objects of substantial value in the Guardianship safe deposit box, unless you determine that the benefits of leaving such property with the Ward outweigh the risks of loss. You should store valuable furs, antiques, art work and excess furniture in an insured warehouse if there is no immediate need for these items at the Ward's residence. You should also determine whether other people hold property that belongs to the Ward. For example, the Ward may have lent to others furniture, art work or other items, and it is necessary for you to determine whether such items should be reclaimed. You should take photographs of all of the Ward's valuable personal and household effects for insurance purposes.

You should get the certificate of ownership of the Ward's automobile. You should make sure that no unauthorized person drives the automobile and no one should drive it unless it is adequately insured. If you decide to store the automobile in a garage, remember to keep the registration current.

Very often the Ward will be entitled to receive payments from the government, insurance companies, (former) employers and trusts. You should contact the Social Security Administration, Civil Service Retirement System and the Veterans Administration to determine whether the Ward is eligible for benefits and arrange for the benefit checks to be sent to you as Guardian. If the Ward is entitled to receive retirement or disability checks from an employer or an insurance company, you should contact the payor and arrange for the benefits to be sent directly to you as Guardian. If the Ward is a beneficiary of a trust, you should review the terms of the trust with the trustee and arrange for the trust distributions to be sent directly to you as Guardian. Call me if the Ward was a trustee.

You should record a copy of your Letters of Guardianship with the County Recorder in each county in which the Ward owns real estate. This will prevent any unauthorized sale or mortgaging of the property. Call me if the Ward owns real estate outside of the State. If the property is rented to others, you should direct the tenants to pay all rent to you as Guardian.

In the case of automobiles, real estate and household effects, you should make sure that the property is insured against fire, theft and other hazards (for its replacement value), as well as against liability to third parties (including workers' compensation claims of household help). You may insure the property, the Ward and yourself without prior Court approval.

You should also consider canceling charge accounts and credit cards in the Ward's name to make sure that no unauthorized purchases are made.

B. Prepare the Inventory

An Inventory of all assets owned by the Ward at the time of your appointment (regardless of where located) must be filed with the Court. [The value of the non-cash assets is then determined ("appraised") by a Court-appointed referee.] The Inventory [and Appraisement]: advises the Court of the extent of the Ward's Estate and indirectly of the income likely to be received for the Ward's support; assists the Court in determining the sufficiency of your bond; serves as the initial listing of property for which you are accountable; and sets the initial minimum sales price and insurable value for the Ward's real estate.

[Unless the Court directs otherwise, the wages of an employed Ward remain in the control of the Ward. You are not accountable to the Court for the wages and they are not to be inventoried. Community/marital property which remains in the control of the Ward's spouse need not be inventoried.]

I will assist you in preparing the final draft of the Inventory and filing it with the [referee and the] Court.

C. Establish a Budget

You should prepare a budget for the Ward in conjunction with the Guardian of the Person and, if possible, with the Ward. The budget should project income from all sources, including income from investments and employment and income from the government, insurance companies, (former) employers and trusts. It should also project all expenses, including housing, food, clothing, personal care, in-home assistants, medical care, transportation, insurance, utilities, taxes, entertainment, Estate administrative costs (such as bond premiums, Guardian fees, accounting fees and attorney fees) and, if authorized, support of the Ward's legal dependents. In establishing a budget, you should remember your *sole* responsibility is to the Ward and those entitled by law to current support from the Ward. You should not deprive the Ward of any reasonable item merely to permit his or her heirs to inherit more property. Your responsibility is to the Ward, not to the heirs.

You will need to discuss with me and the Guardian of the Person how various expenses should be paid. In most cases it is simpler for the Guardian of the Estate to pay the expenses directly, in which case you should arrange to have the bills of regular suppliers of goods and services sent directly to you. However, there may be certain situations, or certain expenses, where it is simpler to pay the money over to the Guardian of the Person, or in certain limited circumstances, to the Ward, to permit that person to pay the expenses. For example, the Ward may enjoy having a small checking account with which to pay monthly utility bills. However, if the Ward will pay the utility bills, you should ask the utility to notify you before any service is cut off for non-payment.

Once a budget has been set, it is often appropriate to receive Court approval of the proposed expenditures, especially if unusual expenditures are anticipated or it is anticipated that funds will be expended for the benefit of persons other than the Ward.

D. Make Suitable Investments

The Ward's investments should be reviewed (perhaps with a qualified financial consultant) to determine whether they are appropriate in light of the Ward's life expectancy, income requirements and size of the Estate. You should review any proposed changes with the Ward and be sensitive to the Ward's perception of what constitutes a risky investment. Before acting on any proposed sale or purchase, you should consult with me to determine whether you need prior Court approval.

[No prior Court approval is required for the purchase of direct obligations of the Federal or State government with a remaining maturity of not more than five years, stocks and bonds listed and purchased on a United States exchange, and registered money market mutual funds invested in Federal obligations. All other proposed investments require prior approval. For example, investments in other mutual funds, in over-the-counter stocks or bonds and in real estate (even a residence for the Ward) require prior Court approval. However, if the Ward had established a dividend reinvestment plan with a mutual fund or corporation prior to the establishment of the Guardianship, the plan may be continued by you without prior Court approval. In general, the Court will not approve investments in unsecured loans, secured loans to relatives, or obligations of foreign countries or foreign corporations.]

When the Guardianship needs cash, you must choose between raising the cash by borrowing, by the sale of assets, or both. [You must obtain prior Court approval to borrow money.] No Court approval is required to withdraw funds from or sell the following investments:

- [Deposits in an insured bank, an insured savings and loan association or an insured credit union located in the state (remember, you should not keep more than $100,000 in any one financial institution);]
- [Federal and State obligations, the obligations of Federal agencies and State political subdivisions (e.g., counties and cities); or]
- [Stocks, bonds and other securities listed and sold on an established stock or bond exchange in the United States.]

Also, no prior Court approval is required for the sale of personal and household effects with an aggregate value of [less than $5,000, provided the Ward agrees or is incapable of agreeing]. However, you should not rush to sell household effects just because it appears likely that the Ward will have to be placed in a nursing home.

Generally, the sale of all other Estate property requires prior Court approval and you should call me before making any final decision to sell. The sale of real estate also normally requires Court confirmation of the specific sale agreement you enter into. You may use an agent to sell the property. [However you must obtain Court approval before you can enter into an exclusive contract to sell. You also need prior Court approval to rent out the property, unless (i) the monthly rental does not exceed $1,500 and the term does not exceed two years, or (ii) the rental term is month-to-month.]

E. Pay Taxes

As Guardian of the Estate, you are responsible for filing tax returns on behalf of the Ward. You may hire and pay a tax preparer to prepare the returns without prior Court approval. If you suspect that the Ward has not filed all required returns, you should contact the Internal Revenue Service and State tax authorities to obtain copies of prior returns that have been filed and to ascertain what returns are missing. There are penalties for both a failure to file a return and a failure to pay the tax. A failure to file penalty generally will not be assessed if it can be shown that the failure was due to reasonable cause and not due to willful neglect. The fact that the Guardianship has been created may be sufficient grounds for waiving the penalty.

You should also make sure that real estate taxes, personal property taxes and employment taxes (e.g., for in-home help) are paid when due. [If the Ward resides in a household that receives less than $_____ in annual income, the State may pay part of the real estate taxes. If the Ward resides in a household that receives more than $_____ but less than $_____ in annual income, part of the real estate taxes may be postponed.]

F. Account to the Court

Unless the Court says otherwise, you must file an accounting with the Court [one year] after your appointment, thereafter at least every [two years], and upon termination of the Guardianship. If possible, you should review the accounting with the Ward prior to the Court hearing on the accounting. In general, the Court must approve the accounting before either you or I may be paid for the work that has been done.

The accounting must show all receipts and expenditures, investment transactions and property on hand at the end of the accounting period. To prepare the accounting properly, you must keep detailed records and documentation. A detailed check register and copies of all bills will usually be sufficient.

As you can see, your responsibilities will be many and will require a significant amount of your time. After you have considered the points discussed above, please call me to arrange a meeting so that we can discuss how to efficiently carry out these responsibilities and discuss any questions that you have that are not covered by this letter.

I look forward to working with you during the coming months to insure that the Ward is provided the best possible help under the circumstances.

Very truly yours,

John B. (or Jacqueline) Lawyer

This sample letter, drafted by W. Scott Thomas, Esq., is derived from his work in the HANDBOOK FOR CONSERVATORS and is in turn reproduced in the booklet, *Guardianship of the Elderly: A Primer for Attorneys*, at pages E-2–E-6 (1990), prepared by the American Bar Association's Commission on Legal Problems of the Elderly and the Young Lawyers Division, Committee on the Delivery of Legal Services to the Elderly. The letter, itself, is based on California conservatorship law; thus, bracketed material may have to be revised in order to reflect local law.

Power of Attorney for Health Care and Instructions for Completion

1 DESIGNATION OF HEALTH CARE AGENT.

I, _____ hereby appoint:
(Principal)

_____
(Attorney-in-fact's name)

_____
(Address)

Home: _____ Work: _____

as my attorney-in-fact (or "Agent") to make health and personal care decisions for me as authorized in this document.

2 EFFECTIVE DATE AND DURABILITY.

By this document I intend to create a durable power of attorney effective upon, and only during, any period of incapacity in which, in the opinion of my agent and attending physician, I am unable to make or communicate a choice regarding a particular health care decision.

3   AGENT'S POWERS.

I grant to my Agent full authority to make decisions for me regarding my health care. In exercising this authority, my Agent shall follow my desires as stated in this document or otherwise known to my Agent. In making any decision, my Agent shall attempt to discuss the proposed decision with me to determine my desires if I am able to communicate in any way. If my Agent cannot determine the choice I would want made, then my Agent shall make a choice for me based upon what my Agent believes to be in my best interests. My Agent's authority to interpret my desires is intended to be as broad as possible, except for any limitations I may state below. Accordingly, unless specifically limited by Section 4, below, my Agent is authorized as follows:

A.   To consent, refuse, or withdraw consent to any and all types of medical care, treatment, surgical procedures, diagnostic procedures, medication, and the use of mechanical or other procedures that affect any bodily function, including (but not limited to) artificial respiration, nutritional support and hydration, and cardiopulmonary resuscitation;

B.   To have access to medical records and information to the same extent that I am entitled to, including the right to disclose the contents to others;

C.   To authorize my admission to or discharge (even against medical advice) from any hospital, nursing home, residential care, assisted living or similar facility or service;

D.   To contract on my behalf for any health care related service or facility on my behalf, without my Agent incurring personal financial liability for such contracts;

E.   To hire and fire medical, social service, and other support personnel responsible for my care;

F.   To authorize, or refuse to authorize, any medication or procedure intended to relieve pain, even though such use may lead to physical damage, addiction, or hasten the moment of (but not intentionally cause) my death;

G.   To make anatomical gifts of part or all of my body for medical purposes, authorize an autopsy, and direct the disposition of my remains, to the extent permitted by law;

H.   To take any other action necessary to do what I authorize here, including (but not limited to) granting any waiver or release from liability required by any hospital, physician, or other health care provider; signing any documents relating to refusals of treatment or the leaving of a facility against medical advice, and pursuing any legal action in my name, and at the expense of my estate to force compliance with my wishes as determined by my Agent, or to seek actual or punitive damages for the failure to comply.

4 STATEMENT OF DESIRES, SPECIAL PROVISIONS, AND LIMITATIONS.

A. The powers granted above do not include the following powers or are subject to the following rules or limitations:

_____
_____
_____
_____

B. With respect to any Life-Sustaining Treatment, I direct the following:

(INITIAL ONLY ONE OF THE FOLLOWING PARAGRAPHS)

 REFERENCE TO LIVING WILL. I specifically direct my Agent to follow any health care declaration or ''living will'' executed by me.

GRANT OF DISCRETION TO AGENT. I do not want my life to be prolonged nor do I want life-sustaining treatment to be provided or continued if my Agent believes the burdens of the treatment outweigh the expected benefits. I want my Agent to consider the relief of suffering, the expense involved and the quality as well as the possible extension of my life in making decisions concerning life-sustaining treatment.

DIRECTIVE TO WITHHOLD OR WITHDRAW TREATMENT. I do not want my life to be prolonged and I do not want life-sustaining treatment:
a. if I have a condition that is incurable or irreversible and, without the administration of life-sustaining treatment, expected to result in death within a relatively short time; or
b. if I am in a coma or persistent vegetative state which is reasonably concluded to be irreversible.

DIRECTIVE FOR MAXIMUM TREATMENT. I want my life to be prolonged to the greatest extent possible without regard to my condition, the chances I have for recovery, or the cost of the procedures.

DIRECTIVE IN MY OWN WORDS: _____
_____
_____

C. With respect to Nutrition and Hydration provided by means of a nasogastric tube or tube into the stomach, intestines, or veins, I wish to make clear that . . .

(INITIAL ONLY ONE)

 I *intend* to include these procedures among the "life-sustaining procedures" that may be withheld or withdrawn under the conditions given above.

 I *do not intend* to include these procedures among the "life-sustaining procedures" that may be withheld or withdrawn.

5   SUCCESSORS.

If any Agent named by me shall die, become legally disabled, resign, refuse to act, be unavailable, or (if any Agent is my spouse) be legally separated or divorced from me, I name the following (each to act alone and successively, in the order named) as successors to my Agent:

    A.   First Alternate Agent _____
          Address: _____
          Telephone: _____

    B.   Second Alternate Agent _____
          Address: _____
          Telephone: _____

6   PROTECTION OF THIRD PARTIES WHO RELY ON MY AGENT.

No person who relies in good faith upon any representations by my Agent or Successor Agent shall be liable to me, my estate, my heirs or assigns, for recognizing the Agent's authority.

7   NOMINATION OF GUARDIAN.

If a guardian of my person should for any reason be appointed, I nominate my Agent (or his or her successor), named above.

8   ADMINISTRATIVE PROVISIONS.

    A.   I revoke any prior power of attorney for health care.
    B.   This power of attorney is intended to be valid in any jurisdiction in which it is presented.
    C.   My Agent shall not be entitled to compensation for services performed under this power of attorney, but he or she shall be entitled to reimbursement for all reasonable expenses incurred as a result of carrying out any provision of this power of attorney.

D.   The powers delegated under this power of attorney are separable, so that the invalidity of one or more powers shall not affect any others.

BY SIGNING HERE I INDICATE THAT I UNDERSTAND THE CONTENTS OF THIS DOCUMENT AND THE EFFECT OF THIS GRANT OF POWERS TO MY AGENT.

I sign my name to this Health Care Power of Attorney on this _____ day of _____ , 19_____ .

My current home address is: _____

Signature: _____

Name: _____

WITNESS STATEMENT

I declare that the person who signed or acknowledged this document is personally known to me, that he/she signed or acknowledged this durable power of attorney in my presence, and that he/she appears to be of sound mind and under no duress, fraud, or undue influence. I am not the person appointed as agent by this document, nor am I the patient's health care provider, or an employee of the patient's health care provider. I further declare that I am not related to the principal by blood, marriage, or adoption, and, to the best of my knowledge, I am not the creditor of the principal nor entitled to any part of his/her estate under a will now existing or by operation of law.

Witness #1:

Signature: _____   Date: _____

Print Name: _____   Telephone: _____

Residence Address: _____

_____

Witness #2:

Signature: _____   Date: _____

Print Name: _____   Telephone: _____

Residence Address: _____

_____

NOTARIZATION

STATE OF _____)

) ss.

COUNTY OF _____)

On this _____ day of _____ , 19_____ , the said _____ , known to me (or satisfactorily proven) to be the person named in the foregoing instrument, personally appeared before me, a Notary Public, within and for the State and County aforesaid, and acknowledged that he or she freely and voluntarily executed the same for the purposes stated therein.

My Commission Expires:

_____   _____

NOTARY PUBLIC

COMPLETION INSTRUCTIONS

The Power of Attorney for Health Care presented herein may or may not fit the requirements of your particular state. A growing number of states have special forms or special procedures for creating health care powers of attorney. If possible, seek legal advice before signing any Power of Attorney. If not clearly recognized by law in your state, a document such as this one may still provide the best evidence of your wishes if you should become unable to speak for yourself.

Section 1 DESIGNATION OF HEALTH CARE AGENT: Print your full name here as the "principal" or creator of the power of attorney.

Print the full name, address and telephone number of the person (over age 18) you appoint as your health care "attorney-in-fact" or "agent." Appoint *only* a person whom you trust to understand and carry out your values and wishes. Do not name any of your health care providers as your agent, since some states prohibit them acting as your agent.

Section 2 EFFECTIVE DATE AND DURABILITY: The sample document is effective if and when you become unable to make health care decisions. That point in time is determined by your agent and your doctor. You can, if you wish, specify other effective dates or other criteria for incapacity (such as requiring two physicians to evaluate your capacity). You can also specify that the power will end at some later date or event before death. In any case, you have the *right to revoke* the agent's authority at any time by notifying your agent or health care provider orally or in writing. If you revoke, it is best to notify both your agent and physician in writing and to destroy the power of attorney document itself.

Section 3 AGENT'S POWERS: This grant of power is intended to be as broad as possible so that your agent will have the authority to make any decision you could make to obtain or terminate any type of health care.

Even under this broad grant of authority, your agent still must follow your desires and directions, communicated by you in any manner now or in the future. You can specifically limit or direct your agent's power, if you wish, in Section 4.

Section 4 STATEMENT OF DESIRES, SPECIAL PROVISIONS, AND LIMITATIONS:

Paragraph A. Here you may include any limitations you think are appropriate, such as instructions to refuse any specific types of treatment that are against your religious beliefs or unacceptable to you for any other reasons, such as blood transfusions, electro-convulsive therapy, sterilization, abortion, amputation, psychosurgery, admission to a mental institution, etc. State law may not allow your agent to consent to some of these procedures, regardless of your health care power of attorney. Be very careful about stating limitations, because the specific circumstances surrounding a future health care decision are impossible to predict. If you do not want any limitations, simply write in "No limitations."

Paragraph B. Because the subject of "life-sustaining treatment" is particularly important to many people, this paragraph provides a place for you to give general or specific directions on the subject, if you want to do so. The different paragraphs are options—choose only *one*, or write your desires or instructions in your own words (in the last option). If you already have a "Living Will," you can simply refer to it by choosing the first option. Or, the instructions you provide here can do what a Living Will would do.

Paragraph C. Because people differ widely on whether nutrition and hydration is something that ought to be refused or stopped under certain circumstances, it is important to make your wishes clear on this topic. Nutrition and hydration means food and fluids provided by a nasogastric tube or tube into the stomach, intestines, or veins. This paragraph allows you to include or not include these procedures among those that may be withheld or withdrawn under the circumstances described in the preceding paragraph. Either choice still permits non-intrusive efforts such as spoon feeding or moistening of lips and mouth.

Section 5 SUCCESSORS: If you wish to name alternate agents in case your first agent becomes unavailable, print the appropriate information in this paragraph. You can name as many successors in the order you wish.

Section 6 PROTECTION OF THIRD PARTIES WHO RELY ON MY AGENT: In most states, health care providers cannot be compelled to follow the directions of your agent, although in some states, they may be obligated to transfer your care to another provider who is willing to comply. This paragraph is intended to encourage compliance with the power of attorney by waiving potential civil liability for good faith reliance on the agent's statements and decisions.

Section 7 NOMINATION OF GUARDIAN: The use of a health care power of attorney is intended to *prevent* the need for a court-appointed guardian for health care decision-making. However, if for any reason, court involvement becomes necessary, this paragraph expressly names your Agent to serve as guardian. A court does not have to follow your nomination, but it will normally comply with your wishes unless there is good reason not to.

Section 8 ADMINISTRATIVE PROVISIONS: These items address miscellaneous matters that could affect the implementation of your power of attorney.

SIGNING THE DOCUMENT: Required procedures for signing this kind of document vary from signature only to very detailed witnessing requirements, or, in some states, simply notarization. The suggested procedure here is intended to meet most of the various state requirements for signing by non-institutionalized persons. The procedure here is likely to be more detailed than is required under your own state's law, but it will help ensure that your Health Care Power is recognized in other states, too. First, sign and date the document in front of *two witnesses*. Your witnesses should know your identity personally and be able to declare that you appear to be of sound mind and under no duress or undue influence. Further, your witnesses should not be:

- Your treating physician, health care provider, or health facility operator, nor an employee of any of these.
- Anyone related to you by blood, marriage, or adoption.
- Anyone entitled to any part of your estate under an existing will or by operation of law. Even a creditor of yours should not be used under these guidelines.

If you are in a nursing home or other institution, be sure to consult state law, because a few states require that an ombudsman or patient advocate be one of your witnesses.

Second, have your signature *notarized*. Some states permit notarization as an alternative to witnessing. Others may simply apply the rules for signing ordinary durable powers of attorney. Ordinary durable powers of attorney are usually notarized. This form includes a relatively typical notary statement, but here again, it is wise to check state law in case a special form of notary acknowledgement is required.

Appendix B is based on a booklet titled, *Health Care Powers of Attorney: An Introduction and Sample Form*, by Charles P. Sabatino, Esquire, (1990) and distributed in cooperation with the American Association of Retired Persons by the American Bar Association. A complete copy of this publication may be obtained by writing AARP, 1909 K Street, N.W., Washington, D.C. 20049.

Three other forms of advance medical directives may be of value and are to be found in: five CONSUMER REPORTS ON HEALTH 93-96 (Sept. 1993) where a check-off list of twelve or more situations (e.g., cardiopulmonary resuscitation, kidney dialysis, chemotherapy) are presented and one may in turn check the appropriate column indicating treatment (with various types) or nontreatment preferences; Conard, Elder Choice, 19 AM. J. L. & MED. 233, 283 (1993) where a listing styled, Patient Preference List, presents four medical states (e.g., irreversible coma, persistent vegetative state, etc.) and allows one to make five levels of treatment—resuscitation, ventilation, tube feeding, transfusion and antibiotics—one wishes or does not wish to receive; and Cantor, Advance Directives and The Pursuit of Death with Dignity: New Jersey's New Legislation, 44 RUTGERS L. REV. 335, 397-403 (1992), for an essentially shortened version of the model proposed by the American Bar Association in *Appendix B*. See generally NORMAN A. CANTOR, ADVANCE DIRECTIVES AND THE PURSUIT OF DEATH WITH DIGNITY (Ind. Univ. Press 1993).

Model Living Will

To my family, my physician, my lawyer, my clergyman

To any medical facility in whose care I happen to be

To any individual who may become responsible for my health, welfare or affairs

Death is as much a reality as birth, growth, maturity and old age—it is the one certainty of life. If the time comes when I, _____, can no longer take part in decisions for my own future, let this statement stand as an expression of my wishes while I am still of sound mind.

If the situation should arise in which there is no reasonable expectation of my recovery from physical or mental disability, I request that I be allowed to die and not be kept alive by artificial means or "heroic measures." I do not fear death itself as much as the indignities of deterioration, dependence, and hopeless pain. I therefore ask that medication be mercifully administered to me to alleviate suffering even though this may hasten the moment of my death.

This request is made after careful consideration. I hope you who care for me will feel morally bound to follow its mandate. I recognize that this appears to place a heavy responsibility upon you, but it is with the intention of relieving you of such responsibility and of placing it upon myself in accordance with my strong convictions that this statement is made.

Signed _____

Date _____

Witness _____   Witness _____

Copies of this request have been given to   _____

_____

This shortened version of a model living will was taken from FORREST J. BERGHORN, DONNA E. SCHAFER et al., THE DYNAMICS OF AGING 95, (Westview Press 1981).

Model Living Will with Comments and Instructions

To my family, doctors, and all those concerned with my care:

I, _____, being an adult of sound mind, wilfully and voluntarily make this statement as a directive to be followed in decisions regarding my health care. I understand that my health care providers are legally bound to act consistently with my wishes, within the limits of reasonable medical practice and other applicable law. I also understand that I have the right to make medical and health care decisions for myself as long as I am able to do so and to revoke this declaration at any time.

Comments and Instructions:

This declaration sets forth your directions regarding health care. You may give your instructions by filling in the blanks in any or all of the following paragraphs or leave these decisions to the discretion of your doctor or proxy (if any), except that you must complete Paragraph 6. You may attach any additional page or pages if more space is needed. You should discuss this with your doctor, if possible.

1 The following are my feelings and wishes regarding my health care (you may state the circumstances under which this declaration applies):

You may state your wishes regarding your care to apply when you have an incurable or irreversible illness or injury with no hope of recovery.

2 I particularly want to have all appropriate health care that will help in the following ways (you may give instructions for care you do want):

You may wish to specify that you want care to provide comfort and control pain and treatment that may substantially improve your condition.

3 I particularly do not want the following (you may list specific treatment you do not want in certain circumstances):

You may or may not wish to list specific types of treatment here. You may state that you do not want treatment if it will not help you recover and will only prolong the dying process.

4 I particularly want to have the following kinds of life-sustaining treatment if I am diagnosed to have a terminal condition (you may list the specific types of life-sustaining treatment that you do want if you have a terminal condition):

You may state that you want certain types of treatment tried for a limited time to determine whether they are beneficial; for example, cardiopulmonary resuscitation (CPR), or mechanical respiration. You may also state that you want all available medical treatment.

5 I particularly do not want the following kinds of life-sustaining treatment if I am diagnosed to have a terminal condition (you may list the specific types of life-sustaining treatment that you do not want if you have a terminal condition):

You may list specific treatment you do not want, such as CPR or long-term mechanical respiration, or any other life-prolonging care that is not necessary to provide comfort or relief from pain.

6 I recognize that if I reject artificially administered sustenance, then I may die of dehydration or malnutrition rather than from my illness or injury. The following are my feelings and wishes regarding artificially administered sustenance should I have a terminal condition (you may indicate whether you wish to receive food and fluids given to you in some other way than by mouth if you have a terminal condition):

Artificially administered sustenance (tube feeding) may prolong your dying indefinitely in a permanently unconscious or persistent vegetative state. You must state either that you want or do not want artificially administered sustenance, or that you want your proxy or doctor to make that decision for you.

7 Thoughts I feel are relevant to my instructions. (You may, but need not, give your religious beliefs, philosophy, or other personal values that you feel are important. You may also state preferences concerning the location of your care):

In addition to religious beliefs, personal values or preferences regarding the location of your care, you may wish to add a provision regarding organ donation or disposition of your remains.

8 Proxy Designation. (If you wish, you may name someone to see that your wishes are carried out, but you do not have to do this. You may also name a proxy without including specific instructions regarding your care. If you name a proxy, you should discuss your wishes with that person.)

If I become unavailable to communicate my instructions, I designate the following person(s) to act on my behalf consistently with my instructions, if any, as stated in this document. Unless I write instructions that limit my proxy's authority, my proxy has full power and authority to make health care decisions for me. If a guardian or conservator is to be appointed for me, I nominate my proxy named in this document to act as guardian of my person. (Form provides space for name, phone number, etc.)

If the person I have named above refuses or is unable or unavailable to act on my behalf, or if I revoke that person's authority to act as my proxy, I authorize the following person to do so. (Form provides space for name, phone number, etc.)

I understand that I have the right to revoke the appointment of the persons named to act on my behalf at any time by communicating that decision to the proxy or my health care provider.

You are encouraged to name a proxy to make health care decisions for you when you cannot do so. Your proxy must honor your wishes as expressed in this declaration, or act in your best interests if your wishes are unknown. If you name a proxy here but do not complete Paragraph 6 above as required, your proxy may not be able to make a decision for you regarding artificially administered sustenance.

This provision ensures that your proxy will be able to make health care decisions for you to the fullest extent permitted by law.

9 Notarization or witnessing. Your declaration should either be notarized or witnessed. (You may sign and date in the presence of two adult witnesses, neither of whom is entitled to any part of your estate under a will or by operation of law, and neither of whom is your proxy.)

If you choose to have your declaration notarized, the Notary Public cannot be named as a proxy in your declaration.

This more detailed living will, with commentary, derives originally from a booklet prepared by the Minnesota Living Will Coalition titled, *Questions and Answers About the Adult Health Care Decisions Act* and excerpted in GOOD AGE at 25 (Mar.–April, 1991).

Nolo Press of Berkeley, California, has produced a software computer program called *Will Maker 5,* which includes modules for creating three basic estate documents: an enhanced will with flexible bequest package; a living will (or health care directive); and a final arrangements document, including complete funeral planning.

The Dying Person's Bill of Rights

I have the right to be treated as a living human being until I die.

I have the right to maintain a sense of hopefulness, however changing its focus may be.

I have the right to be cared for by those who can maintain a sense of hopefulness, however changing this might be.

I have the right to express my feelings and emotions about my approaching death, in my own way.

I have the right to participate in decisions concerning my care.

I have the right to expect continuing medical and nursing attention even though "cure" goals must be changed to "comfort" goals.

I have the right not to die alone.

I have the right to be free from pain.

I have the right to have my questions answered honestly.

I have the right not to be deceived.

I have the right to have help from and for my family accepting my death.

I have the right to die in peace and dignity.

I have the right to retain my individuality and not be judged for my decision, which may be contrary to the beliefs of others.

I have the right to discuss and enlarge my religious and/or spiritual experiences, regardless of what they may mean to others.

I have the right to expect that the sanctity of the human body will be respected after death.

I have the right to be cared for by caring, sensitive, knowledgeable people who will attempt to understand my needs and will be able to gain some satisfaction in helping me face my death.

This appendix is reproduced from an article by Whitman & Lukes titled, ''Behavior Modification for Terminally Ill Patients,'' as it appeared in 75 AM. J. NURSING 98 at 99 (1975).

Notes

PREFACE

1. GEORGE P. SMITH, II, BIOETHICS AND THE LAW: MEDICAL, SOCIO-LEGAL AND PHILOSOPHICAL DIRECTIONS FOR A BRAVE NEW WORLD, Ch. 1, (Univ. Press Am. 1993).

2. LEGAL AND ETHICAL ASPECTS OF HEALTH CARE FOR THE ELDERLY 4 (Marshall B. Kapp, Harvey E. Pies, Jr., et al., eds.), (Health Adm. Press 1985). See also, Barnard, Ethics Issues at the End of Life: Dying, Death and the Care of the Aged, in THE CLINICAL CARE OF THE AGED PERSON, Ch. 10 (David G. Satin ed.), (Ox. Univ. Press 1994).

3. PAUL T. MENZEL, STRONG MEDICINE: THE ETHICAL RATIONING OF HEALTH CARE 195–197, (Ox Univ. Press 1990); Callahan, Health Care in the Aging Society: A Moral Dilemma in OUR AGING SOCIETY: PARADOX AND PROMISE at 332, 333 (Alan Pifer & Lydia Bronte eds.), (W.W. Norton 1986).

4. See generally, HANDBOOK OF THE HUMANITIES AND AGING, Chs. 1–4, 15, 16 (Thomas R. Cole, David D. Van Tassel, & Robert Kastenbaum eds.), (Springer Pub. 1992).

5. ROBERT C. ATCHLEY, SOCIAL FORCES AND AGING, Ch. 13, (Wadsworth, 6th ed. 1991).

6. Id. at p. 3.

7. FORREST J. BERGHORN, DONNA E. SCHAFER, et al., THE DYNAMICS OF AGING 343, (Westview Press 1981).

8. Supra note 5, at ps. 4, 9, 17–18.

9. Cohen, Realism, Law and Aging, 18 L. MED. & HEALTH CARE 183, 186 (1990).

10. KENNETH R. PELLETIER, LONGEVITY: FULFILLING OUR BIOLOGICAL POTENTIAL 3–5, (Dell 1981).

11. Id. at 24, 31.

12. Goleman, A Modern Tradeoff: Longevity for Health, N.Y. TIMES, May 16, 1991, at B8.

13. Guralnik, La Croix, Branch, et al., Morbidity and Disability in Older Persons in the Years Prior to Death, 81 AM. J. PUB. HEALTH 443 (1991).

14. Supra note 5, at 27.

15. Supra note 13.

16. Rovner, A Younger Generation Measures the Worth of Old Age, WASH. POST HEALTH MAG., Oct. 17, 1989, at 11.

17. Casswell, The Sorcerer's Broom: Medicine's Rampant Technology, 23 HASTINGS CENTER RPT. 32 (1993).

18. DANIEL CALLAHAN, WHAT KIND OF LIFE: THE LIMITS OF MEDICAL PROGRESS 22, 81, (Simon & Schuster 1989). See Kalb, Controlling Health Care Costs by Controlling Technology: A Private Contractual Approach, 99 YALE L. J. 1109 (1990).

19. Priest, The Road to Health Care Reform, WASH. POST, Jan. 26, 1993, at 12.

20. Euthanasia: What is the Good Death?, THE ECONOMIST, 15, 17 (July 20, 1991).

21. Callahan, supra note 17, at 253.

22. See Morreim, Cost Containment and The Standard of Medical Care, 75 CAL. L. REV. 1719 (1987).

23. TOM BEAUCHAMP & JAMES F. CHILDRESS, PRINCIPLES OF BIOMEDICAL ETHICS 106–47, (Ox. Univ. Press 2d ed.1983).

24. Callahan, supra note 17, at 264.

CHAPTER 1

1. Begley & Hager, The Search for The Foundation of Youth, NEWSWEEK, Mar. 5, 1990, at 44.

2. Gelman, A Kiss is Still a Kiss, NEWSWEEK, Mar. 5, 1990, at 53. See generally, GROWING OLD IN THE TWENTIETH CENTURY (Margot Jeffreys ed.), (Routledge 1989).

3. LEWIS THOMAS, THE FRAGILE SPECIES 71, 72, 77, (Macmillan 1992).

4. Id. at 76.

5. Id.

See GEORGES MINOIS, HISTORY OF OLD AGE: FROM ANTIQUITY TO THE RENAISSANCE, (Univ. Chi. Press 1989).

6. ROBERT BUTLER, WHY SURVIVE? BEING OLD IN AMERICA, Ch. 1, (Harper Collins 1975). See generally, THOMAS R. COLE, THE JOURNEY OF LIFE: A CULTURAL HISTORY OF AGING IN AMERICA, (Camb. Univ. Press 1992).

7. Id.

8. HERMAN J. LOETHER, PROBLEMS OF AGING: SOCIOLOGICAL AND SOCIAL PSYCHOLOGICAL PERSPECTIVES 3, (Dickerson Pub. Co. 1967).

9. Butler, supra note 6, Preface, 47; BETTY FRIEDAN, THE FOUNTAIN OF AGE 31, (Simon & Schuster 1993).

10. Friedan, id. at 49.—See also, McKendie, Equality Between Age Groups 21 PHIL. & PUB. AFFAIRS 275 (1992).

11. Butler, supra note 6, Preface; HAROLD G. COX, LATERLIFE: THE REALITIES OF AGING 243, (Prentice Hall 2d ed. 1988). See also, AGING IN SOCIETY: AN INTRODUCTION TO SOCIAL GERONTOLOGY, Ch. 12 (John Bond & Peter Coleman eds.), (Sage 1990); AN AGING WORLD: DILEMMAS AND CHALLENGES FOR LAW AND SOCIAL POLICY (John M. Eekelaar & David Pearl eds.), (Ox. Univ. Press 1989).

12. KATHLEEN WOODWARD, AGING AND ITS DISCONTENTS: FREUD AND OTHER FICTIONS 193, (Ind. Univ. Press. 1991).

13. Id. at 194.

14. Id. at 193.

15. Id. at 21.

16. Butler, Ageism: Another Form of Bigotry, 9 THE GERONTOLOGIST 243 (1969).

17. Kapp, Options for Long Term Financing: A Look to the Future, 42 HASTINGS L.J. 719, 735 (1991). See also, HARRY R. MOODY, ETHICS IN AN AGING SOCIETY, Ch.10 (Johns Hopkins Univ. Press 1992); Rovner, Truce Between Generations May Be Smoke, WASH. POST. HEALTH MAG., Jan. 30, 1990, at 14.

18. SHERWIN B. NULAND, HOW WE DIE: REFLECTIONS ON LIFE'S FINAL CHAPTER 71, (Knopf 1994).

19. KENNETH R. PELLETIER, LONGEVITY: FULFILLING OUR BIOLOGICAL POTENTIAL 75, (Dell 1981).

20. Id. See also, Strehler, The Understanding and Control of The Aging Process in CHALLENGING BIOLOGICAL PROBLEMS at 140 (John A. Behnke ed.), (Ox. Univ. Press 1972).

21. SIMONE de BEAUVOIR, OLD AGE 9, 13, 285 (Patrick O'Brien transl.), (Putman 1972).

22. FORREST J. BERGHORN, DONNA E. SCHAFER, et al., THE DYNAMICS OF AG-ING 333, 334, (Westview Press 1981). See Warnes, Being Old, Old People and the Burdens of Burden, 13 AGEING & SOCIETY 297, (Camb. Univ. Press 1993).

23. LUCILLE GRESS & ROSE T. BAHR, THE AGING PROCESS: A HOLISTIC PER-SPECTIVE 146, (Mosby Yr. Bk., Inc. 1984). See NATHAN BILLIG, GROWING OLDER AND WISER: COPING WITH EXPECTATIONS, (Lexington Books 1993); WILLIAM F. MAY, THE PATIENT'S ORDEAL, Ch. 7, (Ind. Univ. Press 1991).

See generally JOSEPH L. ESPOSITO, THE OBSOLETE SELF: PHILOSOPHICAL DIMEN-SIONS OF AGING (Univ. Cal. Press 1987).

24. AGING AMERICA: TRENDS AND PROJECTIONS ANN., An Information Paper to the Special Committee on Aging, U.S. Senate, No. 101–J (Feb. 1990), at 1.

See MARSHALL B. KAPP, GERIATRICS AND THE LAW, Ch. 1, (Springer Pub. 2d ed. 1992).

25. AGING AMERICA, id. at 2.

26. Id. at 3.

27. Id. at 6.

28. Id. at 9.

29. Id. at 11.

30. Id. at 12, 13.

31. Id. at 13.

32. Cohen, Realism, Law, and Aging, 18 L. MED. & HEALTH CARE 183, 191 (1990).

33. Supra note 24, at 95, 96.

34. Id. at 96.

35. Id.

36. Id. at 97.

An especially comprehensive consideration of aging is to be found in a two-volume report of the U.S. Senate's Special Committee on Aging entitled, DEVELOPMENTS IN AGING: 1990, #102–28 (1991).

Every 3 years, the U.S. Senate Special Committee on Aging, in association with the American Association of Retired Persons, the Federal Council on the Aging and the U.S. Administration on Aging publishes a statistical report on AGING AMERICA: TRENDS AND PROJECTIONS. It, too, is quite good as a resource tool. The current edition is 1994.

37. WASH. POST HEALTH MAG., Mar. 22, 1994, at 5.

38. See Lifelong Learning for an Aging Society, Info. Paper for Special Comm. on Aging, U.S. Senate, #102–J (Dec. 1991).

See generally Siegenthaler & Silva, The Aged in the World Constitutions, 4 J. AGING & SOC. POL'Y 199 (1992).

CHAPTER 2

1. Furrow, The Ethics of Cost Containment: Bureaucratic Medicine and The Doctor as Patient-Advocate, 3 NOTRE DAME J. L. ETHICS & PUB. POL'Y 187, 209–210 (1988).

2. Id. at 200 *passim*; Pellegrino, Rationing Health Care: The Ethics of Medical Gatekeeping, 2 J. CONTEMP. HEALTH L. & POL'Y 23 (1986). See generally E. GINSBURG, THE MEDICAL TRIANGLE: PHYSICIANS, POLITICIANS AND THE PUBLIC (Harv. Univ. Press 1990).

3. Callahan, What is a Reasonable Demand on Health Care Resources? Designing a Basic Package of Benefits, 8 J. CONTEMP. HEALTH L. & POL'Y 1, 9–10 (1992).

4. Podolsky & Silverner, How Medicine Mistreats the Elderly, U.S. NEWS & WORLD REPORT, Jan. 18, 1993, at 72.

5. Id. at 72, 73.

6. Id. at 75.

7. Id. at 75, 76.

8. Wetle, Age as a Risk Factor for Inadequate Treatment, 258 J. AM. MED. ASSN. 516 (1987). See also, Jecker, Age-Based Rationing and Women, 266 J. AM. MED. ASSN. 3012 (1991).

9. Schapira, Studnicki, et al., Intensive Care, Survival, and Expense of Treating Critically Ill Cancer Patients, 269 J. AM. MED. ASSN. 783 (1993). See Byrne, Vernon, & Cohen, Effect of

Age and Diagnosis on Survival of Older Patients Beginning Chronic Dialysis, 271 J. AM. MED. ASSN. 34 (1994); Ifudu, Mayers, Matthew, et al., Dismal Rehabilitation in Geriatric Inner-City Hemodialysis Patients, 271 J. AM. MED. ASSN. 29, (1994).

10. Lentzner, Pamuk, Rhodenhiser, et al., The Quality of Life in the Year Before Death, 82 AM. J. PUB. HEALTH 1093 (1992). See generally Fink, Siu, Brook, et al., Assuring the Quality of Health Care for Older Persons, 258 J. AM. MED. ASSN. 1905 (1987).

11. 1 Developments in Aging: 1990, Rpt. 102–28 of Special Comm. on Aging, U.S. Senate, Ch. 8 (1991). See generally IRENE POLLIN & SUSAN K. GOLART, TAKING CHARGE— OVERCOMING THE CHALLENGES OF LONG-TERM ILLNESS, (Random House 1994).

12. Schneider & Guralink, The Aging of America: Impact on Health Care Costs, 263 J. AM. MED. ASSN. 2335, 2337 (1990).

13. Id. at 2338.

14. Id. at 2238–2239.

15. NATHAN BILLIG, GROWING OLDER AND WISER, (Lexington Books 1993).

Beginning at age 25, a steady deterioration of the brain occurs to the point that at 70, it will be 11% smaller than that of a 40 year old. Bazell, The Infancy of Aging, THE NEW REPUBLIC, Dec. 22, 1986, at p. 17.

16. See generally ALZHEIMER'S DEMENTIA AND DILEMMAS IN CLINICAL RE- SEARCH (Vijaya L. Melnick & Nancy N. Dubler eds.), (Humana 1985); Norberg, Ethics in the Care of the Elderly with Dementia in PRINCIPLES OF HEALTH CARE ETHICS at 721 (Raanan Guillon ed.) (John Wiley & Sons, 1994).

17. Supra note 12, at 2338.

18. Id. at 2339. See Morgan, When Long Term Means Life Time, WASH. POST, Feb. 1, 1994, at A3.

19. Supra note 12, at 2339–2340.

20. Id. at 2340.

21. President's Commission for the Study of Ethical Problems in Medicine and Biomedical and Behavioral Research, SECURING ACCESS TO HEALTH CARE: THE ETHICAL IMPLI- CATIONS OF DIFFERENCES IN THE AVAILABILITY OF HEALTH SERVICES (1983).

22. Wing, The Right to Health Care in the United States, 2 ANNALS HEALTH L. 161 (1993); Callahan, supra note 3. See Childress, Ensuring Care, Respect and Fairness for the Elderly, 14 HASTINGS CENTER RPT. 27, 29 (1984) where he argues the two moral principles of beneficence (care or compassion) and justice provide a social obligation to acknowledge a health care right for all.

23. Scholes, La Croix, Wagner, et al., Tracking Progress Toward National Health Objectives in the Elderly: What Do Restricted Activity Days Signify?, 81 AM. J. PUB. HEALTH 485 (1991).

24. DANIEL CALLAHAN, SETTING LIMITS 241, (Simon & Schuster 1987). Editorial, Kovar & Feinleib, Older Americans Present a Double Challenge: Preventing Disability and Providing Care, 81 AM. J. PUB. HEALTH 237 (1991).

25. Id.

26. CALLAHAN, supra note 24, at 146.

27. EZEKIEL J. EMANUEL, THE ENDS OF HUMAN LIFE 91, (Harv. Univ. Press 1991).

28. Id.

29. CALLAHAN, supra note 24, at 247–48.

30. Id. at 248.

Stated otherwise, physicians should have a presumptive duty to strive to provide treatments that are potentially beneficial, i.e., they are empirically demonstrated such, are part of the standard of care for a given condition, or are recommended by established clinical guidelines and that are chosen by an informed patient or proper surrogate. Wolf, Health Care Reform and The Future of Physician Ethics, 24 HASTINGS CENTER RPT. 28 (1994).

31. Lindgren, Death by Default, 56 L. & CONTEMP. PROBS. 185, 228–29 (1993).

See The Multi-Society Task Force on Persistent Vegetative Status, 330 NEW ENG. J. MED. 1499, 1576 (1994).

32. Id. at 229.

33. Id.

34. Id. See also, Emanuel & Emanuel, Decisions at The End of Life: Guided by Communities of Patients, 23 HASTINGS CENTER RPT. 6 (1993).

CHAPTER 3

1. Piktialis & Koocher, The Economics of the Health Care System: Financing Health Care for the Aged Person in THE CLINICAL CARE OF THE AGED PERSON, Ch. 13 (David G. Satin ed.), (Ox. Univ. Press 1994).

2. Id. at 385.

3. Id. See generally Lundberg, National Health Care Reform: The Aura of Inevitability Intensifies, 267 J. AM. MED. ASSN. 2521 (1992).

4. Supra note 1, at 364.

5. See Brown, The Medically Uninsured: Problems, Policies and Politics, 15 J. HEALTH POLITICS, POLICY & L. 413 (1990); Blendon, The Problem of Cost, Access and Distribution of Medical Care, 115 DAEDALUS 119 (1986).

6. Kinney, Rule and Policy Making for the Medicaid Program: A Challenge to Federalism, 51 OHIO STATE L. J. 855 (1990).

7. Id.

8. Supra note 1, at 374.

9. MARSHALL B. KAPP, GERIATRICS AND THE LAW 62, (Springer Pub. 2d ed. 1992). A study by the Alliance for Aging has reported that Medicare costs will increase six fold by the year 2040. Vobejda, Baby Boomers Could Trigger Huge Health Care Crisis, WASH. POST, Jan. 4, 1993, at A3.

10. Hearn, Curing the Health Care Industry: Government Response to Medicare Fraud and Abuse, 5 J. CONTEMP. HEALTH L. & POL'Y 175 (1989). See generally, RENEWING THE PROMISE: MEDICARE AND ITS REFORM (David Blumenthal, Mark Schlesinger, et al., eds.), (Ox. Univ. Press 1988).

11. Id.

12. Sharkey & Buckle, The Medicare Prospective Payment System: Impact on the Frail, Elderly and Alternative Reimbursement Formula, 3 NOTRE DAME J. L. ETHICS & PUB. POL'Y 227, 231 (1988).

13. Supra note 11.

14. Supra note 12, at 232. See also, Dougherty, Ethical Perspectives on Prospective Payment, 19 HASTINGS CENTER RPT. 5 (1989).

15. Supra note 12, at 233.

16. Id.

17. WASH. POST HEALTH MAG., July 28, 1992, at 19.

18. Supra note 12, at 233; Gilbert, Is America Abandoning Sick Patients?, N.Y. TIMES MAG., April 29, 1990, at 22.

19. Schwartz & Mendelson, Hospital Cost Containment in the 1980s, 324 N. ENG. J. MED. 1037 (1991).

20. Gilbert, supra note 18. See generally Gibbs, Income Capital and The Cost of Care in Old Age, 11 AGEING & SOCIETY 373 (1991).

21. Id.

22. 42 U.S.C.A. §3001 et seq. (1973).

23. 1 DEVELOPMENTS IN AGING: 1990, Rpt. of Special Comm. on Aging #102–28, U.S. Senate (1991).

24. Jette, Disability Trends and Community Long Term Health Care in THE CLINICAL CARE OF THE AGED PERSON at 353, (David G. Satin ed.), (Ox. Univ. Press 1994). See Weitzman, Legal and Policy Aspects of Home Care Coverage, 1 ANNALS HEALTH L. 1 (1992).

25. ROBERT C. ATCHLEY, SOCIAL FORCE AND AGING 371, 372, (Wadsworth 6th ed. 1991).

26. Supra note 1, at 375. See generally Feder, Health Care of The Disadvantaged: The Elderly, 15 J. HEALTH POLITICS, POL'Y & L. 259 (1990).

27. Piktialis & Koocher, supra note 1, at 367.

28. Id.

29. Id.

30. Id. at 368.

For example, it includes diagnostic laboratory tests—including x-rays, kidney dialysis treatment and supplies, radiology therapy, and nonroutine podiatry care. Id.

31. Id. at 367.

32. Id. at 370. See Rubin & Koelin, Out-of-Patient Expenditure Differentials between Elderly and Non Elderly Households, 33 THE GERONTOLOGIST 595 (1993).

33. Id.

See MEDIGAP POLICIES: FILLING GAPS OR EMPTYING POCKETS?, Hearings before Special Comm. on Aging, U.S. Senate, Mar. 7, 1990.

34. Supra note 1, at 375.

35. Williams, Rules of Living in Connecticut Change . . . , HARTFORD COURANT, Sept. 29, 1992, at A1. See Beck, Hager, Springen, & Barrett, Planning to be Poor, NEWSWEEK, Nov. 30, 1992, at 66.

36. 42 U.S.C.A. §1396a(k)(2) (1992).

37. See Sanders, The King Lear Strategy, FORBES, Dec. 9, 1991, at 164.

38. See Sartain, Probate Code Section 15306: Discretionary Trusts as a Financial Solution for the Disabled, 37 U.C.L.A. L. REV. 595 (1990).

39. See generally Russ, Eligibility for Welfare Benefits as Effected by Claimant's Status as Trust Beneficiary, 21 AM. L. RPTs. 4th 729 (1993).

40. Lohr & Donaldson, Assuring Quality of Care for the Elderly, 18 L. MED. & HEALTH CARE 244, 247–48 (1990).

41. DAVID HABER, HEALTH CARE FOR AN AGING SOCIETY: COST CONSCIOUS COMMUNITY CARE AND SELF-CARE APPROACHES 12–13, (Hemisphere 1989).

42. Supra note 40, at 248.

43. Burke, Medicaid-HMOs: A Device for Delivering Health-Care Service to the Poor?, 3 NOTRE DAME J. L. ETHICS & PUB. POL'Y 281, 284 (1988).

44. Supra note 41, at 8.

See Schickich, Legal Characteristics of the Health Maintenance Organization, in HEALTH-CARE FACILITIES LAW, Ch. 16 (Anne M. Dellinger ed.), (Little Brown 1991).

45. Id.

See Fleck, Justice, HMOs, and The Invisible Rationing of Health Care Resources, 4 BIOETH-ICS 97 (1990).

46. Supra note 43, at 287–88.

47. Supra note 1, at 382–83.

48. Id.

49. See generally HEALTHCARE FACILITIES LAW: CRITICAL ISSUES FOR HOSPITALS, HMOS, AND EXTENDED CARE FACILITIES (Anne M. Dellinger ed.), (Little, Brown 1991). Reinhardt, Reflections on the Meaning of Efficiency: Can Efficiency Be Separated from Equity?, 10 YALE L. & POL'Y REV. 302 (1992).

50. Supra note 41, at 9; MICHAEL D. ROSKO & ROBERT W. BROYLES, THE ECONOMICS OF HEALTH CARE 328 passim, (Greenwood 1988).

51. ALISTAIR McGUIRE, PAUL FENN, & KEN MAYHEW, PROVIDING HEALTH CARE: THE ECONOMICS OF ALTERNATIVE SYSTEMS OF FINANCE AND DELIVERY 231–232, (Ox. Univ. Press 1991). See generally BRADFORD H. GRAY, THE PROFIT MOTIVE AND PATIENT CARE, (Harv. Univ. Press 1991).

52. Rosko & Broyles, supra note 50, at 327.

53. Rich, With Easy Cuts Exhausted, Hospital Costs Could Jump, WASH. POST, April 11, 1991, at A3.

54. Supra note 25, at ps. 12, 378. See Lundberg, supra note 3; Gibbs, supra note 20.

55. DANIEL CALLAHAN, WHAT KIND OF LIFE: THE LIMITS OF MEDICAL PROGRESS 75–78, (Simon & Schuster 1989).

56. Id.

See Symposium, America's Health Care: Which Road to Reform?, 10 YALE L. & POL'Y REV. 205 (1992).

57. White & Fletcher, The Patient Self-Determination Act: On Balance, More Help than Hindrance, 266 J. AM. MED. ASSN. 410, 412 (1991).

58. Lubitz, Beebe, & Baker, Longevity and Medical Expenditures, 332 NEW ENG. J. MED. 999 (1995).

59. Kramer, Health Care for Elderly Persons—Myths and Realities, 332 NEW ENG. J. MED. 1027 (1995).

CHAPTER 4

1. PAUL T. MENZEL, STRONG MEDICINE: THE ETHICAL RATIONING OF HEALTH CARE 3, (Ox. Univ. Press 1990).

See Pellegrino, Rationing Health Care: The Ethics of Medical Gatekeeping, 2 J. CONTEMP. HEALTH L. & POL'Y 23 (1986).

See generally Mehlman, The Patient-Physician Relationship for an Era of Scarce Resources: Is There a Duty to Treat?, 25 CONN. L. REV. 349 (1993).

It has been suggested that physicians should be modern advocates on their patients behalf for both medical *and* monetary resources to which they may be entitled. Building upon a standard of resource use, it is argued that all patients accepted for medical care are entitled to assert they, in turn, receive a minimum quality of care which of necessity requires a minimum level of access to medical technology. Morreim, Stratified Scarcity: Redefining The Standard of Care, 17 L. MED. & HEALTH CARE 356 (1989).

2. MENZEL, supra note 1.

3. ALISTAIR McGUIRE, PAUL FENN, & KEN MAYHEW, PROVIDING HEALTH CARE: THE ECONOMICS OF ALTERNATIVE SYSTEMS OF FINANCE AND DELIVERY 172, (Ox. Univ. Press 1991).

4. HENRY J. AARON & WILLIAM B. SCHWARTZ, THE PAINFUL PRESCRIPTION: RATIONING HEALTH CARE 83, 89, (Brookings 1984).

5. MENZEL, supra note 1, at 4.

6. Supra note 4.

7. Id. at 84.

8. MENZEL, supra note 1, at 5.

9. Id. at 7.

10. See Dubler & Sabatino, Age-based Rationing and The Law: An Exploration, in TOO OLD FOR HEALTH CARE? CONTROVERSIES IN MEDICINE, LAW, ECONOMICS AND ETHICS at 92 (Nancy Dubler & Charles Sabatino eds.), (Johns Hopkins Univ. Press 1991).

11. Abrams, Shades of Meaning, 7 FRONTLINES 2 (May, 1990), Center for Health, Ethics & Policy, Univ. Colorado, Denver.

12. Id. See also, supra note 3, at 230.

13. Supra note 11.

14. Id.

15. Id. See Comment, The Oregon Basic Health Services Act: A Model for State Reform?, 45 VANDERBILT L. REV. 977 (1992).

16. Supra note 11, at 3.

17. Hirshfeld, Should Ethical and Legal Standards for Physicians Be Changed to Accommodate New Models of Rationing Health Care?, 140 U. PA. L. REV. 1809, 1843 (1992).

18. Hadorn & Brook, The Health Care Resource Allocation Debate: Defining Our Terms, 266 J. AM. MED. ASSN. 3328 (1991).

19. Waymark, Old Age and The Rationing of Scarce Health Care Resources in AGING AND ETHICS: PHILOSOPHICAL PROBLEMS IN GERONTOLOGY at 248, 249 (Nancy S. Jecker ed. 1991).

20. Id.; supra note 1, at 195–97.

21. Supra note 10, at 114.

22. Id. at 115.

23. Maguire & McFadden, The Ethics of Health Care Rationing: The Missing Value in HEALTH CARE RATIONING: DILEMMA AND PARADOX at 149–54 (Kathleen Kelly ed.), (Mosby Yr. Bk. Inc. 1994).

24. Sultz, Health Policy: If You Don't Know Where You Are Going, Any Road Will Take You, 81 AM. J. PUB. HEALTH 418, 420 (1991).

25. Haddad, Ethical Issues in Health Care Rationing in HEALTH CARE RATIONING, supra note 23.

26. Id.

27. Smith, *Triage*: Endgame Realities, 1 J. CONTEMP. HEALTH L. & POL'Y 143 (1985).

28. Supra note 25, at 12.

29. See generally Callahan, Symbols, Rationality and Justice: Rationing Health Care, 18 AM. J. L. & MED. 1 (1992).

Interestingly, a continuing study of the practices of over 900 hospitals supported by Genetech is showing that one quarter of all patients over 75 are not being given clot-dissolving drugs (which become one of the front-line therapies for minimizing the damage of heart attacks) because of their age. These elderly heart attack victims are denied standard kinds of care—including aspirin. WASH. POST HEALTH MAG., March 23, 1993, at 5.

30. Supra note 1, at 38. See Perett, Valuing Lives, 6 BIOETHICS 185, 193 passim (1992).

31. MENZEL, supra note 1, at 79.

See generally Symposium, Quality of Care and Health Reform: Complementary or Conflicting, 20 AM. J. L. & MED. 1 (1994).

32. MENZEL, supra note 1, at 80.

33. Id.

34. Id.

35. Id. at 81.

36. Id. at 80, 81. See also, Koppel & Sandoe, QALYS, Age and Fairness, 6 BIOETHICS 297 (1992) where it is argued QALYS are not ageist, yet fairness bespeaks treating the young before the old; and La Puma & Lawlor, Quality-Adjusted Life-Years: Ethical Implications for Physicians and Policymakers, in BIOETHICS at 404–418 (Thomas A. Shannon ed.), (Paulist Press 4th ed. 1993).

37. 42 U.S.C. §§ 12201–12213 (Supp. III 1991); Comment, The Use of Quality of Life Measures to Ration Health Care: Reviving a Rejected Proposal, 93 COLUM. L. REV. 1985, 2020–21 (1993).

38. Comment, id. See generally Thomasma, Ethical Judgments of Quality of Life in The Care of the Aged, Ch. 19, in QUALITY OF LIFE (James J. Walter & Thomas A. Shannon eds.), (Paulist Press 1991).

39. Rich, AMA Official Suggests Risk-Benefit Rationing, WASH. POST HEALTH MAG., Jan. 23, 1990, at 5.

40. LARRY R. CHURCHILL, RATIONING HEALTH CARE IN AMERICA 122 *passim*, (U. Notre Dame Press 1988).

41. Daniels, A Lifespan Approach to Health Care in AGING AND ETHICS: PHILOSOPHICAL PROBLEMS IN GERONTOLOGY at 237 *passim*, (Nancy S. Jecker ed.), (Humana 1991).

42. Supra note 19, at 253.

43. DANIEL CALLAHAN, WHAT KIND OF LIFE: THE LIMITS OF MEDICAL PROGRESS 175–183, (Ox. Univ. Press 1989).

44. Id.

45. Id. at 182.

46. Supra note 10, at 116. See Smith & Rother, Older Americans and The Rationing of Health Care, 140 U. PA. L. REV. 1847 (1992).

CHAPTER 5

1. HARRY R. MOODY, ETHICS IN AN AGING SOCIETY 134–35, (Johns Hopkins Univ. Press 1992); ETHICAL CONFLICTS IN THE MANAGEMENT OF HOME CARE: THE CASE MANAGER'S DILEMMA 37, 47 (Rosalie A. Kane & Arthur L. Caplan eds.), (Springer 1993).

See Hegeman & Tobin, Enhancing the Autonomy of Mentally Impaired Nursing Home Residents, 28 THE GERONTOLOGIST 71 (Supp. 1988).

2. MOODY, id. at 135.

3. Id. at 179–80; KANE & CAPLIN, supra note 1, at Ch. 3.

See O'Hare, Legal Issues in the Care of the Aged in THE CLINICAL CARE OF THE AGED PERSON, Ch. 11 (David G. Satin ed.), (Ox. Univ. Press 1994). See also, GEORGE J. AGICH, AUTONOMY AND LONG-TERM CARE (Ox. Univ. Press 1993).

4. MOODY, supra note 1, at 145.

5. See generally JAMES F. CHILDRESS, WHO SHOULD DECIDE: PATERNALISM IN HEALTH CARE (Ox. Univ. Press 1982).

6. Komrad, A Defense of Medical Paternalism: Maximizing Patient's Autonomy 9, J. MED. ETHICS 38 (1983).

7. Barnes, Beyond Guardianship Reform: A Reevaluation of Autonomy and Beneficence for a System of Principled Decision-Making in Long Term Care, 41 EMORY L. J. 633, 672 (1992).

8. Id. at 673.

9. Id. at 674.

See generally MARK R. WICCLAIR, ETHICS AND THE ELDERLY (Ox. Univ. Press 1993).

10. Id. at 675. See RUSSELL A. WARD, MARK L. GORY, & SUSAN R. SHERMAN, THE ENVIRONMENT FOR AGING: INTERPERSONAL, SOCIAL AND SPATIAL CONTEXTS (Univ. Alabama Press 1988).

11. Supra note 7, at 679.

See MARSHALL B. KAPP, GERIATRICS AND THE LAW, Ch. 8 (Springer 2d ed. 1992).

12. Lo, Assessing Decision-Making Capacity, 18 L. MED & HEALTH CARE 193 (1990).

In the case of *In re Von Bulow*, it was held by the New York Supreme Court that a determination of incapacity could not be based upon a physician's affidavit alone—even with a concurrence by all parties to its conclusions. Rather, the issue of capacity was reserved to a court as a viable issue of fact based as such upon medical evidence. 2 Misc. 2d, 129 N.Y.2d 72 (Sup. Ct. 1983).

13. Lo, id. at 194.

14. Id.

15. Id.

16. See Margolis, The Doctor Knows Best?: Patient Capacity for Health Care Decisionmaking, 42 OR. L. REV. 909, 913 (1992).

17. Id. at 923–25; supra note 12, at 197.

18. Supra note 16, at 923–25. See Appleman & Grisso, Assessing Patient's Capacities to Consent to Treatment, 319 NEW ENG. J. MED. 1635 (1988).

See Murphy, Older Clients of Questionable Competency: Making Accurate Competency Determinations Through the Utilization of Medical Professionals, 4 GEO. J. LEGAL ETHICS 899 (1991).

19. Appleman & Grisso, id., at 1636–38. See generally Altman, Parmelee, & Smyer, Autonomy, Competence, and Informed Consent in Long Term Care: Legal and Psychological Perspectives, 37 VILL. L. REV. 1671 (1992).

20. Regan, Protecting the Elderly: The New Paternalism, 32 HASTINGS L. J. 1111 (1981).

21. Id. at 1112.

22. Id. at 1113, 1120–1127.

See Kapp, Adult Protective Services: Convincing the Patient to Consent in LEGAL AND ETHICAL ASPECTS OF HEALTH CARE FOR THE ELDERLY at Ch. 20 (Marshall B. Kapp, Harvey Pies, et al. eds.), (Health Admin. Press 1985).

23. Supra note 20, at 1114; Kapp, id., at 233–236.

See DECISION-MAKING, INCAPACITY, AND THE ELDERLY: A PROTECTIVE SERVICES PRACTICE MANUAL, Legal Counsel for the Elderly & Am. Assoc. of Retired Persons (1987).

24. Iris, Threats to Autonomy in Guardianship Decision Making, GENERATIONS 39 (Supp. 1990).

25. Id.

26. See generally Beyer, Enhancing Self-Determination Through Guardian Self-Declaration, 23 IND. L. REV. 71 (1990).

27. Supra note 24, at 40.

28. das Neves, The Role of Counsel in Guardianship Proceedings for The Elderly, 4 GEO. J. LEGAL ETHICS 855, 858–59 (1991).

29. See ROBERT N. BROWN, THE RIGHTS OF OLDER PERSONS 328, (So. Ill. Univ. Press 2d ed. 1989).

30. Dubler, The Dependent Elderly: Legal Rights and Responsibilities in Agent Custody in ETHICAL DIMENSIONS OF GERIATRIC CARE at 148–49 (Stuart F. Spicker, Stanley R. Ingman, & Ian R. Lawson eds.), (Kluwer Academic 1987). See also, Hommel, Wang, & Bergman, Trends in Guardianship Reform: Implications for the Medical and Legal Professions, 18 L. MED. & HEALTH CARE 213 (1990).

31. Supra note 24, at 41.

32. Id. See generally ALLEN E. BUCHANAN & DAN W. BROCK, DECIDING FOR OTHERS: THE ETHICS OF SURROGATE DECISIONMAKING, Ch. 6 (Camb. Univ. Press 1989).

33. See Appendix A for a comprehensive model attorney's letter to a client appointed as a guardian detailing as such the complex duties he will have to perform in this capacity.

34. Supra note 28, at 865. See also, Hommel, Wang, & Bergman, supra note 26, at 219–223.

See generally COURT-RELATED NEEDS OF THE ELDERLY AND PERSONS WITH DIS-ABILITIES, Am. Bar Assoc. & Nat'l Judicial College (1991); Fentiman, Privacy and Personhood Revisited: A New Framework for Substitute Decisionmaking for the Incompetent Incurably Ill Adult, 57 GEO. WASH. U. L. REV. 801 (1989).

35. Court-Related Needs of the Elderly and Persons with Disabilities: A Blueprint for the Future at 11 (ABA 1991).

36. GUARDIANSHIP: AN AGENDA FOR REFORM at iii, ABA Commission on the Mentally Disabled, Comm. on Legal Problems of the Elderly (1989).

37. Id.

38. See generally Roundtable Discussion on Guardianship, WORKSHOP BEFORE THE SPECIAL COMMITTEE ON AGING, U.S. Senate, June 2, 1992, #102–22.

39. Coleman & Dooley, Making the Guardianship System Work, GENERATIONS 47 at 50 (Supp.1990).

40. Id.; Venessy, 1990 Guardianship Law Safeguards Personal Rights Yet Protects Vulnerable, 24 AKRON L. REV. 161 (1990). See generally supra note 38.

CHAPTER 6

1. JOHN STUART MILL, ON LIBERTY, at 68 (Gertrude Himmelfarb ed.), (Knopf 1974).

2. See Hinckle, Informed Consent and The Family Physician, 12 J. FAM. PRACT. 109 (1981).

3. MARSHALL B. KAPP, GERIATRICS AND THE LAW 15–16, (Springer 2d ed. 1992); see Deardorff, Informed Consent, Termination of Medical Treatment, and the Federal Tort Claims Act—A New Proposal for the Military Health Care System, 115 MILITARY L. REV. 5 (1987). See also, *Schloendorff v. Society of New York Hospital*, 211 N.Y. 125, 105 N.E. 9 (1914) (Affirmation of the ideal of personal autonomy by Justice Cardozo, who stated "[e]very human being of adult years and sound mind has a right to determine what shall be done with his own body."). See generally GEORGE P. SMITH, II, GENETICS, ETHICS AND THE LAW, Ch. 3, (Assoc. Faculty Press 1981).

4. Moody, From Informed Consent to Negotiated Consent, 28 THE GERONTOLOGIST 64 (Supp. 1988); see KAPP, supra note 3, at 15. (The word "autonomy" originates from Greek, meaning self law or rule and has been defined, inter alia, as being the moral right to choose one's own plan of life and action). See also, *Canterbury v. Spence*, 464 F.2d 772 (D.C. Cir.), cert. denied, 409 U.S. 1064 (1972); *Cobbs v. Grant*, 8 Cal. 3d 229, 502 P.2d 1, 104 Cal. Rptr. 505 (1972); *Nathanson v. Kline*, 186 Kan. 393, 350 P.2d 1093, clarified, 187 Kan. 186, 354 P.2d 670 (1960); *Schloendorff v. Society of New York Hospital*, 211 N.Y. 125, 105 N.E. 92 (1914), overruled on other grounds by *Bing v. Thunig*, 2 N.Y.2d 656, 143 N.E.2d 3, 163 N.Y.S.2d 1 (1957).

5. Id.

See Katz, Informed Consent—Must It Remain a Fairy Tale, 10 J. CONTEMP. HEALTH L. & POL'Y, 69 (1994). See also, ERIC J. CASSELL, TALKING WITH PATIENTS (MIT Press 1985).

6. See Meisel, The "Exceptions" to the Informed Consent Doctrine: Striking a Balance Between Competing Values in Medical Decisionmaking, 1979 WIS. L. REV. 413, 413–29. Ac-

cording to Meisel, the doctrine of informed consent is a source of conflicting viewpoints. He asserts that even though the doctrine has been "condemned by the medical profession as a 'myth' and a 'fiction,' it has been generally praised by legal scholars for promoting significant individual rights and has also been well regarded by the plaintiff's bar, though perhaps for less altruistic reasons." Id. at 413. See also, JAMES E. LUDLAM, INFORMED CONSENT 1, (Am. Hosp. Pub. Inc. 1978); BERNARD BARBER, INFORMED CONSENT IN MEDICAL THERAPY AND RE-SEARCH (Rutgers Univ. Press 1980); Heckert, Informed Consent in Pennsylvania—The Need for a Negligence Standard, 28 VILL. L. REV. 149 (1982–83).

7. Ludlam, supra note 6, at 2; see Barber, supra note 6. "For the longest part of their history, professional medical codes have been paternalistically nonegalitarian . . . . The Hippocratic Oath required that physicians refuse requests in certain cases . . . . The oath also stipulated that it is the doctor's right to determine what confidences to keep in his dealings with his patients. So, from the beginning in the practice of medicine, informed consent has not been an accepted norm." Id. at 28 (citing JEFFREY L. BERLANT, PROFESSION AND MONOPOLY: A STUDY OF MEDICINE IN THE UNITED STATES AND GREAT BRITAIN (Univ. Cal. Press 1975) and Pelegrino, Medical Ethics, Education and the Physician's Image, 235 J. AM. MED. ASSN. 1043, 1043–44 (1976)). See JAY KATZ, THE SILENT WORLD OF DOCTOR AND PATIENT (Free Press 1984).

8. Dubler, Some Legal and Moral Issues Surrounding Informed Consent for Treatment and Research Involving the Cognitively Impaired Elderly, in LEGAL & ETHICAL ASPECTS OF HEALTH CARE FOR THE ELDERLY, 247–248 (MARSHALL B. KAPP, HARVEY PIES, JR., et al., eds.), (Health Adm. Press 1985).

9. 95 Eng. Rep. 860 (K.B. 1767).

10. Id.

11. Id. at 862.

12. See, e.g., Burroughs v. Crichton, 48 App. D.C. 596 (1919); Pratt v. Davis, 224 Ill. 300, 79 N.E. 562 (1906); State v. Housekeeper, 70 Md. 162, 16 A. 382 (1889); Mohr v. Williams, 95 Minn. 261, 104 N.W. 12 (1905), overruled on other grounds by Genzel v. Halvorson, 248 Minn. 527, 80 N.W.2d 854 (1957); Schloendorff v. Society of New York Hospital, 211 N.Y. 125, 105 N.E. 92 (1914), overruled on other grounds by Bing v. Thunig, 2 N.Y.2d 656, 143 N.E.2d 3, 163 N.Y.S.2d 1 (1957); Rolater v. Strain, 39 Okla. 572, 137 P.96 (1913); Hunter v. Burroughs, 123 Va. 113, 96 S.E. 360 (1918); Hively v. Higgs, 120 Or. 588, 253 P. 363 (1927). See also, Note, Consent as a Prerequisite to a Surgical Operation, 14 UNIV. CIN. L. REV. 161, 181–183 (1940).

13. See Meisel, The Expansion of Liability for Medical Accidents: From Negligence to Strict Liability by Way of Informed Consent, 56 NEB. L. REV. 51 (1977).

14. There were cases that recognized the consent requirement, yet found implied consent in the patients presentation for treatment. See, e.g., Knowles v. Blue, 209 Ala. 27, 95 So. 481 (1923); Barfield v. South Highland Infirmary, 191 Ala. 553, 68 So. 30 (1915); O'Brien v. Cunard S.S. Co., 154 Mass. 272, 28 N.E. 266 (1891); McGuire v. Rix, 118 Neb. 434, 225 N.W. 120 (1929); Brennan v. Parsonnet, 83 N.J.L. 20, 83 A.948 (1912); Boydston v. Giltner, 3 Or. 1138 (1869); Dicenzo v. Berg, 340 Pa. 305, 16 A.2d 15 (1940).

15. See e.g., Schloendorff v. Society of New York Hospital, 211 N.Y. 125, 105 N.E. 92, (1914), overruled on other grounds by Bing v. Thunig, 2 N.Y.2d 656, 143 N.E.2d 3, 163 N.Y.S.2d 1 (1957); Mohr v. Williams, 95 Minn. 261, 104 N.W. 12 (1905), overruled other grounds by Genzel v. Halvorson, 248 Minn. 527, 80 N.W.2d 854 (1957); Rolater v. Strain, 39 Okla. 572, 137 P. 96 (1913); State v. Housekeeper, 70 Md. 162, 16 A. 382 (1889); see also, Pratt v. Davis, 224 Ill. 300, 79 N.E. 562 (1906) (basis of liability resting on trespass to the person). See generally, Plante, An Analysis of "Informed Consent," FORDHAM L. REV. 639, 648–53 (1968); Comment, New Trends in Informed Consent?, 54 NEB. L. REV. 66, 67 (1975). In those cases where a physician was found liable for battery, the physician was also deemed to be responsible for any physical ill effects that resulted from the treatment, regardless of whether the treatment was within the standard of care usually observed by members of the profession. See Comment, Informed Consent in Medical Malpractice, 55 CAL. L. REV. 1396, 1399 n.18 (1967).

16. See e.g., Wojciechowski v. Coryell, 217 S.W. 638 (Mo. App. 1920); Hunter v. Burroughs, 123 Va. 113, 96 S.E. 360 (1918); Theodore v. Ellis, 141 La. 709, 75 So. 655 (1917).

17. See Comment, The Evolution of the Doctrine of Informed Consent, 12 GA. L. REV. 581, 582–83 (1978). See, e.g., Pratt v. Davis, 224 Ill. 300, 79 N.E. 562 (1906) (patient agreed to an operation involving her womb but was not aware that her ovaries and uterus would be removed); Zoetree v. Repp, 187 Mich. 319, 153 N.W. 692 (1915) (patient's consent was for hernia operation

and patient did not consent to having her ovaries removed, which the physician did); *Bang v. Charles T. Miller Hosp.*, 251 Minn. 427, 88 N.W. 12 (1905) (patient was not informed that a prostate operation involving the tying off of his spermatic cords would result in sterility); *Mohr v. Williams*, 95 Minn. 261, 104 N.W. 12 (1905) (patient consented to an operation on the right ear but instead, the physician operated on the left ear); *Schloendorff v. Society of New York Hospital*, 211 N.Y. 125, 105 N.E. 92 (1914) (patient's consent was for an examination of a lump in her stomach; instead, the physician removed it); *Rolater v. Strain*, 39 Okla. 572, 137 P. 96 (1913) (patient's sesamoid bone was removed even though patient's consent was limited to allowing the operation on her big toe so long as no bones were removed).

18. Deardorff, supra note 3, at 8, citing Meisel, supra note 13, at 79–80.

These responses have been recognized generally in the courts as authorizing a physician to proceed with treatment and thereby provided a defense to an action for battery. Id.

19. Barber, supra note 6, at 29–30; see also, Beecher, Some Guiding Principles for Clinical Investigation, 195 J. AM. MED. ASSN. 1135, 1135–36 (1966). It was the Nuremberg Trials that first endorsed the notion of informed consent as an ethical and legal doctrine. Tancredi, Competency for Informed Consent, Conceptual Limits of Empirical Data, 5 INT'L J. L. & PSYCH. 51 (1982). See generally, Meisel, Assuring Adequate Consent 209–10, in ALZHEIMER'S DEMENTIA, DILEMMAS IN CLINICAL RESEARCH (Vijaya L. Melnick & Nancy N. Dubler, eds.), (Humana 1985); JAY KATZ, EXPERIMENTATION WITH HUMAN BEINGS 305–306, (Russell Sage 1972).

20. Deardorff, supra note 3, at 8. It was not until 1964 that the World Medical Association, in its 1964 Declaration of Helsinki, also subscribed to the requirement of informed consent, however, only for the limited extent of experimental procedures. See Meisel, id. at 209.

21. Id.

22. Id.

23. LUDLAM, supra note 6, at 8.

24. Deardorff, supra note 3, at 9. It should be noted, however, that merely mentioning the procedure to the patient generally continued to operate as a shield for physicians, id. See Meisel, supra note 13; see also, *Corn v. French*, 71 Nev. 280, 289 P.2d 173 (1955), where, while discussing exploratory surgery with a patient, the physician mentioned the possibility of removing the patient's breast. The patient's response made clear that she did not want her breast removed. The physician, in turn, stated that he had no intention of removing the patient's breast, and at a later date, the patient signed a consent form for a "mastectomy," not knowing the meaning of the word. Before being anesthetized, the patient reiterated her desire not to have her breast removed, yet when she recovered, she discovered that her breast had indeed been removed. The court upheld the validity of her consent, and the only issue raised by the court was whether the patient had revoked her consent.

25. Deardorff, supra note 3, at 9, quoting Meisel, supra note 13, at 80.

26. Meisel, supra note 6, at 419. See supra notes 3–8 and accompanying text.

27. See Fox, The Medicalization and Demedicalization of American Society, in DOING BETTER AND FEELING WORSE—HEALTH IN THE UNITED STATES at 5, 9–22 (John H. Knowles ed.), (Norton 1977). Fox notes the asserted rights to which patients feel an entitlement, expressed as "health," "quality of life," and "quality of death." Id. at 12–14.

28. Fox, supra note 27, at 14; see Heckert, supra note 6, at 151.

29. See Heckert, supra note 6, at 151.

30. Heckert, supra note 6, at 151. See McThenia, Deciding for Others: Issues of Consent, in BIOETHICS at 261–279 (Thomas A. Shannon ed.), (Paulist Press 4th ed. 1993).

31. 154 Cal.App.2d 560, 317 P.2d 170 (1957).

32. Id. at 578, 317 P.2d at 181 (emphasis added). Although the court clearly places an affirmative duty to disclose on the physician, the case fails to specify exactly what type of information the duty requires to be disseminated. The court simply stated that the physician was obligated to disclose "all the facts which materially affect [the patients] rights and interests and of the surgical risk, hazard and danger if any."

33. 251 Minn. 427, 88 N.W.2d 186 (1958).

34. Id.

35. Id. at 434, 88 N.W.2d at 190.

36. See *Lester v. Aetna Casualty Surety Co.*, 240 F.2d 676 (5th Cir. 1957). Even though the court did assert that physicians must generally advise patients of the diagnosis and proposed treat-

ment, it did not go so far as to grant the patient relief on the grounds that the physician failed to advise him of the danger involved with the medical procedure. Id. at 679.

37. See *Steele v. Woods*, 327 S.W.2d 187 (Mo. 1959). Here the court ruled that the physician should have informed the patient of available alternative treatments. Id. at 198–99.

38. See Deardorff, supra note 3, at 10.

39. See *Wood v. Pommerening*, 44 Wash. 2d 867, 271 P.2d 705 (1954).

40. See *Hall v. United States*, 136 F.Supp. 187 (W.D. La. 1955), aff'd, 234 F.2d 811 (5th Cir. 1956) (In this affirmation, the issue of consent was not addressed by the Fifth Circuit Court).

41. See Meisel, supra note 13, at 75. According to Meisel, in the more contemporary informed consent cases, the courts began to focus on the "conduct of the physician in obtaining the patient's consent." Id. See also, PAUL S. APPLEBAUM, CHARLES W. LIDZ, & ALAN MEISEL, IN-FORMED CONSENT: LEGAL THEORY AND CLINICAL PRACTICE 12, (Ox. Univ. Press 1987); BARBER, supra note 6, at 36; LUDLAM, supra note 6, at 21.

42. *Nathanson v. Kline*, 186 Kan. 393,350 P.2d 1093.

43. *Mitchell v. Robinson*, 334 S.W.2d 11 (Mo. 1960).

44. 186 Kan. 393 (1960).

45. Id. at 410. The court did, however, limit disclosure to what a reasonable medical practitioner would make under the same or similar circumstances. Id.

46. 334 S.W.2d 11 (Mo. 1960).

47. Id. at 19.

48. See Ludlam, supra note 6, at 23; Deardorff, supra note 3, at 11.

49. Deardorff, supra note 3, at 12.

50. Id.

51. GEORGE P. SMITH, II, BIOETHICS AND THE LAW 85, (Univ. Press Am. 1993).

52. MARSHALL B. KAPP, GERIATRICS AND THE LAW 26–29, 51–54, (Springer 2d ed. 1992).

53. See Tancredi, supra note 19, at 51.

54. Id. (emphasis added); see also, Allen R. Dyer, Assessment of Competence to Give Informed Consent, in ALZHEIMER'S DEMENTIA, supra note 19, at 228; MARGARET BRAZIER, MEDICINE, PATIENTS AND THE LAW 94–111, (Penguin 2d ed. 1992).

55. Tancredi, supra note 19, at 51; see Barnhardt, Pinkerton & Roth, Informed Consent to Organic Behavior Control, 17 SANTA CLARA L. REV. 39–83 (1977).

56. Hollowell & Eldridge, The Nurse's Role in Informed Consent, in 39 J. PRACTICAL NURSING 28 (1989).

57. See Tancredi, supra note 19, at 51–52. The identified groups include primarily children, the elderly, the mentally ill, the retarded, prisoners, and other institutionalized individuals. Id. at 52. See also, IRVING GOFFMAN, ASYLUMS: ESSAYS ON THE SOCIAL SITUATION OF MENTAL PATIENTS AND OTHER INMATES, (Doubleday 1961). (The author studied the regressive changes that occur as a result of long-term institutionalization).

58. Meisel, Assuring Adequate Consent, in ALZHEIMER'S DEMENTIA, supra note 19, at 208.

59. See Tancredi, supra note 19, at 52.

60. Id.

61. Id.

62. See *Canterbury v. Spence*, 464 F.2d 772 (D.C. 1972); *Cobbs v. Grant*, 8 Cal. 3d 229, 04 Cal. Rptr. 505, 502 P.2d 1 (1972); see also, Tancredi, supra note 19, at 52.

63. Meisel, supra note 58. He also points out that "patients need not be given information that they already know or that they can reasonably be assumed to know either by virtue of their own experience or by virtue of the fact that the information is common knowledge." Furthermore, he delineates those particular issues that a physician must inform a patient about, including the material risk of treatment, the anticipated benefits and alternative forms of treatment. Id. See Meisel & Kabnick, Informed Consent to Medical Treatment: An Analysis of Recent Legislation, 41 U. PITT. L. REV. 407, 427 (1980).

64. Id. It should usually be the physician who performs the informed consent discussion, including mentioning alternatives to the treatment and the possible outcome. A clerical worker can then get the necessary signatures after the interactive discussion has occurred. Hudson, Informed Consent Problems Become More Complicated, in 65 HOSPITALS 38, 40 (1991).

65. Schuck, Rethinking Informed Consent, 103 YALE L. J. 899, 943 (1994).

66. Id. 943 at n. 174.

67. Id. at 948.

68. Taub, Baker, & Sturr, Informed Consent for Research: Effects of Readability, Patient Age and Education, 34 J. AM. GERIATRICS SOC. 601 (1986). See also, Fitten, Lusky & Hamann, Assessing Treatment Decision-Making Capacity in Elderly Nursing Home Residents, 38 J. AM. GERIATRICS SOC. 1097 (1990).

69. Stanley, The Elderly Patient and Informed Consent, 252 J. AM. MED. ASSN. 1302 (1984).

70. Supra note 1, at 949, 950.

71. Id. at 950, 959.

72. See Fitten & Waite, Impact of Medical Hospitalization on Treatment Decision-Making in the Elderly, 150 ARCH. INTERN. MED. 1717 (1990); see also, RUTH FADEN & TOM BEAU-CHAMP, A HISTORY AND THEORY OF INFORMED CONSENT (Ox. Univ. Press 1986).

73. Tancredi, supra note 19, at 53.

74. See Tancredi, supra note 19, at 53; Hawkins, Consent and Confidentiality, in 103 TRANS. MED. SOC. LONDON 67, 69 (1986–87). Hawkins points out that a cynic may view informed consent as merely a form of ritual deception, since it is never completely possible for there to be an informed exchange, except in those instances where the patient is another doctor. Indeed, according to Hawkins, if it takes a physician 6 years to qualify and another 10 years to reach the level of knowledge that a surgeon possesses, how can a patient be so informed in a 10-minute dialogue with the physician. Id., citing JAMES CALNAN, TALKING WITH PATIENTS—A GUIDE TO GOOD PRACTICE (MIT Press 1983).

75. See Tancredi, supra note 19, at 53; Fitten & Waite, supra note 72, at 1717.

In actual practice, it may not be feasible to obtain informed consent from presumably competent medically ill individuals who are suffering from decisional impairments during a period of hospital-ization for acute illness. Fitten & Waite, id. See also, Scofield, Is Consent Useful When Resuscitation Isn't, in BIOETHICS at 342–357 (Thomas A. Shannon ed.), (Paulist Press 4th ed. 1993).

76. Tancredi, supra note 19, at 53.

77. See Fitten & Waite, supra note 72, at 1717.

Any determination of the capacity of an individual to decide on a course of treatment requires that person to possess a set of values and goals, have an ability to communicate and understand information, and be able to reason and deliberate about choices. MAKING HEALTH CARE DE-CISIONS: A REPORT OF THE ETHICAL AND LEGAL IMPLICATIONS OF INFORMED CON-SENT IN THE PATIENT-PRACTITIONER RELATIONSHIP 57–60 (President's Commission for the Study of Ethical Problems in Medicine and Biomedical and Behavioral Research (1982)).

78. See Tancredi, supra note 19, at 53. Tancredi also points out that it is conceivable for an individual to understand one type of risk, such as an especially severe one, without being able to comprehend other risks or benefits and alternatives to treatment. Id.

79. See Moody, supra note 4, at 64; see Hofland, Autonomy in Long Term Care: Background Issues and a Programmatic Response, 28 THE GERONTOLOGIST 3 (Supp. 1988). Hofland points out that patient autonomy is not a value indigenous to medical contexts, but one imported into medicine from extrinsic social agendas such as that of constitutional law and the evolution of individual rights. Id. at 4. See also, Komrad, A Defense of Medical Paternalism: Maximizing Patient Autonomy, 9 J. MED. ETHICS, 38 (1983).

80. Id.

81. Id.

82. Id.; see DONALD VANDEVEER, PATERNALISTIC INTERVENTION: THE MORAL BOUNDS OF BENEVOLENCE (Princeton Univ. Press 1986).

83. See Moody, supra note 4, at 64.

84. Id.

85. See Moody, Ethical Dilemmas of Nursing Home Placement, 11 GENERATIONS 16–23 (1987). The difficulties are heightened by professional interventions that verge on being more social than medical (e.g., eating, bathing, exercise), the patients' need for a degree of regimentation in their lifestyles, and the continuous fluctuation in competency or decisional capacity of the patients. See Moody, supra note 4, at 64–65.

86. Moody, supra note 4, at 65.

87. Id.

88. Id. at 67.

89. Id. Instead, negotiated consent proposes the structure of a team decision-making process, allowing for greater influence and more effective communication. Id.

90. Moody, supra note 4, at 67.

91. Id.

92. Id.

93. Krynaki, Tymchuk, & Ouslander, How Informed Can Consent Be? New Light on Comprehension Among Elderly People Making Decisions About Enteral Tube Feeding, 34 THE GERONTOLOGIST 36 (1994).

94. Moody, supra note 4, at 67. The notion exists, particularly with elderly patients, that a patient ought to be aware that negotiations are underway. Furthermore, the patient should know which parties are active participants in the negotiation process and ultimately, any decision derived at should be presented in such a manner as to be publicly defensible on a wide-scale basis. Id.

95. Id.

96. See id. at 68.

97. Id. (Emphasis added). Moody recognizes that typically, the physician and patient are unequal because physicians have vastly more knowledge at their disposal. Id; see supra note 78 and accompanying text. The patient, contrariwise, has the option of noncompliance with any particular regimen recommended by the physician and thereby retains an element of power for himself. Therefore, the situation may so develop in which both patient and physician each use the resources available to them, resulting in, at a minimum, the reduction of the inequality. See id. at 68.

98. See Moody, supra note 4, at 68, citing President's Commission for the Study of Ethical Problems in Medicine and Biomedical and Behavioral Research, MAKING HEALTH CARE DECISIONS: A REPORT ON THE ETHICAL AND LEGAL IMPLICATIONS OF INFORMED CONSENT IN THE PATIENT-PRACTITIONER RELATIONSHIP (1982). Moody recognizes the attractiveness of shared decision-making under ideal circumstances, however, fails to see its applicability in those situations far from ideal. Id. at 68.

99. See Moody, supra note 4, at 69. Unfortunately, all to often, the patient's rights, including the right to self-determination, are merely hypothetical. Moreover, Moody does point out that too strong an adherence to virtues is equally detrimental in attempting to find an equitable resolution to the consent issue. Specifically, virtue ethics and the traditional language of medical codes of ethics can often be used to support unlimited professional discretion on the part of physicians. Id.

100. Dubler, The Dependent Elderly: Legal Rights and Responsibilities in Agent Custody, in ETHICAL DIMENSIONS OF GERIATRIC CARE, 137 (Stuart F. Spicker, Stanley R. Ingman, & Ian R. Lawson eds.), (Kluwer Academic 1987).

101. Id.

102. See id. Their rights to choose require the cooperation of others and this often invites strangers to scrutinize prospective plans. Id.

103. Fitten & Waite, supra note 72, at 1717.

104. Id.

105. Riffer, Elderly 21% of the Population by 2040, 59 HOSPITALS 41–44 (1985); see Fitten & Waite, supra note 72, at 1717.

106. See Fitten & Waite, supra note 72, at 1717.

107. See id.; see also, Kokmen, Okazaki, & Schoenberg, Epidemiologic Patterns and Clinical Features of Dementia in a Defined US Population, 105 TRANS. AM. NEUROLOGICAL ASS'N. 334–336 (1980); Rocca, Ammaducci, & Schoenberg, The Epidemiology of Dementia, 19 ANN. NEUROLOGY 415–424 (1986); Neurological Disorders in the Elderly at Home, in 39 J. NEUROLOGIC NEUROSURGERY PSYCHIATRY 362–366 (1976).

108. See Fitten & Waite, supra note 72, at 1717. The attitude often prevalent among the elderly requiring medical treatment occasionally plays a role in excluding them from decision making as well. Id.

109. See id.; see also, supra note 47 and accompanying text.

110. See Fitten & Waite, supra note 72, at 1717.

111. Dubler, supra note 100, at 137. See Fitten, Lusky & Hamann, Assessing Treatment Decision-Making Capacity in Elderly Nursing Home Residents, 38 J. AM. GERIATRICS SOC. 1097 (1990).

112. Dubler, supra note 100, at 137.

113. Id.

114. Id.

115. See supra note 88 and accompanying text. An additional benefit of involving the family, physician, and friends reveals itself in the situation where both the memory and comprehension of the elderly may be reduced. These skills are very much involved in the communication process, and having parties who share an attachment to the patient involved in the decision-making process may ultimately allow for better representation of the elderly patient's desires. See Tymchuk, Ouslander, & Rader, Informing the Elderly, A Comparison of Four Methods, in 34 J. AM. GERIATRIC SOC. 818 (1986).

116. Hes, Hect, & Levy, Some Psychological and Legal Considerations in the Determination of Incompetence in the Elderly, 7 MED. LAW 151, 153 (1988).

117. Stanley, Guido, Stanley, et al., The Elderly Patient and Informed Consent, 252 J. AM. MED. ASSN. 1302, 1305 (1984).

118. Id. The study revealed that, in comparison to their younger counterparts, older patients did show poorer comprehension, yet generally also seemed to make equally reasonable decisions. Thus, the quality of decision making was not noted to be significantly adversely affected until comprehension ability was deemed to be severely impaired, as in severe senile dementia. Id.

119. Moody, supra note 4, at 69.

120. Id. Moody points out that, especially with elder patients, it is possible to provide opportunities and to safeguard rights, but without motivation, they will derive no benefits from these acts. It is essentially their own liberty that they must exercise in order to take advantage of the opportunities being made available to them. Id.

121. Moody, supra note 4, at 68. Full recording of information is usually wise but not always required by moral principle. In the case of litigation, however, a physician armed with clear written records has a much better chance of having his good-faith judgment upheld in court. Id.

122. See id. A basic example of what should be recorded is as follows: "Family talked it over and decided in favor of trying the new treatment, Patient agreed it was best." Id.

123. Moody is aware of the view that the "proposed C's, Communication, Clarification, and Consensus-Building" amount to only a procedural standard for conduct. Moody, supra note 4, at 69.

124. HARRY R. MOODY, ETHICS IN AN AGING SOCIETY 183, (Johns Hopkins Univ. Press 1992).

125. Id. at 180.

126. Id. at 174. See generally Smith, The Ethics of Ethics Committees, 6 J. CONTEMP. HEALTH L. & POL'Y 157 (1990).

See also, Caplan, Informed Consent and Provider-Patient Relationships in Rehabilitative Medicine, 69 ARCH. MED. REHABIL. 312 (1988).

127. PROTECTING PRIVACY IN COMPUTERIZED MEDICAL INFORMATION at 70, U.S. Cong. Off. Tech. Assessment (1993) (hereinafter PROTECTING PRIVACY).

See Dellinger, Medical Records, Ch. 8, in HEALTHCARE FACILITIES LAW (Anne M. Dellinger ed.), (Little Brown 1991).

128. PROTECTING PRIVACY, id. at 71.

129. Id. at 72. See EVAN HENDRICKS, TRUDY HAYDEN & JACK D. NOVIK, YOUR RIGHT TO PRIVACY: A BASIC GUIDE TO LEGAL RIGHTS IN AN INFORMATION SOCIETY (So. Ill. Univ. Press 2d ed. 1990).

130. 5 U.S.C. §552a (1988).

131. PROTECTING PRIVACY, supra note 127, at 72.

132. Id. at 73.

133. Id.

134. Id. at 5. See Squires, Federal Protection of Patients' Privacy Urged, WASH. POST HEALTH MAG., Feb. 8, 1994, at 8; HENDRICKS, HAYDEN, & NOVIK, supra note 129.

135. The address for MIB is P.O. Box 105, Essen, Massachusetts 02112, telephone 617-329-4500.

136. The address for AHIMA is 919 North Michigan Avenue, Chicago, Illinois 60611, telephone 800-335-5535.

137. Squires, Who Has Access to Medical Records?, WASH. POST HEALTH MAG., Feb. 8, 1994, at 9. See also, Alpert, Smart Cards, Smarter Policy: Medical Records, Privacy and Health Care Reform, 23 HASTINGS CENTER RPT. 13 (1993).

138. Moody, supra note 4, at 69.

139. Id. at 69. See Tomlinson, The Physician's Influence on Patients' Choices, 7 THEORETICAL MAG. 105–122 (1986).

See generally GEORGE J. ANNAS, THE RIGHTS OF PATIENTS: THE BASIC ACLU GUIDE TO PATIENTS RIGHTS, Ch. VI, (Humana 2d ed. 1989).

140. Nancy N. Dubler, Some Legal and Moral Issues Surrounding Informed Consent for Treatment and Research Involving the Cognitively Impaired Elderly, in LEGAL AND ETHICAL ASPECTS OF HEALTH CARE FOR THE ELDERLY 247, 248 (Marshall B. Kapp, Harvey E. Pies, et al., eds.), (Health Admin. Press 1985).

141. Id.

142. Id.

143. Tymchuk, Ouslander, Rohbar, & Fitten, Medical Decision-Making Among Elderly People in Long Term Care, 28 THE GERONTOLOGIST 59 (Supp. 1988).

144. Moody, supra note 4, at 70.

145. Id. at 69.

CHAPTER 7

1. Lindgren, Death by Default, 56 L. & CONTEMP. PROBS. 185 at notes 112, 122 (1993).

Advance directive means a written instruction such as a living will or durable power of attorney recognized by state law and relating to the provision of such care when an individual is incapacitated. Durable powers of attorney are also referred to as health care proxies. For a discussion of the various types of advance directives, see Conard, Elder Law, 19 AM. J. L. & MED. 233, 242–281 (1993).

2. Haman, Family Surrogate Laws: A Necessary Supplement to Living Wills and Durable Powers of Attorney, 38 VILL. L. REV. 103, n. 7 (1993).

3. Suman, More Find Peace of Mind in Living Wills, MIAMI HERALD, Feb. 10, 1994, at 1 BR. See generally Cantor, Prospective Autonomy: On the Limits of Shaping One's Post Competence Medical Forte, 8 J. CONTEMP. HEALTH L. & POL'Y 13 (1992).

4. Ganey, Living Wills Cited in Rise in Death: Many Forego Extra Measures, ST. LOUIS DISPATCH, April 29, 1994, at 1A.

5. Last Rights: Why a Living Will is Not Enough, 5 CONSUMER RPTS. HEALTH 93 (Sept. 1993). See also, Stone, Advance Directives, Autonomy and Unintended Death, 8 BIOETHICS 223 (1994).

6. Supra note 1.

7. Comment, Protecting the Right to Die: The Patient Self-Determination Act of 1990, 28 HARV. J. LEG. 609 (1991).

Under clinical standards, a futile case is one for which a cure is physiologically impossible, treatment is nonbeneficial and unlikely to produce a desired benefit for which a treatment, while plausible, has not been validated. Miles, Medical Futility, 20 L. MED. & HEALTH CARE 310 (1992).

8. Supra note 1.

9. See Areen, Advance Directives Under State Law and Judicial Decisions, 19 L. MED. & HEALTH CARE 91 (1991).

10. Virmani, Schneiderman, & Kaplan, Relationship of Advance Directives to Physician-Patient Communication, 154 ARCH. INTERN. MED. 909 (1994).

See Jecker & Schneiderman, Medical Futility: The Duty Not to Treat, 2 CAMB. Q. HEALTHCARE ETHICS 151 (1993). See also, Danis, Southerland, et al., A Prospective Study of Advance Directives for Life-Sustaining Care, 324 NEW ENG. J. MED. 882 (1991), where a study showed physicians routinely acted in ways which contradicted advance directives!

Another common reason for not executing an advanced directive is because of an inability to choose a proxy—owing to the absence of a trusted friend or relative or because there were too many and choosing one would cause conflicts. Markson & Steel, Using Advance Directive in The Home Care Setting, 14 GENERATIONS 25, 27 (Supp. 1990).

11. Id. at 913.

12. Id.

See Alexander, Time for a New Law on Health Care Advance Directives, 42 HASTINGS L. J. 775 (1991).

13. See Schneiderman, Kaplan, & Pearlman, Do Physicians' Own Preferences for Life-Sustaining Treatment Influence Their Perceptions of Patients' Preferences?, 4 J. CLIN. ETHICS 28 (1993). See also, Emmanuel & Emmanuel, The Medical Directive, 261 J. AM. MED. ASSN. 3288 (1989).

14. Emmanuel & Emmanuel, Decisions at the End of Life: Guided by Communities of Patients, 23 HASTINGS CENTER RPT. 6 (1993).

15. 110 S.Ct. 2841 (1990).

16. See generally Rouse, The Role of State Legislatures After Cruzan: What Can—and Should—State Legislatures Do?, 19 L. MED. & HEALTH CARE 83 (1991). At note 50 in this article, the citations to the 50 state statutory provisions for appointment of general durable powers of attorney statutes are listed.

17. 42 U.S.C. §§1395cc(f)(1), 1396a(a) (1991).

18. Comment, supra note 7, at 628.

19. McCloskey, Between Isolation and Intrusion, The Patient Self-Determination Act, 19 L. MED. & HEALTH CARE 80 (1991).

20. Supra note 18, at 626.

21. Supra note 18, at 615, n. 28 (quoting Prof. John C. Fletcher).

22. Supra note 18, at 628.

23. President's Commission for the Study of Ethical Problems in Medicine and Biomedical and Behavioral Research, DECIDING TO FOREGO LIFE-SUSTAINING TREATMENT: ETHICAL, MEDICAL, AND LEGAL ISSUES IN TREATMENT DECISIONS 139 (1983).

See generally, Kutner, Euthanasia: Due Process for Death with Dignity: The Living Will, 54 IND. L. J. 201 (1979).

See Appendix C and Appendix D for models of living wills. A very thorough example of an annotated living will is to be found in Cantor, My Annotated Living Will, 18 L. MED. & HEALTH CARE 114 (1990).

24. President's Commission, supra note 23, at 140.

25. Id.

One jurisdiction, the New Jersey Supreme Court, held in *In re Conroy*, 98 N.J. 321, 351, 486 A.2d 1209, 1224 (1985) that declining life sustaining medical treatment should not be viewed as an attempt to commit suicide.

26. For a current listing of the statutes, see supra note 2, at 125, n.122.

27. JOHN E. NOWAK, RONALD D. ROTUNDA, & J. NELSON YOUNG, CONSTITUTIONAL LAW 765, (West Pub. Co. 2d ed.1983).

28. Id.

29. Forty-one states and the District of Columbia have either natural death or death with dignity legislation. See Alexander, supra note 12, at 758, n.15 for a complete listing of statutory citations.

No statutes authorize lethal injection and many physician directive statutes forbid the termination of hydration and nutrition even when, by intubation, food and liquids are administered. Alexander, id. at 761, n.61.

30. President's Commission, supra note 23, at 141.

31. Id.

32. See CAL. HEALTH & SAFETY CODE §§ 7185–7195 (West Supp. 1993).

In *Bartling v. Superior Court of Los Angeles County (Glendale Adventist Center)*, 163 Cal. App. 3d 186, 209 Cal. Rptr. 226 (1984), the court observed that even with a set of statutory guidelines as those found in the California Natural Death Act, such guidelines were "so cumbersome that it is unlikely that any but a small number of high educated and motivated patients will be able to effectuate their desires." 163 Ca. App. 3d at 194, n. 5, 209 Cal. Rptr. at 224, n. 5 (quoting *Barber v. Superior Court of Los Angeles County*, 147 Cal. App. 3d 1006 at 1015, 195 Cal. Rptr. 484 at 489 (1983).

33. President's Commission, supra note 23, at 144.

34. Id.

35. Id.

36. Id.

37. See e.g., Natural Death Act, CAL. HEALTH & SAFETY CODE §7188 (West Supp. 1993); Natural Death Act, KAN. STAT. ANN. §§65–28, 101–109 (1985); Withholding or Withdrawal of Life Sustaining Procedures, NEV. REV. STAT. §499.590.610 (1991); Natural Death Act, WASH. REV. CODE ANN. §70.122.010 (1994).

38. N.C. GEN. STAT. §§90.320 to 323 (1990).

39. VA. CODE ANN. §54-325.8:1 (Michie Supp. 1992).

See generally, Comment, Proxy Decisionmaking for the Terminally Ill: The Virginia Approach, 70 VA. L. REV. 1269 (1984).

40. N.M. STAT. ANN. §24-7-4 (Michie 1991).

41. ARK. CODE ANN. §82-3803 (Michie 1991).

42. President's Commission, supra note 23, at 145, 146.

43. For a complete listing of the state statutory citations, see Rouse, The Role of State Legislatures After Cruzan: What Can—and Should—State Legislatures Do?, 19 L. MED. & HEALTH CARE 83 at n. 32 (1992).

See generally, Martyn & Jacobs, Legislating Advance Directives for the Terminally Ill: The Living Will and Durable Power of Attorney, 63 NEB. L. REV. 779 (1984).

44. President's Commission, supra note 23, at 147.

45. Id.

46. Id. at 146.

47. Id. at 147.

48. Id.

49. Stigel, Hurme, & Stone, Durable Powers of Attorney: An Analysis of State Statutes, CLEARINGHOUSE REV. 690, 693 (Oct. 1991).

50. Id.

51. Id.

52. Id. at 694.

53. Unif. Rights of the Terminally Ill Act, 9B UNIF. LAWS ANN. 96 (West Supp. 1992). Only 13 states have adopted—to one degree or other—the Act. See supra note 2, at 124, n. 114.

54. Defined as ''any medical procedure or intervention that, when administered to a qualified patient, will serve only to prolong the process of dying.'' Sec. 1(4).

55. Defined as ''an incurable or irreversible condition that, without the administration of life-sustaining treatment, will, in the opinion of the attending physician, result in death within a relatively short time.'' Sec. 1(9).

56. See Marzen, The Uniform Rights of the Terminally Ill Act: A Critical Analysis, 1 ISSUES L. & MED. 441 (May 1986).

57. See Standards for Cardiopulmonary Resuscitation (CPR) and Emergency Cardiac Care (ECC), 227 J. AM. MED. ASSN. 837 (1974).

See generally, Evans & Brody, The Do Not Resuscitate Order in Teaching Hospitals, 253 J. AM. MED. ASSN. 2236 (1985).

58. Id.

59. Id.

See Miller, Death with Dignity and the Right to Die: Sometimes Doctors Have a Duty to Hasten Death, 13 J. MED. ETHICS 81 (1987).

60. PAUL RAMSEY, THE PATIENT AS PERSON 239–246, (Yale Univ. Press 1970).

See also, Smith, Death Be Not Proud: Medical, Ethical and Legal Dilemmas in Resource Allocation, 3 J. CONTEMP. HEALTH L. & POL'Y 47 (1987).

61. Capron, Legal and Ethical Problems in Decisions for Death, 14 L. MED. & HEALTH CARE 141 (1986).

62. Id.

63. Id.

64. Id.

65. See generally, Comment, A Structural Analysis of the Physician-Patient Relationship in No-Code Decisionmaking, 93 YALE L. J. 362 (1983).

66. Id.

67. See, e.g., In re Quinlan, 70 N.J. 10, 355 A.2d 647, 664 (1976).

68. See, e.g., *Lane v. Candura*, 6 Mass. App. 377, 376 N.E.2d 1232 (1978); *matter of Quackenbush*, 156 N.J. Super. 282, 383 A.2d 785 (1978).

69. See e.g., *Custody of a Minor*, 383 Mass. 697, 434 N.E.2d 601, 604–605, 607 n. 9 (1982); *In re Dinnerstein*, 6 Mass. App. 466, 380 N.E.2d 134, 135–36 (1978); *Brophy v. New Eng. Sinai Hosp.*, 398 Mass. 417 (1986).

For some groups of chronically ill, the right to refuse treatment ought to be offered as an option from the inception of treatment, itself. Knowing this option would be particularly reassuring for the unsophisticated who might be unaware of it. Applebaum & Roth, Patients Who Refuse Treatment in Medical Hospitals, 250 J. AM. MED. ASSN. 1296 (1983).

See Scofield, Is Consent Useful When Resuscitation Isn't, in BIOETHICS at 342–357 (Thomas A. Shannon ed. 4th ed.), (Paulist Press 1993).

70. Report of the Clinical Care Committee of the Massachusetts General Hospital, Optimum Care for Hopelessly Ill Patients, 295 NEW ENG. J. MED. 362 (1976).

71. Smith, *Triage*: Endgame Realities, 1 J. CONTEMP. HEALTH L. & POL'Y 143 (1985).

72. Report of the Clinical Care Committee of the Massachusetts General Hospital, Optimum Care for Hopelessly Ill Patients, 295 NEW ENG. J. MED. 362 (1976).

73. Id.

74. DO NOT RESUSCITATE ORDERS: THE PROPOSED LEGISLATION AND REPORT OF THE NEW YORK STATE TASK FORCE ON LIFE AND THE LAW (1986).

See generally, Mooney, Deciding Not to Resuscitate Hospital Patients: Medical and Legal Perspectives, 1986 ILL. L. REV. 1025.

75. The Proposed Legislation, "Orders Not to Resuscitate," numbers 12 actual pages in the Report, itself at 59–71.

Governor Mario Cuomo signed into law, on August 7, 1987, Chapter 818 of the Laws of New York, that adopted in major part the findings and legislative proposals of this Report. It became effective April 1, 1988, and was codified as N.Y. Pub. Health Law §§2960–2978 (McKinney 1987).

For a comparison of the new law with the proposals of the New York State Task Force on Life and the Law, see Comment, Do Not Resuscitate Orders: A Matter of Life or Death in New York, 4 J. CONTEMP. HEALTH L. & POL'Y 449 (1988).

76. §§2(6), 3, 4. N.Y. Pub. Health Law §2962 (McKinney 1993). This secondary cite to McKinney is the correlative citation to the Task Force Proposal. Both citations are presented in footnotes 72–96. Hereinafter, the New York Health Law Code citation will be McKinney §.

77. Id. at §5. McKinney §2964.

78. Id. at §4. McKinney §2964(2)(a)(b).

79. Id. at §5. McKinney §2964.

80. Id. McKinney §2964(2)(b).

81. Id. at §5(3). McKinney §2964(3).

82. Id. Id.

83. Id. at §§3, 4, 5. McKinney §2962(1).

84. Id. at §5. See McKinney §2961(3).

85. Id. at §6. McKinney §2965.

86. Id. McKinney §2965(2), (3).

87. Id. Id.

88. Id. McKinney §2965(5)(c).

89. Id. at §6(5). McKinney §2965(5)(a).

90. Id. at §7. McKinney §2966(1).

91. Id. at §9. McKinney §2968.

92. Id. at §10. McKinney §2969(1).

93. Id. McKinney §2969(2).

94. Id. McKinney §2969(3).

95. Id. at §13. See McKinney §2972.

96. Id. at §14. McKinney §2973(1).

97. Id. at §14(2). McKinney §2973(3).

98. Id. at §15. McKinney §2974.

99. Id. Id.

100. Id. at §16. McKinney §2975.

101. Park, Krone, et al., Use of the Medical Futility Rationale in Do-Not-Attempt-Resuscitation Orders, 273 J. AM. MED. ASSN. 124 (1995).

102. Hackler & Hackler, Family Consent to Orders Not to Resuscitate: Reconsidering Hospital Policy, 264 J. AM. MED. ASSN. 1281 (1990).

103. Teno, Hakim, et al., Preference for Cardiopulmonary Resuscitation: Physician-Patient Agreement and Hospital Resource Use, 10 J. GEN. INTERN. MED. 179 (1995).

104. Id.

105. Younger, Do-Not-Resuscitate Orders: No Longer Secret, But Still a Problem, 17 HASTINGS CENTER RPT. 24, 32 (1987).

See MARSHALL B. KAPP, GERIATRICS AND THE LAW 221–224, (Springer 2d ed. 1992).

CHAPTER 8

1. Younger, Do-Not-Resuscitate Orders: No Longer Secret, But Still a Problem, 17 HASTINGS CENTER RPT. 24, 33 (1987).

2. Malcolm, Reassessing Care of Dying: Policy Seen Evolving from A.M.A. Opinion, N.Y. TIMES, Mar. 17, 1986, at 1.

3. Capron, Legal and Ethical Problems in Decisions for Death, 14 L. MED. & HEALTH CARE 141 (1986).

4. Id.

5. Supra note 2.

6. TIME, Mar. 31, 1986, at 60.

See Cohn, Doctor and Patient, Facing Death Together, WASH. POST HEALTH MAG., Mar. 15, 1988, at 14.

7. Am. Medical News, Nov. 28, 1986, at 13.

8. Id.

9. Id.

10. See TIME, Mar. 31, 1986, at 60; supra note 2.

11. Id.

Previously, the AMA had acknowledged that, "When a terminally ill patient's coma is beyond doubt irreversible and there are adequate safeguards to confirm the accuracy of the diagnosis, all means of life support may be discontinued, but also acknowledged that most patients of this nature were probably given basic measures such as hygiene and artificial nutrition," 1982 AMA's Judicial Council, CURRENT OPINIONS, AMA 9–10 (1982), as reported in, President's Commission for the Study of Ethical Problems in Medicine and Biomedical and Behavioral Research, supra note 23, ch. 7, at 186, 187.

See Colburn, Withholding Food, WASH. POST HEALTH MAG., Jan. 26, 1988, at 15.

12. President's Commission for the Study of Ethical Problems in Medicine and Biomedical and Behavioral Research, DECIDING TO FOREGO LIFE-SUSTAINING TREATMENT: ETHICAL, MEDICAL AND LEGAL ISSUES IN TREATMENT DECISIONS at 90, 288 (1983).

See also, Lynn & Childress, Must Patients Always be Given Food and Water?, 13 HASTINGS CENTER RPT. 17, 20 (1983).

13. Annas, Do Feeding Tubes Have More Rights than Patients, 16 HASTINGS CENTER RPT. 16 (1986).

14. Colburn, AMA Ethics Panel Revises Rules on Withholding Food, WASH. POST HEALTH MAG., April 2, 1986, at 9.

15. 70 N.J. 10, 355 A.2d 647, cert. denied sub nom, Garger v. New Jersey, 429 U.S. 922 (1976).

16. Id.

17. Supra note 13.

18. TIME, Mar. 31, 1986, at 60.

See, Somerville, 'Should the Grandparents Die?': Allocation of Medical Resources with an Aging Population, 14 L. MED. & HEALTH CARE 158 (1986).

19. Id.

20. Id.

21. Supra note 14.

22. Id.

23. Id.

24. Statement of the Council on Ethical and Judicial Affairs, Am. Med. Assoc., March 15, 1986, "Withholding or Withdrawing Life Prolonging Medical Treatment."

25. Id.

26. Id.

27. Id.

28. Doctor Sees Trend Not to Resuscitate, WASH. POST, June 13, 1982, at A1.

29. Brown & Thompson, Nontreatment of Fever in Extended-Care Facilities, 300 NEW ENG. J. MED. 1246 (1979).

30. Id.

31. Id.

32. DIANA CRANE, THE SANCTITY OF SOCIAL LIFE: PHYSICIAN'S TREATMENT OF CRITICALLY ILL PATIENTS 58-61, (Russell Sage 1975); Noyes, Jochimsen, & Travis, The Changing Attitudes of Physicians Toward Prolonging Life, 25 J. AM. GERIATRIC SOC. 470 (1977).

33. Weiner, New VA Policy Allows Right-to-Die Instructions, WASH. POST, Sept. 20, 1983, at 1.

34. Id.

35. Id.

36. Id.

See generally, Kuhse, The Case for Active Voluntary Euthanasia, 14 L. MED. & HEALTH CARE 125 (1986).

37. Cohen, Ethical Problems of Intensive Care, 47 ANESTHESIOLOGY 217 (1977).

38. McCormick, To Save or Let Die and The Dilemma of Modern Medicine in HOW BRAVE A NEW WORLD 339 at 349 (Richard A McCormick ed.), (Georgetown Univ. Press 1981).

39. Supra notes 24–27.

40. Supra note 33.

41. Supra note 32.

42. Fletcher, Love is the Only Measure, 83 COMMONWEALTH 427 (1966).

43. See GEORGE P. SMITH, II, GENETICS, ETHICS AND THE LAW 2, 8, 164 (Assoc. Faculty Press 1983).

44. President's Commission for the Study of Ethical Problems in Medicine and Biomedical Research, supra note 12, at 288.

45. TIME, Mar. 31, 1986, at 60.

46. Paris & McCormick, The Catholic Tradition on the Use of Nutrition and Fluids, AMERICA 356, 358 (1987).

47. Id.

48. Id. at 361.

See generally, DAVID F. KELLY, THE EMERGENCE OF ROMAN CATHOLIC MEDICAL ETHICS IN NORTH AMERICA (Cath. Hosp. Assn. 1979).

49. Gostin, The Right to Choose Death: The Judicial Trilogy of Brophy, Bouvia, and Conroy, 14 L. MED. & HEALTH CARE 198, 201 (1986).

50. Id. at 200.

51. Id.

52. Childress, When Is It Morally Justifiable to Discontinue Medical Nutrition and Hydration? in BY NO EXTRAORDINARY MEANS at 81 (Joanne Lynn ed.), (Ind. Univ. Press 1986).

53. Id. at 81.

See Hilfiker, Allowing the Debilitated to Die: Facing Ethical Choices, 308 NEW ENG. J. MED. 716 (1983).

54. Supra note 49, at 201.

55. Id.

56. Id. at 201.

57. Williamson, Prolongation of Life or Prolonging the Act of Dying?, 202 J. AM. MED. ASSN. 162 (1967).

58. *Guidelines*, pp. 46–52.

59. Id. at 35–42.

60. Id. at 43–56.

61. Id. at 57–62.

62. Id. at 63–68.

63. Id. at 69–75.

64. Id. at 6–8.

65. Id. at 119–125.

66. Id. at 122.

67. 50 Fed. Register 14873 (1985). Child Abuse Amendments of 1984, Pub. L. No.98–457, 98 Stat. 1749, 42 U.S.C. §701 *passim*.

68. Id.

69. See generally Smith, Quality of Life, Sanctity of Creation: Palliative or Apotheosis?, 63 NEB. L. REV. 709 (1984); HELGA KUHSE & PETER SINGER, SHOULD THE BABY LIVE, (Ashgate 1994).

70. Moskop & Saldanha, The Baby Doe Rule: Still a Threat, 16 HASTINGS CENTER RPT. 8, 9 (1986).

71. Id. at 14.

The Governor's Task Force on Life and the Law of New York has urged a detailed procedural system structured in legislation allowing for the identification and appointment of surrogate decision makers, and setting forth the standards by which they can be guided in those cases where incapacitated (i.e., mentally disabled, newborns, and children) individuals requiring medical decisions to be made regarding their health—have neither executed advance directives nor formally designated a decision maker for this purpose. See the Report of the Task Force, WHEN OTHERS MUST CHOOSE: DECIDING FOR PATIENTS WITHOUT CAPACITY (1992) analyzed in Symposium, Giving Life to Patient to Self-Determination, 23 HASTINGS CENTER RPT. 12 (1993). See generally, appointment of health care agent by incompetent adults, N.Y. PUBLIC HEALTH LAW §2980 et. seq. (1990).

72. Supra note 70, at 14.

73. See Pellegrino, Rationing Health Care: The Ethics of Medical Gatekeeping, 2 J. CONTEMP. HEALTH L. & POL'Y 23 (1986).

Admitting the strong inference from the literature that the terminally ill receive proportionately more expensive treatment than do other patients, and that—consequently—the issue of extended care should be made within the reasonable context of cost containment, a distinguished group of researchers has set three basic goals for cost-containment policies for the terminally ill: develop more reasonable criteria for the admission of patients to intensive or critical care units; promote the autonomy of patients and their families as decision makers in healthcare issues of this nature; and develop and promote alternative forms of institutional care such as the hospice. Bayer, Callahan, Fletcher, et al., The Case of The Terminally Ill: Morality and Economics, 309 NEW ENG. J. MED. 1490 (1983).

See also, Fries, Aging, Natural Death and the Compression of Morbidity, 303 NEW ENG. J. MED. 130, 131, 135 (1980). It is predicted that the mean average age at death by the year 2009 will be 82.4 years. Id. at 131.

74. See, The President's Commission for the Study of Ethical Problems in Medicine and Biomedical and Behavioral Research, supra note 12, at 5, n. 3 and p. 228.

See also, Englehardt, Ethical Issues in Aiding the Death of Young Children in BENEFICENT EUTHANASIA at 180, 187 (Marvin Kohl ed.), (Prometheus 1975) where he proposed a concept of injury for continuance of existence as an analogue of the concept of the tort of wrongful life.

"It seems reasonable . . . that the life of children with diseases that involve pain and no hope of survival should not be prolonged." Id. at 189.

See generally, ROBERT F. WEIR, SELECTIVE NON TREATMENT OF HANDICAPPED NEWBORNS, (Ox. Univ. Press 1984).

75. Survey, Euthanasia: Criminal, Tort, Constitutional and Legislative Considerations, 48 NOTRE DAME L. REV. 1202, 1203 (1973); Cantor, Conroy: Best Interests, and the Handling of Dying Patients, 37 RUTGERS L. REV. 543, 549 (1985).

76. Clarke, The Choice to Refuse or Withhold Medical Treatment: The Emerging Technological and Medical-Ethical Consensus, 13 CREIGHTON L. REV. 813, 815 (1980).

77. See, e.g., *In re President & Directors of Georgetown College Inc.*, 331 F.2d, 1000, 1009 (D.C. Cir. 1964), *reh. en banc denied*, 331 F.2d 1010 (D.C. 1964); *John F. Kennedy Memorial Hosp. v. Hestor*, 58 N.J. 576, 279 A.2d 670, 674 (1971).

78. See, e.g., *In re Conroy*, 98 N.J. 321, 351, 486 A.2d 1209, 1224 (1985); *Satz v. Perlmutter*, 362 So.2d 160, 162 (Ct. App. Fla. 1978).

79. See, e.g., *In re Melidio*, 88 Misc. 2d 974, 309 N.Y.S.2d 524 (Sup. Ct. 1976).

80. 4 ENCYCLOPEDIA OF BIOETHICS 1502 (1976).

81. Byrn, Compulsory Lifesaving Treatment for the Competent Adult, 44 FORDHAM L. REV. 1, 35 *passim* (1975).

82. See *Jacobson v. Massachusetts*, 197 U.S. 11 (1905), the leading case where state interest—in preventing the spread of smallpox—was held to supersede the right of a person to refuse treatment inoculation. See generally, GERMAIN GRIEZ & JOSEPH M. BOYLE, JR., LIFE AND DEATH WITH LIBERTY AND JUSTICE, (Univ. Notre Dame Press 1977).

83. *Bartling v. Superior Court (Glendale Adventist Medical Center)*, 163 Cal. App. 2d 186, 196, 209 Cal. Rptr. 220, 225 (1984).

84. *Satz v. Perlmutter*, 362 So.2d 160, 162 (Fla. Dist. Ct. App.), *aff'd* 370 So.2d 359 (Fla. 1980). See also, *Superintendent of Belchertown State School v. Saikewicz*, 373 Mass. 728, 370 N.E.2d 417 (1977); *In re Quinlan*, 70 N.J. 10, 355 A.2d 647, *cert. denied* 429 U.S. 922 (1976); *In re Colyer*, 99 Wash. 2d 114, 660 P.2d 738 (1983).

85. *In re Quinlan*, 70 N.J. 10, 23–29, 355 A.2d 647, 655–657, *cert. denied* 429 U.S. 922 (1976); *Superintendent of Belchertown State School v. Saikewicz*, 373 Mass. 728, 737–740, 370 N.E.2d 417, 423–424 (1977); *Eichner v. Dillon*, 72 A.D.2d 431, 468–469 (1980) *modified sub. nom.*, *In re Storar*, 52 N.Y.2d 363, 420 N.E.2d 64, 438 N.Y.S.2d 266 (1981).

86. *In re Quackenbush*, 156 N.J. Super. 282, 290, 383 A.2d 785 (Morris County Ct. 1978); *John F. Kennedy Memorial Hosp. v. Heston*, 58 N.J. 576, 270 A.2d 670 (1971).

87. PAUL RAMSEY, ETHICS AT THE EDGES OF LIFE: MEDICAL AND LEGAL IN-TERSECTIONS 1–14, (Yale Univ. Press 1978).

88. Sherlock, For Everything There Is a Season: The Right to Die in the United States, 1982 BRIGHAM YOUNG UNIV. L. REV. 545, 560 (1982).

Although, in itself, the principle of beneficence could arguably support a course of medical treatment against the wishes of a patient, it is restricted or conditioned by the principles of respect for persons or recognition, simply, of one's autonomy. This principle of personal respect mandates full attention be given to the competency of the patient who disclaims the use of prolongation of life-sustaining therapies. JAMES F. CHILDRESS, WHO SHOULD DECIDE? PATERNALISM IN HEALTH CARE 175, (Ox. Univ. Press 1982).

89. Comment, Balancing the Right to Die with Competing Interests: A Socio-Legal Enigma, 13 PEPPERDINE L. REV. 109 (1985).

90. Id. at 127, 128.

For example, a patient might be classified as terminal because it is expected that he will live for 9 months even though there are other significant variables: his treatment may be intrusive and painful and he has expressed a desire to be removed from life-sustaining mechanisms in order to ensure his certain death in a more dignified manner. Another case might find a patient with a more terminal condition in that he has but a 5-month life expectancy and his treatment is less intrusive and thus less painful and, furthermore, his desire to be taken off life-supporting treatment has wavered. Here, the condition of the patient would have to be more serious in order to meet or overcome the competing state interest in preserving life. Id. A set of additional interesting hypotheticals are posed at 125 *passim*, id.

91. ROBERT M. VEATCH, DEATH, DYING AND THE BIOLOGICAL REVOLUTION 146, (Yale Univ. Press 1976).

92. JOHN E. NOWAK, RONALD D. ROTUNDA, & J. NELSON YOUNG, CONSTITU-TIONAL LAW 764, (West Pub. Co. 2d ed. 1983).

93. Id.

94. See, e.g., *In re Conroy*, 98 N.J. 321, 486 A.2d 1209, (1985); *Bartling v. Superior Court*, 163 Cal. App. 2d 186, 209 Cal. Rptr. 220 (1984).

95. See Jonas, The Right To Die, 8 HASTINGS CENTER RPT. 31 (1978).

96. See, e.g., *In re Conroy*, 98 N.J. 321, 348; 486 A.2d 1209, 1222 (1985); *Bartling v. Superior Court*, 163 Cal. App. 2d 186, 195 209 Cal. Rptr. 220, 225 (1984); *In re Colyer*, 99 Wash.

2d 114, 132–33, 660 P.2d 738 (1983); *In re Storar*, 52 N.Y.2d 363, 420 N.E.2d 266, 276, *cert. denied*, 454 U.S. 858 (1981).

97. *Bartling v. Superior Court*, supra; *In re Storar*, supra; *In re Quinlan*, 70 N.J. 10, 40, 355 A.2d 647, 663, *cert. denied*, 429 U.S. 922 (1976); *Superintendent of Belchertown State School v. Saikewicz*, 373 Mass. 728, 370 N.E.2d 417, 425–427 (1977); *Matter of Spring*, 380 Mass. 629, 405 N.E.2d 115 (1980).

The Court in *In re Yetter* held that " . . . the right of privacy includes a right to die with which the State should not interfere where there are no minor or unborn children and no clear and present danger to public health, welfare or morals." 62 Pa. D. & C. 619, 623 (1973).

See also, GRIEZ & BOYCE, supra note 82, at 98 *passim*; Delgado, Euthanasia Reconsidered— The Choice of Death as an Aspect of the Right to Privacy, 17 ARIZ. L. REV. 474 (1975).

98. See, e.g., *In re Osborne*, 294 A.2d 372 (D.C. 1972); *In re Estate of Brooks*, 32 Ill. 2d 361, 205 N.E.2d 435 (1965).

See JAMES E. NOWAK & RONALD D. ROTUNDA, CONSTITUTIONAL LAW 1236– 1238, (West Pub. Co. 4th ed. 1991); LAURENCE H. TRIBE, AMERICAN CONSTITUTIONAL LAW, Ch. 14, (Foundation Press 2d ed. 1988).

99. See, e.g., *In the Matter of the Guardianship of Joseph Hamlin, an Incompetent Person*, 102 Wash. 2d 810, 689 P.2d 1372 (1984).

100. Friendly, The Courts and Social Policy: Substance and Procedure, 33 U. MIAMI L. REV. 21 (1978).

101. See *Truman v. Thomas*, 27 Cal. 3d 285, 611 P.2d 902, 165 Cal. Rptr. 308 (1980); *Crisher v. Spak*, 122 Misc. 2d 355, 471 N.Y.S.2d 741 (1983).

102. *In re Conroy*, 98 N.J. 321, 486 A.2d 1209 (1985).

CHAPTER 9

1. ROBERT N. BROWN, THE RIGHTS OF OLDER PERSONS, Ch. 9, (So. Ill. Univ. Press 2d ed. 1989).

2. HARRY R. MOODY, ETHICS IN AN AGING SOCIETY 183, (Johns Hopkins Univ. Press 1992).

3. Id. at 286.

4. Id.

See also, MARSHALL B. KAPP, GERIATRICS AND THE LAW, Ch. 9, (Springer 2d ed. 1992).

5. KAPP, id.

6. Omnibus Budget Reconciliation Act of 1987, Pub. L. 100–20 (1987), 42 U.S.C. § 1395 *passim* (1992).

7. Supra note 1; KAPP, supra note 4.

8. See also, Bishop, Competition in the Market for Nursing Home Care, 13 J. HEALTH POLITICS POL'Y & L. 341, 341 (1988); Kapp, State of the Law: Nursing Homes, 18 L. MED. & HEALTH CARE 282 (1990).

9. Coleman & Karp, Recent State and Federal Developments in Protective Services and Elder Abuse, 1 J. ELDER ABUSE & NEGLECT 51 (1989); Elder Abuse: The Hidden Problem: Briefing by the Select Committee on Aging, U.S. House of Representatives, #96-220 (1980).

10. BARRY R. FURROW, et al., HEALTH LAW 75, (West Pub. Co. 2d ed. 1991).

11. Davitt, Nursing Homes' Top Priority: Caregiving or Profitmaking, 4 DEL. LAW. 14, 14– 16 (1985).

12. Bishop, supra note 8, at 344.

13. Id. See LONG–TERM CARE: ECONOMIC IMPACTS AND FINANCING DILEM- MAS—A REPORT (R.W. Weltge ed.), (Am. Health Care Assoc. 1990).

14. Characteristic of modern nursing homes is a high staff turnover rate and an operational style more akin to fast food outlets or hospitals rather than residences designed to care for the elderly. FORREST J. BERGHORN, DONNA E. SCHAFER, et al., THE DYNAMICS OF AGING 447, (Westview Press 1981).

15. BERGHORN & SCHAEFER, id. at 452.

16. Id.

17. Supra note 10, at 76.

Acting under a Congressional mandate, the Department of Health and Human Services has developed new regulations designed to correct substandard care and abuse in the administration of nursing homes. For serious violations of these regulations that endanger the patient, heavy fines of up to $10,000 a day may be imposed. Additionally, all nursing homes are mandated to conduct initial and annual assessments of the condition of every resident to develop and update individual plans of care. These regulations also set new qualifications for the training of nursing staffs. Furthermore, inspections of nursing home facilities are to be conducted an average of once a year, but not less than once every 15 months. 50 FED. REGISTER 56116 (1994). 42 CODE OF FED. REGULATIONS Pts. 401, 431, 435, 440, 441, 442, 447, 483, 488, 489, 498 (1994) (eff. July 1, 1995).

18. BERGHORN & SCHAEFER, supra note 14, at 451.

19. Bishop, supra note 8, at 345.

20. Id. at 344.

21. Id. at 349.

22. See Palmer & Gould, Economic Consequences of Population Aging at 377 *passim*, and Callahan, Health Care in the Aging Society at 330 in OUR AGING SOCIETY (Alan Pifer & Lydia Bronte eds.), (W.W. Norton 1986).

23. Supra note 10, at 77.

24. Bishop, supra note 8, at 245–46.

25. Jones, Restructuring Health Care Services, in HEALTH CARE RATIONING: DILEMMA AND PARADOX at 133 (Kathleen Kelly ed.), (Mosby Yr. Bk., Inc. 1994).

26. Wetle, Levkoff, Cwikel & Rosen, Nursing Home Resident Participation in Medical Decisions: Perceptions and Preferences, 28. THE GERONTOLOGIST 32 (1988 Supp.).

27. ETHICAL CONFLICTS IN THE MANAGEMENT OF HOME CARE: THE CASE MANAGERS DILEMMA Chs. 2, 14 (Rosalie A. Kane & Arthur L. Caplan eds.), (Springer 1993).

28. Id., Ch. 14.

29. Brooks, Warshaw, et al., The Physician Decision-Making Process in Transferring Nursing Home Patient to the Hospital, 154 ARCH. INTERN. MED. 902 (1994).

30. Dooley, Resolving Dispute Outside the Courtroom, in COURT-RELATED NEEDS OF THE ELDERLY AND PERSONS WITH DISABILITIES: A BLUEPRINT FOR THE FUTURE at 165 (ABA 1991).

31. Kosberg & Cairl, The Cost of Care Index: A Case Management Tool for Screening Informal Care Providers, 26 THE GERONTOLOGIST 273 (1986).

See also, Resident Assessment: The Springboard to Quality of Care and Quality of Life for Nursing Home Residents, WORKSHOP BEFORE SPECIAL COMM. ON AGING, U.S. Senate, Oct. 22, 1990, #101-30 (1991).

See generally Sturm & Wells, How Can Care for Depression Become More Cost-effective?, 273 J. AM. MED. ASSN. 51 (1995).

32. Barnes, Beyond Guardianship Reform: A Reevaluation of Autonomy and Beneficence for a System of Principles Decision-Making in Long Term Care, 41 EMORY L. J. 633, 635 (1992).

33. Id. at 640, 641.

34. Temkin-Greener, Meiners, et al., The Use and Cost of Health Services Prior to Death: A Comparison of the Medicare-only and the Medicare-Medicaid Elderly Populations, 70 MILBANK Q. 679, 700 (1992).

35. Rich, How Much Can Americans Pay for Nursing Homes?, WASH. POST HEALTH MAG., Feb. 6, 1990, at 5.

36. Moody, Ethical Dilemmas in Nursing Home Placement, 11 GENERATIONS 16, 17 (Summer, 1987).

37. Id.

38. Id.

39. Kane, Everyday Life in Nursing Homes: The Way Things Are, in EVERYDAY ETHICS: RESOLVING DILEMMAS IN NURSING HOMES at 10 (Rosalie A. Kane & Arthur L. Caplan eds. 1990), (hereinafter cited as EVERYDAY ETHICS); supra note 36, at 18–19.

40. Kane, id. at 11.

See also, GEORGE J. ANNAS, THE RIGHTS OF PATIENTS, Ch. V, (Humana, 2d ed. 1989).

41. Kane, supra note 125, at 21–22.

See generally Ambrogi, Legal Issues In Nursing Home Admissions, 18 L. MED. & HEALTH CARE 254 (1990).

42. Kane, supra note 125, at 22.

43. 42 C.F.R. §§ 405.1121(k)(4), 442.311(c) (1993).

44. Sabatino, Nursing Home Admission Contracts: Undermining Rights the Old-Fashioned Way, CLEARINGHOUSE REV. 553, 555 (Oct. 1990).

45. Id.

46. See 42 U.S.C. §§ 1395i-3(c)(2), 1395i-3(e)(3), 1396r(c)(2), 1396r(e)(3), (Supp. 1990).

47. Supra note 44, at 555.

48. Id. at 558.

49. JACK M. ZIMMERMAN, HOSPICE: COMPLETE CARE FOR THE TERMINALLY ILL 1–20, (Urban & Schwarbenberg 1981).

50. Comment, The Hospice Movement: A Renewed View of The Death Process, 4 J. CONTEMP. HEALTH L. & POL'Y 295 (1988). See THE FUTURE OF PALLIATIVE CARE: ISSUES OF POLICY AND PRACTICE (David Clark ed.), (Taylor & Francis 1993).

51. Supra note 179, at 8. See PAUL M. DUBOIS, THE HOSPICE WAY OF DEATH (Human Science 1980).

52. Comment, Don't Make Them Leave Their Rights at the Door: A Recommended Model State Statute to Protect the Rights of The Elderly In Nursing Homes, 4 J. CONTEMP. HEALTH L. & POL'Y 321 at 333, n's 69, 70 (1988).

53. Comment, supra note 50, at 9–10.

It is thought generally that hospices and hospice attitudes serve as a strong antidote to arguments for active euthanasia.

54. Supra note 14, at 96, 97.

55. Id. at 97.

56. MARSHALL B. KAPP, GERIATRICS AND THE LAW 228–230 (Springer 2d ed. 1992).

57. 42 C.F.R. §418.309 (1993).

58. 42 C.F.R. §418.60 (1993).

59. 42 C.F.R. §418.21 (1993).

Actually, a fourth subsequent period of extension—of unlimited duration—may be granted during the lifetime of the terminal individual. Id., 42 C.F.R. §418.21 (1993).

60. 42 C.F.R. §418.24 (1993).

61. Kane, Caplan, Freeman et al., Avenues to Appropriate Autonomy: What Next in EVERY-DAY ETHICS at 380. See also, Ethical and Policy Implications of Cost-Containment Strategies, 10 J. HEALTH POLITICS, POL'Y & L. 565 (1985).

62. See GEORGE P. SMITH, II, FINAL CHOICES: AUTONOMY IN HEALTH CARE DECISIONS (Charles C Thomas Pub. 1989).

63. See Crowley, No Pain, No Gain? The Agency for Health Care Policy and Research's Attempt to Change Inefficient Health Care Practice of Withholding Medication from Patients in Pain, 10 J. CONTEMP. HEALTH L. & POL'Y 383 (1994).

64. Comment, supra note 125, at 313.

65. KENNETH P. COHEN, HOSPICE—A PRESUMPTION FOR TERMINAL CARE 56–57 (Aspen Pub. 1979).

66. See generally, ELIZABETH KUBLER-ROSS, ON DEATH AND DYING (Macmillian 1970).

67. ETHICAL CONFLICTS IN THE MANAGEMENT OF HOME CARE: THE CASE MANAGER'S DILEMMA at 139 (Rosalie A. Kane & Arthur L. Caplan eds.), (Springer 1993).

CHAPTER 10

1. See Palmer & Gould, Economic Consequences of Populating Aging at 377 *passim* and Callahan, Health Care in the Aging Society at 330 in OUR AGING SOCIETY (Alan Pifer & Lydia Bronte eds.), (W.W. Norton 1986).

2. Pub. Law No. 100–203. 52 Fed. Reg. 38582, 38584 (Oct. 16, 1987).

See 1 DEVELOPMENTS IN AGING: 1990, Rpt. of Special Comm. on Aging, U.S. Senate, #102-28 at 237 *passim* (1991).

3. H.R. 391, 100th Cong., 1st Sess. (1987).

4. 42 U.S.C. §1395i-3(g)(1) (1992); 42 U.S.C. §1396r(g) (1992).

5. 42 U.S.C. §1395i-3(c)(1)(A) (1992); 42 U.S.C. §1396r(e)(1)(A) (1992).

See Comment, Don't Make Them Leave Their Rights at the Door: A Recommended Model State Statute to Protect the Rights of the Elderly in Nursing Homes, 4 J. CONTEMP. HEALTH L. & POL'Y 321, 325 (1988).

6. 42 U.S.C. §1395i-3(c)(1)(A) (1992); 42 U.S.C. §1396r(c)(1)(A) (1992).

See Ackerman, A Bill of Responsibilities for Nursing Home Residents, 14 GENERATIONS 81 (Supp. 1990); GEORGE J. ANNAS, THE RIGHTS OF PATIENTS: THE BASIC ACLU GUIDE TO PATIENTS RIGHTS 283–291, (Humana 2d ed. 1989).

7. ANNAS, id., Ch. XV at 259.

8. 42 U.S.C. §1395i-3(2) (1992); 42 U.S.C. §1396r(b)(2) (1992).

9. 42 U.S.C. §§1395i-3(3)(A),(C) (1992); 42 U.S.C. §1396r(b)(3) (1992).

10. Id.

11. Id.

12. 42 U.S.C. §§ 1395i-3(b)(4)(A),(C) (1992); 42 U.S.C. §1396r(b)(4) (1992).

13. Jost, Legal Characteristics of the Extended Care Facility, in HEALTHCARE FACILITIES LAW at Ch. 15 ps. 1022–1025 (Anne M. Dellinger ed.), (Little Brown 1991).

14. 42 U.S.C. § 1395i-(3)(b)(5) (1992); 42 U.S.C. §1396r(b)(5) (1992).

15. Comment, supra note 5, at 326.

16. Id. at 327.

17. Id. at 330.

18. Ackerman, supra note 6, at 81.

19. Id.

20. The general premise of such responsibilities is the tenet that no one nursing home resident's right should supersede the rights of any other resident or staff member. As such, responsibilities of residents include those to themselves, to other residents, and to the staff and facility. For example, a resident may be responsible for providing "accurate medical, physical and social history so that a therapeutic care plan may be formulated by the health care team"; for accepting "responsibility for [their] actions if [they] refuse treatment or medication"; "to be cooperative and respectful in [their] behavior toward other residents"; "to cooperate with the [nursing home] staff's efforts to help [the resident] as they provide care and treatment; to be respectful of the rights of staff members in [the resident's] words and actions." Ackerman, supra note 30, at 82.

See MARSHALL B. KAPP, GERIATRICS AND THE LAW, Ch. 9, (Springer 2d ed. 1992).

21. Vobejda, Elderly Find Alternatives to Institutions, WASH. POST, June 28, 1993, at A9.

22. BETTY FRIEDAN, THE FOUNTAIN OF AGE 511, (Simon & Schuster 1993), quoting Dr. Robert N. Butler, former director of the National Institute on Aging and Chairman of the Geriatrics Department of Mount Sinai Medical Center in New York City.

See also, MENTAL HEALTH AND THE AGING, Forum by the Special Comm. on Aging, U.S. Senate, July 15, 1993, #103-10.

23. Supra note 21.

Additional alternative to institutional care would include segregated adult house sharing, congregate housing, and adult day care. DAVID HABER, HEALTH CARE FOR AN AGING SOCIETY (Hemisphere 1989).

24. Supra note 21.

See Correll, Aging and Care for the Aged: Misguided Concepts Lead to Poor Practices, 20 J. INT'L FEDERATION AGING 60 (1993).

25. Id.

See DAVID A. WISE, ISSUES IN THE ECONOMICS OF AGING, Chs. 6, 10, (Univ. Chic. Press 1990).

26. Council on Scientific Affairs, Elder Abuse and Neglect, 257 J. AM. MED. ASSN. 966 (1987). For example, in pre-industrial European agricultural settings, peasants often secured property rights on the transfer of their assets to the next generation through annuity contracts. These contracts

would commonly contain provisions granting rights to an elder parent, including the right to sit at the family table or use the front door of the house. Id.

27. Shanas, Social Myth as Hypothesis: Case of the Family Relations of Old People, 19 GERONTOLOGIST 3–9 (1979).

28. Rosenmayr, Socio-cultural Change in the Relation of the Family to its Older Members: Towards an Integration of Historical, Sociological and Psychiatric Perspectives, in 2 PROCEEDINGS, Tenth International Conference of Social Gerontology 49–63, Int'l Center Social Gerontology (Paris 1984).

See ROBERT N. BUTLER, WHY SURVIVE? BEING OLD IN AMERICA, Ch. 1, (Harper Collins 1985).

29. Id.

A divided California Supreme Court, clarifying the duty to care for aged parents, has ruled that adult children can be prosecuted for neglect only if they have control over the elder's care. *People v. Heitzman*, 9 Cal. 4th 189 (1994).

30. Lau & Kosberg, Abuse of the Elderly by Informal Care Providers, 299 AGING 10–15 (Sept./Oct. 1979).

31. Generally, physical abuse can be defined as an act of hysterical violence against an elderly victim. Such acts could include beating, pushing, shoving, shooting, and threatening the victim with a weapon. See Lupinski, Elder Abuse: A Pressing Need for Federal Assistance, 5 PUBLIC L. FORUM 137–77 (1986).

32. Physical abuse or neglect can involve the intentional failure to provide the elder with necessities such as nourishment or to assist a physically disabled elder in movement, or failing to supervise an elder incapable of taking care of himself due to infirmities. See id. at 141.

33. Financial or material abuse usually involves the theft or misuse of the elder's money or property and usually occurs through the use of threats or violence or through the use of undue influence with respect to wills. Id.

34. Elder Abuse: A National Disgrace: Report by the Subcommittee on Health and Long Term Care of the Select Committee on Aging, U.S. House of Representatives, Committee Publication 99–506 (1985). See Pillemer & Finkelhor, The Prevalence of Elder Abuse: A Random Sample Survey, 28 THE GERONTOLOGIST 51 (1988).

35. Steve Bates, Elderly Abuse Rises Sharply, WASH. POST, Mar. 7, 1993, at A1.

36. Supra note 26, at 966.

37. Report D of the Board of Trustees, HEALTH CARE FOR THE AGED POPULATION, Am. Med. Ass'n (1984).

38. O'Malley et. al., Identifying and Preventing Family-Mediated Abuse and Neglect of Elderly Persons, 98 ANNALS INTERN. MED. 998–1005 (1983).

39. Steuer & Austin, Family Abuse of the Elderly, 28 J. AM. GERIATRIC SOC'Y 372–76 (1980).

40. USA Today, May 30, 1990, at 10–A. The study even admitted that due to reluctance on the part of state inspectors to disclose the problems, the problems could in fact be ten times worse than reported.

41. Id.

Nationally, 18% failed to meet federal standards.

42. Id. Nationally, 36% failed to handle food under sanitary conditions.

43. Id.

44. Warren, Fatal Lapses in Rest Home Care Cited, L.A. TIMES, Aug. 5, 1993, at A3.

45. Hill, Claims of Nursing Home Abuse Rise, TIMES-PICAYUNE, Mar. 21, 1993, at A1.

46. WASH. POST HEALTH MAG., Feb. 12, 1991, at 7.

47. Johnson, The Fear of Liability and the Use of Restraints in Nursing Homes, 18 L. MED. & HEALTH CARE 263 (1990).

48. One nursing home administrator attributed the use of restraints to his perception that attorneys and families are " 'wanting and willing to sue if a home doesn't use protective devices to protect the resident.' " Indicative of this fact is the situation at the administrator's facility, which was originally designed as a "restraint free" institution. According to the administrator, since opening 12 years ago, his institution restrains 20%–30% of its residents "under pressure from insurance carriers, doctors and families." Johnson, id., at 264.

49. WASH. POST HEALTH MAG., supra note 46, at 7.

50. A recent case in Ohio illustrates this very point. A 78-year-old Alzheimer's patient suffocated to death because of restraints attaching her to her bed. Grant, Coroner Says Patient Killed by Restraints, THE PLAIN DEALER, Sept. 16, 1993, at 1A.

51. Johnson, supra note 47, at 263.

52. 506 F. Supp. 915 (N.D. Ohio 1980).

53. Id. at 925. See generally, Comment, An Involuntary Mental Patient's Right to Refuse Treatment with Antipsychotic Drugs: A Reassessment, 48 OHIO ST. L. J. 1135 (1987) (arguing that a qualified right to refuse treatment is more consistent with the mental health system as a whole).

54. In support of their arguments, plaintiffs claimed that compulsory treatment implicated three legal rights: 1) the patient's interest in bodily integrity and personal dignity; 2) the patient's interest in independence in making decisions of importance to the patient; and 3) the patient's interest in maintaining his or her ability to think and communicate freely. Id. at 930.

55. Id. at 934.

56. Id. at 935.

57. Id.

58. Id.

59. Id. at 938.

60. 476 F. Supp. 1294 (D.N.J. 1979).

61. Id. at 1307. The court enumerated several requirements that, as a matter of law, it deemed essential prior to administering psychotropic drugs. First, a hospital must obtain specific written consent from patients before they are medicated with a psychotropic drug. Second, a neutral, independent decision-maker must be provided in the treatment context (a role possibly fulfilled by an ombudsman). Third, due to the possibilities of excessive costs to the state without a significant decrease in the risk of erroneous determinations, the court refused to require either a formal hearing or even the presence of an attorney for forcible drug administration. Id. at 1307–08.

62. 653 F.2d 836 (1981).

63. Id. at 842.

64. Id. at 843 (citing *Vitek v. Jones*, 445 U.S. 480 (1980)).

65. 720 F.2d 266 (3rd Cir. 1983).

66. 644 F.2d 147 (3rd Cir. 1980), vacated, 457 U.S. 307 (1982). Youngberg involved the physical restraining of a mentally retarded patient in a state institution.

67. 457 U.S. at 321.

68. *Rennie v. Klein*, 720 F.2d 266, 269 (3rd Cir. 1983).

69. Id.

70. Compare *Project Release v. Prevost*, 722 F.2d 960 (2d Cir. 1983) (involving a plaintiff's claim of alleged violations of the plaintiff's rights under the Fourteenth Amendment of the Federal Constitution) with *Rivers v. Katz*, 504 N.Y.S.2d 485, 495 N.E.2d 337 (N.Y. 1986) (involving a plaintiff's allegation that rights were violated under the common law and the state constitution).

71. 165 Ill. App. 3d 498, 531 N.E.2d 64 (1988).

72. 531 N.E.2d at 73. In *Orr*, the state circuit court involuntarily committed pursuant to a hearing the patient, Jeffrey Orr, because of his mental illness and the court's reasonable expectation that his illness would cause him to seriously harm himself or others. The court further authorized the state to administer medication. Id. at 67.

73. Id. at 73, citing Ill. Rev. Stat. ch. 1101/2, para. 11a-3 (1985).

74. Id. at 73–74. The court noted that informed consent and the right to refuse medical treatment were grounded in the common law right to be free of nonconsensual bodily invasions, the individual liberty interest of bodily integrity, and the right to privacy protected by both the state and federal constitutions. Id., citing *Davis v. Hubbard*, 506 F. Supp. 915, 929–939 (N.D. Oh. 1980).

75. (Emphasis added). There are, however, two recognized exceptions: emergencies that threaten life or property when drugs are administered to temporarily control someone's violent behavior; and to manage the dangerous behaviors of someone who has been committed to a nursing home or institute involuntarily. See MARSHALL B. KAPP, supra note 2, at 34–39.

76. Reducing Antipsychotic Drug Use in Nursing Homes: A Controlled Trial in Provider Education, 153 ARCHIVES INTERN. MED. 713 (1993).

77. Id.

78. USA Today, supra note 40.

79. Romano, Unshackling the Elderly, 17 CONTEMP. LONG TERM CARE 36 (1994).

80. See GERALD BENNETT & PAUL KINGSTON, ELDER ABUSE: CONCEPTS, THE-
ORIES & INTERVENTIONS (Singular Press 1993).

81. Supra note 114, at 37–38.

82. Id. at 42. See Colburn, Nursing Homes Try Restraint Removal, WASH. POST, April 12,
1994, at 5.

83. Colburn, Patients Who Wander Worry VA Hospitals, WASH. POST HEALTH MAG.,
Mar. 22, 1994, at 5.

84. Klonoff, The Problems of Nursing Homes: Connecticut's Response, 31 ADMIN. L. REV.
1, 5–6 (1979).

85. Kimsey et. al., Abuse of the Elderly—The Hidden Agenda, 29 J. AM. GERIATRIC
SOC'Y 465–72 (1981).

86. Supra note 26, at 966–71.

87. Kane, Caplan, Freeman et al., Avenues to Appropriate Autonomy: What Next in EVERY-
DAY ETHICS: RESOLVING DILEMMAS IN NURSING HOMES at 307 (Rosalie A. Kane &
Arthur L. Caplan eds.), (Springer 1990), (hereinafter cited as EVERYDAY ETHICS).

88. Caplan, The Morality of The Mundane: Ethical Issues Arising in the Daily Lives of Nursing
Home Residents, supra note 87, in EVERYDAY ETHICS at 45.

See Ambrogi, The Impact of Nursing Home Admission Agreements on Resident Autonomy,
28 THE GERONTOLOGIST 82 (Supp. 1988).

89. Caplan, id., at 47.

90. Kane, Everyday Life in Nursing Homes: The Way Things Are, supra note 87, in EVERY-
DAY ETHICS at 8–9.

91. Caplan, supra note 88, at 49.

92. Freeman, Developing Systems That Promote Autonomy: Policy Considerations, supra note
87, in EVERYDAY ETHICS at 292.

93. Supra note 87, at 345.

94. Id. at 317.

95. Id. at 307.

96. Supra note 92, at 302.

97. Id. at 302–303.

98. Id.

99. Supra note 92, at 299.

100. 42 U.S.C. §3001 et seq. (1988).

101. See id. §3120.

102. LEGAL SERVICES FOR THE ELDERLY—WHERE THE NATION STANDS: A
ROLE FOR THE BAR, (ABA 4th ed. 1988).

103. Id.

104. Id.

105. 42 U.S.C. §§3021(c), 3027(a)(12)(A) (1990); Lisa Tudisco Evren, Longterm-Care Om-
budsmen; A National Survey of Their Views, 11 GENERATIONS 43 (Summer 1987). Specifically,
the ombudsman was charged with five activities: "(1) to investigate complaints regarding 'administrative action which may adversely affect the health, safety, welfare, and rights' of residents of
longterm-care facilities; (2) to monitor the development and implementation of federal, state, and
local laws, regulations, and policies regarding longterm-care facilities; (3) to provide information to
public agencies regarding the problems of facilities' residents; (4) to train volunteers and promote
the involvement of citizen organizations in the ombudsman program; and (5) to carry out 'other
activities' as the commissioner of aging deems appropriate." Id.

106. 42 U.S.C. §§3021(c), 3027(a)(12)(A) (1990). In pertinent part, Section 3027(a)(12)(A)
provides:

(A) The State agency will establish and operate, either directly or by contract or other arrangement with any public agency or other appropriate private nonprofit organization, other than an agency
or organization which is responsible for licensing or certifying long-term care services in the State
. . . an office of the State Long-Term Care Ombudsman . . . and shall carry out through the Office
a long-term care ombudsman program which provides an individual who will on a full-time basis

(i) investigate and resolve complaints made by or on behalf of older individuals who are
residents of long-term care facilities relating to action, inaction, or decision or providers, or their

representative of long-term care services of public agencies, or of social service agencies, which may adversely affect the health, safety, welfare, or rights of such residents;

(ii) provide for training staff and volunteers and promote the development of citizen organizations to participate in the ombudsman program; . . . .

(B) The State will establish procedures for appropriate access by the Ombudsman to long-term care facilities and patient's records, . . . and ensure that the identity of any complainant or resident will not be disclosed without the written consent of such complainant or resident, or upon court order. . . . Id.

See Coleman, Advocacy in The Older Americans Act, GENERATIONS, 43 (Summer/Fall 1991).

107. Carol O'Shaughnessy, Older Americans Act Amendments in 1987: P.L. 100–175—A Summary of Provisions 1 (Mar. 1988).

See Older American Act Amendments of 1987, U.S. House of Representatives, #100-427, (1987); and U.S. Senate, #100-36, (1987).

See generally, Sinclair, Focus of Programs for Elderly Reassessed, WASH. POST, Aug. 24, 1987, at 1.

108. Toshio Tatara, Nat'l Aging Resource Center, Elder Abuse in the United States: An Issue Paper 9 (1990). The trigger provision for federal funding of the elder abuse program terminated in 1990 and as such, Congress was able to provide funding for fiscal year 1991. In October 1990, Congress appropriated $3 million to support initial funding of the program in the Older Americans Act. This funding lasted only through fiscal year 1991 and was again addressed in the 1991 Reauthorization Amendments.

109. The authorized funding ranges from $10 million in fiscal year 1992, gradually increasing to approximately $11.5 million for fiscal year 1995. S. 243, §702(b).

110. Conway, Patient Care Advocacy Program Ages Well, L.A. TIMES, Nov. 29, 1993, at E1. See ANNAS, supra note 6, at 263 *passim*.

111. Institute of Medicine, IMPROVING THE QUALITY OF HEALTH CARE IN NURSING HOMES 177 (1986); See Frank, State Ombudsman Legislation in the United States, 29 U. MIAMI L. REV. 397 (1975).

112. Evren, supra note 105, at 43.

113. See Woolfolk, Civil Aspects of Patient Abuse, 7 DEL. LAW. 12, 13 (1989); Wooleyhan, Restrictions v. Rights, Disability v. Dignity: The Long-Term Care Ombudsman Program, 7 DEL. LAW. 24, 25 (1989).

114. Jost, LEGAL CHARACTERISTICS OF THE EXTENDED CARE FACILITY, IN HEALTHCARE FACILITIES LAW at Ch. 15 ps. 1017–1018 (Anne Dellinger ed.), (Little Brown 1991).

115. Accordingly, whereas Alaska receives over $600 per nursing home bed, Washington State is providing funding at a rate of $90, a mere 15% of its northern counterpart. See National Association of Statute Units on Aging, COMPREHENSIVE ANALYSIS OF STATE LONGTERM-CARE OMBUDSMAN OFFICES 7–9 (1990).

116. See In the Matter of Conroy, 486 A.2d at 1237–38 (1985); N.J.S.A. 30:13-1 to 13-11.

117. D'Ambrosio, Office of the Ombudsman for the Institutionalized Elderly, NEW JERSEY LAW. 45 (Winter 1985). See Price & Armstrong, New Jersey 'Granny Doe' Squad: Arguments about Mechanisms for Protection of Vulnerable Patients, 17 L. MED. &HEALTH CARE 255 (1989).

118. New Jersey Stat. Ann., §52:27G-7.2 (1986).

119. New Jersey Stat. Ann., §§52:27G-5b; 52:27G-8d (1986).

120. D'Ambrosio, supra note 117, at 45.

121. New Jersey Office of the Ombudsman for the Institutionalized Elderly, 1988/89 ANNUAL REPORT at 2 (1989).

122. Id. at 3–4. New Jersey does, however, establish a volunteer program designed to train assistants and to provide visitors with communication skills and expertise to understand problems faced by institutionalized elderly.

123. See Rhoden, Litigating Life and Death, 102 HARV. L. REV. 375, 435 (1988).

124. Harshbarger, A Prosecutor's Perspective on Protecting Older Americans, 1 J. ELDER ABUSE & NEGLECT 5 (1989).

125. Am. Public Welfare Assoc., A COMPREHENSIVE ANALYSIS OF STATE POLICY AND PRACTICE RELATED TO ELDER ABUSE, at 143, 145 (July, 1986).

126. Heisler, The Role of the Criminal Justice System in Elder Abuse Cases, 3 J. ELDER ABUSE & NEGLECT 86–87 (1991).

127. Power, Two Charged in Abuse of Home Patient, BOSTON GLOBE, June 23, 1993, at 20.

128. Power, Push Is On to Punish Abusers of Elderly, BOSTON GLOBE, Aug. 1, 1993, at 29.

129. Id. at 7.

CHAPTER 11

1. See generally, MARVIN KOHL, THE MORALITY OF KILLING, (Humanities 1974).

2. Id.

3. Kass, Man's Right to Die, 35 THE PHAROS 73, 74 (1972).

4. Id.

5. Id. See also, MARGARET BRAZIER, MEDICINE, PATIENTS AND THE LAW, 443–465, (Penguin 2d ed. 1992).

6. Ladd, Introduction, in ETHICAL ISSUES RELATING TO DEATH at 4 (John Ladd ed.), (Ox. Univ. Press 1979).

Machines have a tendency to de-personalize death and thus alleviate human responsibility for it. Annas, Killing Machines, 21 HASTINGS CENTER RPT. 33, 35 (1991).

7. Supra note 1, at 76.

8. Id. at 75, 76.

9. ROBERT M. VEATCH, DEATH, DYING AND THE BIOLOGICAL REVOLUTION 77 (Yale Univ. Press 1976).

Positive euthanasia has been stated as doing something that ends life deliberately and is the form in which the issue of suicide is brought into question (as a voluntary or direct choice of death). The end-goal of both direct or positive and indirect or negative euthanasia is precisely the same—the end of a patient's life and a release from pointless misery and dehumanizing loss of bodily functions. Fletcher, In Defense of Suicide, in SUICIDE AND EUTHANASIA: THE RIGHTS OF PERSONHOOD 38 at 47 (Samuel E. Wallace & Albin Eser eds.), (Univ. Tenn. Press 1981).

10. VEATCH, supra note 9.

11. Kuhse, The Case for Active Voluntary Euthanasia, 14 L. MED. & HEALTH CARE 145, 147 (1986).

12. Id.

13. Id.

14. Id.

15. Id.

16. Id.

17. VEATCH, supra note 9 at 135.

18. Supra note 1, at 95.

19. Id. at 95–96.

20. Id. at 96.

21. Id. at 99.

22. Id.

23. Id. at 100.

24. EIKE-HENNER W. KLUGE, THE PRACTICE OF DEATH 149, (Yale Univ. Press 1975).

25. Supra note 1, at 103, 106.

26. Id. at 107.

National attention was drawn to the poignancy and humaneness of euthanasia when—in its January 8, 1988, issue—the American Medical Association printed an anonymous column entitled, "It's Over Debbie," written by a physician who described the manner in which he deliberately injected a 20-year-old woman suffering from ovarian cancer with an overdose of morphine, 259 J. AM. MED. ASSN. 272 (1988). Subsequently, citing confidentiality and First Amendment issues, the American Medical Association refused to provide the Cook County State Attorney's request to provide a grand jury in Chicago with the name of the physician who authored the column. Specter, AMA Won't Identify Mercy Killer, WASH. POST, Feb. 17, 1988, at A3. The Chief Judge of the Cook County Court ruled later that no crime had been proved and dismissed a later grand jury subpoena demanding the physician author's identity. Wilkerson, Judge Stalls Inquiry into a Mercy Killing Case, N.Y. TIMES Mar. 19, 1988, at 6. See also, WASH. POST HEALTH MAG., April 12, 1988, at 10; Cohn, Saving Lives, Ending Lives, WASH. POST HEALTH MAG., Mar. 1, 1988, at 13.

27. Supra note 24 at 161.

28. Id.

29. Id.

The longest record for survival with nutrition from a feeding tube is 37 years. *Brophy v. New England Sinai Hospital Inc.*, 497 N.E.2d 626, 637 (Mass. 1986).

30. Supra note 27.

31. Id. at 162.

32. Id.

33. Id. at 162.

34. Id., Ch. 4, notes 1–7.

35. McCormick, To Save or Let Die: The Dilemma of Modern Medicine in HOW BRAVE A NEW WORLD? at 339–349 (Richard A. McCormick ed.), (Georgetown Univ. Press 1981).

36. Rachels, Euthanasia, Killing and Letting Die in ETHICAL ISSUES RELATING TO DEATH at Ch. 7, p. 148 (John Ladd ed.), (Ox. Univ. Press 1979).

See also, JAMES RACHELS, THE END OF LIFE, (Ox. Univ. Press 1986).

37. Applebaum & Klein, Therefore Choose Death?, 81 COMMENTARY 23, 27 (1986).

38. Rachels, supra note 36.

For example, if someone were to see that an infant were drowning in a bathtub, would it make any difference whether an act of active or passive euthanasia were followed? It could be perceived "just as bad to let it drown as to push its head under water," for one act is as iniquitous as the other. Foot, Euthanasia in ETHICAL ISSUES RELATING TO DEATH 28, at 29, supra note 36.

39. FRANK HARRON, JOHN BURNSIDE, & TOM BEAUCHAMP, HEALTH AND HUMAN VALUES 48, (Yale Univ. Press 1983).

40. Id.

See also, Rachels, Active and Passive Euthanasia, 292 NEW ENG. J. MED. 78 (1975).

41. Id. at 42.

42. Id.

43. Id.

44. 140 MED. J. AUST. 431 (1981).

45. Kuhse, Euthanasia—Again, 142 MED. J. AUST. 610, 611 (1985).

46. Id.

47. Fearing condonation or actual use of "poisons or similar lethal agents" upon request by a patient would "risk serious abuse," the President's Commission for the Study of Ethical Problems in Medicine and Biomedical and Behavioral Research refused to sanction such usage. See DECIDING TO FOREGO LIFE-SUSTAINING TREATMENT: ETHICAL, MEDICAL AND LEGAL ISSUES IN TREATMENT DECISIONS, 62 *passim* (1983). Yet, the Commission did recognize the treatment refusals for dying patients should be honored. Id. at 63.

The Law Reform Commission of Canada has concluded euthanasia should not be legalized because such a condonation would severely weaken respect for all human life. Rather, it suggests a better answer to the sufferings of terminally ill would be to develop more effective palliative care and to search for equally effective pain control therapies. Report 20, EUTHANASIA, AIDING SUICIDE AND CESSATION TREATMENT, REPORT OF THE LAW REFORM COMMISSION OF CANADA 17, 18, 21, 31 (1983). The Commission did recognize that patients are autonomous decision makers and, acting within this role, have a right to make a decision regarding the discontinuation of treatment either already in progress or not to even commence any type of treatment at all; and that this expression of one's will is but a simple question of fact. Id.

48. Kuhse, The Case for Active Voluntary Euthanasia, 14 L. MED. & HEALTH CARE 145, 147 (1986).

49. Id.

50. Amundsen, The Physician's Obligation to Prolong Life: A Medical Duty Without Classical Roots, 8 HASTINGS CENTER RPT. 23 (1978).

51. Id. at 27.

52. Id.

53. Id. at 25.

54. Id.

55. Id. at 27, 28.

56. Supra note 50, at 27.

57. Id.

58. Id.

59. President's Commission, supra note 47, at 300–307 (1983).

See Hansen, Doctors Assert Patient's Right to Die: Court Rules Man Can Keep Comatose Wife on Respirator Despite Hospital's Wishes, 77 AM. BAR ASSN. J. 26 (Oct. 1991).

60. Id. at 305.

61. Id.

62. Id. Emphasis provided.

63. Id. Emphasis provided.

See Hansen, Right to Die: A Consensus is Emerging with Assistance of Catholic Theologians, NAT'L CATHOLIC RPTR, Dec. 11, 1987, at 1.

64. Id.

65. Id. Emphasis provided.

66. Id.

67. See generally, Smith, *Triage*: Endgame Realities, 1 J. CONTEMP. HEALTH L. & POL'Y 143 (1985).

One prominent Jesuit theological, Fr. Edwin J. Healey, has implied that the maximum amount of money that could be expended on an ordinary course of treatment *before* it became extraordinary, was $2,000. Kelly, The Duty of Using Artificial Means of Preserving Life, 11 THEOLOGICAL STUDIES 203 at 206 f.n. 9 (citing Fr. Healey), (1950).

68. Supra note 59, at 307.

69. RICHARD A. McCORMICK, NOTES ON MORAL THEOLOGY, 1965 THROUGH 1980, at 565, (Univ. Press Am. 1981).

70. JAMES F. CHILDRESS, WHO SHOULD DECIDE: PATERNALISM IN HEALTH CARE 166, (Ox. Univ. Press 1982).

71. Hilfiker, Allowing the Debilitated to Die: Facing Our Ethical Choices, 308 N. ENG. J. MED. 716 (1983).

72. Childress, When is it Morally Justifiable to Discontinue Medical Nutrition and Hydration? in BY NO EXTRAORDINARY MEANS at 81 (Joanne Lynn ed.), (Ind. Univ. Press 1986).

73. Id.

74. Smith, Quality of Life, Sanctity of Creation: Palliative or Apotheosis?, 63 NEB. L. REV. 707, 734 (1984).

75. GEORGE P. SMITH, II, GENETICS, ETHICS AND THE LAW 1–4, (Assoc. Faculty Press 1981).

See also, GEORGE P. SMITH, II, THE NEW BIOLOGY, Ch. 8, (Plenum 1989).

76. Supra note 74.

77. Supra note 75.

78. Supra note 74, at 738.

79. The ultimate morality of an action or inaction in cases of this nature being considered here can never be evaluated properly without reference to the quality of life being extended by the heroic measures. WILL, When Homicide is Noble, in THE MORNING AFTER: AMERICAN SUCCESSES AND EXCESSES 1981–86 at 84, 85 (George F. Will ed.), (Free Press 1986).

80. Supra note 75, at 9.

A recent study of procedures followed by upstate New York hospitals found prolonged use of artificial ventilators to treat patients over 80 years of age in an intensive care unit is not cost effective. Specifically, it was found that when the sum of a patient's age and the number of days on a respirator reached at least 100, the chances of survival were near zero. Thus, a 90-year-old person on a respirator for 10 days had a very minimal chance of survival. Cohen, Lambrinos & Fein, Mechanical

Ventilation for the Elderly Patient in Intensive Care: Incremental Changes and Benefits, 269 J. AM. MED. ASSN. 1025 (1993).

81. Beall, Mercy for the Terminally Ill Cancer Patient, 249 J. AM. MED. ASSN. 2883 (1983).

See Schneiderman & Jecker, Futility in Practice, 153 ARCH. INTERN. MED. 437 (1993); Miles, Medical Futility, 20 L. MED. & HEALTH CARE 310 (1992).

82. 1982 A.M.A. JUDICIAL COUNCIL CURRENT OPINIONS, Am. Med. Assoc. 9–10 (1982); President's Commission for the Study of Ethical Problems in Medicine and Biomedical and Behavioral Research, supra note 47, at 288 (1983).

See Multi-Society Task Force on PVS, Medical Aspects of The Persistent Vegetative State, 330 NEW ENG. J. MED. 1499, 1592 (1994).

83. Kelly, The Duty of Using Artificial Means of Preserving Life, 11 THEOLOGICAL STUD-IES 203, 206, (1950).

84. Id. at 207.

85. H. TRISTRAM ENGELHARDT, JR., THE FOUNDATIONS OF BIOETHICS 307, (Ox. Univ. Press 1986).

86. GERALD A. KELLY, MEDICO-MORAL PROBLEMS 129, (Cath. Hosp. Assn. 1958).

87. DANIEL MAGUIRE, DEATH BY CHOICE 123, (Schocken 1975).

Only when there is hope of health (*si sit spes salutis*) or where hope of recovery appeared (*ubi spes affulget convalescendi*) is treatment required. Futile treatments (*nemo ad inutile*) or treatments that only postponed death or blunted briefly the illness (*parum pro nihilo reputatur moralitier*) are not required to be undertaken. An obligation to accept treatment is defeated if the at-risk individual has an aversion to the particular form of treatment (*horror magnus*). Supra note 85, at 332, f.n. 122.

88. Supra note 85, at 225.

89. Id.

90. Supra note 83, at 214.

91. Id. at 210.

Another fascinating case is to be found in considering the duty to use or administer insulin with reference to a patient who has both diabetes and cancer. The patient would be required to use the insulin because it is the normal, ordinary manner to combat or stabilize the diabetes. The interesting problem here is whether one who suffers from two lethal diseases is obligated to pursue ordinary treatments in order to check one when there is no hope of checking the other disease that is lethal. Stated otherwise, given the presence of the terminable cancer, can insulin injections be regarded as a reasonable hope of success? Should the diseases be considered separately or would it be better to evaluate the total patient condition? It is argued that for the clear duty to use insulin to exist, two factors must exist: it must be both an ordinary means as well as offer a reasonable hope of success. Obviously, the presence of cancer casts some serious doubt on this second factor. Id. at 216.

92. 380 N.E.2d 134, 137 n. 7 (Mass. App. Ct. 1978).

93. 373 Mass. 728, 370 N.E.2d 417, 424 (1977). Emphasis provided.

94. 70 N.J. 10, 335 A.2d 647, 668 cert. denied 429 U.S. 922 (1976). Emphasis provided.

In 1991, New Jersey became the first state to enact a statute recognizing a personal religious exemption or conscience clause that has the effect of requiring a physician to declare death upon the basis of cardiorespiratory criteria (or, the cessation of all circulatory and respiratory functions) rather than brain, or neurological death, in those cases where he knows or has reason to believe such action is consistent with a patient's religious belief. 26 N.J. REV. STAT. §§6A1–6A8 (1991 Supp.). See Olick, Brain Death, Religious Freedom and Public Policy: New Jersey's Landmark Legislative Initiative, 1 KENNEDY INST. ETHICS J. 275 (1991).

95. Ramsey, Euthanasia and Dying Well Enough, 44 LINACRE Q. 43 (1977).

96. Id.

See also, Ramsey, Prolonged Dying: Not Medically Indicated, 6 HASTINGS CENTER RPT. 16 (1976).

97. VEATCH, supra note 9, at 110.

98. Id.

99. Id.

100. Id. at 112.

See McCORMICK, supra note 35 at Ch. 21.

101. Supra note 70, at 166.

102. Id.

103. Id.

104. Id.

105. ROBERT M. VEATCH, A THEORY OF MEDICAL ETHICS 37, 39, (Basic Bks. 1981).

106. Id. at 39.

107. Martin, Suicide and Self Sacrifice in SUICIDE: THE PHILOSOPHICAL ISSUES 48 at 58 (Margaret P. Battin & David J. Mayo eds.), (Dufour 1980).

108. Supra note 106. See McCORMICK, supra note 35, at 412–429.

See also, President's Commission supra note 47, at 80, n. 10 (1983).

109. Supra note 106, at 39.

110. Id. at 235.

Where treatment offered to extend life would be unreasonably burdensome or simply useless to a terminally ill patient, the principle would permit non treatment. Id. at 40.

111. Louisell, Euthanasia and Biathanasia, 22 CATH. UNIV. L. REV. 723, 742 (1973).

112. Id.

113. Id.

114. See Smith, supra note 67.

115. Engelhardt, Suicide and the Cancer Patient, 36 CA-A Cancer Journal for Clinicians 105, 108 (1986).

116. Id.

117. Id.

118. Id.

Interestingly, a recent study showed that many surviving elderly heart attack victims do not receive potentially life saving treatments such as clot-busting drugs and blood thinners—and some are not even told to stop smoking. Ellerbeck, Jencks, et al., Quality of Care for Medical Patients with Acute Myocardial Infarction, 273 J. AM. MED. ASSN. 1509 (1995).

119. Supra note 115.

120. CICELY SAUNDERS & MARY BAINES, LIVING WITH DYING: THE MANAGE-MENT OF TERMINAL DISEASE 4, (Ox. Univ. Press 1983).

121. Id.

122. Id.

123. Id.

The double effect principle was validated in the case of Rex v. Bodkin-Adams (1957). Here, Dr. John Bodkin-Adams was acquitted of murder after having administered narcotics that apparently caused the death of his patient. The judge held (in this unreported case) that a physician who administers narcotics in order to relieve pain is not guilty of murder merely because the measures he takes incidentally shortens life. O. RUTH RUSSELL, FREEDOM TO DIE 255, (Human Science 1977).

124. WILLIAM L. PROSSER, THE LAW OF TORTS § 56 at 373–74, (West Pub. Co. 5th ed. 1984).

125. Fletcher, Prolonging Life, 42 WASH. L. REV. 909 (1967).

126. Id. at 1009–1012.

127. Id.

128. See ROBERT H. WILLIAMS, TO LIVE AND TO DIE: WHEN, WHY AND HOW (Springer-Verlag 1973); Fletcher, Legal Aspects of the Decision Not to Prolong Life, 203 J. AM. MED. ASSN. 65 (1968).

See also, Angell, The Case of Helga Wanglie: A New Kind of Right to Die Case, 325 NEW ENG. J. MED. 511 (1991).

129. Comment, The Right to Die, 7 HOUSTON L. REV. 654, 659 (1970).

130. Fletcher, supra note 128.

131. Id.

132. Supra note 125.

Truly, the bounds of moral judgment are strained to the point of collapse when an ultimate decision is sought as to whether switching off a respirator is an act of active euthanasia or merely passive euthanasia! Rachels, Active and Passive Euthanasia, 292 NEW ENG. J. MED. 78 (1975).

In a 1983 California case, Barber v. Superior Court of Los Angeles County, 147 Cal. App. 3d 1006, 195 Cal. Rptr. 484, the court recognized that there was a difference between killing and letting die and that actions by two doctors in turning off a respirator of a patient who was vegetative, with permission from the patient's wife, was not an act of killing.

133. Supra note 24, at 171.

134. Id.

135. Id.

136. Id.

137. Id.

138. Id.

139. *People v. Beardsley*, 150 Mich. 206, 113 N.W. 1128, 1129 (1907).

140. Survey, Euthanasia: Criminal, Tort, Constitutional and Legislative Considerations, 48 NOTRE DAME L. REV. 1202, 1207 (1973).

141. Id. at 1208.

142. Id.

143. Id.

A new and novel tort action for *wrongful living* has been proposed recently. Under the proposal, the tort would be recognized as personal and hence redressed only by the individual whose right to die was compromised; or, if that individual should die subsequently, by his representative on a survival basis. If the interfering treatment is made and thereupon the patient lives, the interference with the right to die involves compensation for the living. Contrariwise, if the interfering treatment causes death earlier than nontreatment, then there is a clear, casual connection between the interference and the loss: permanent death. Accordingly, wrongful death damages to the beneficiaries of the decedent would be appropriate, but damages could be calculated for that period of time by which the life was shortened by the treatment. Oddi, The Tort of Interference with the Right to Die: The Wrongful Living Cause of Action, 75 GEO. L.J. 625, 641 (1980).

See also, Furrow, Damage Remedies and Institutional Reform: The Right to Refuse Treatment, 12 L. MED. & HEALTH CARE 152 (1982).

144. Supra note 140, at 1213.

145. Id.

146. Id.

147. Id. at 1213, n. 82.

148. VEATCH, supra note 9, at 79.

149. Id. See generally, MacKinnon, Euthanasia and Homicide, 26 CRIM. L. Q. 483 (1984).

150. Keown, The Law and Practice of Euthanasia in The Netherlands, 108 L. Q. REV. 51 (1992).

151. Id. at 78.

152. Id. at 58–60.

153. Id. at 60.

154. Id. at 70.

155. Id.

156. Id. at 66 *passim*. See also, Ciesielski & Kimsma, The Impact of Reporting Cases of Euthanasia in Holland: A Patient and Family Perspective, 8 BIOETHICS 151 (1994).

157. Fenigsen, The Report of The Dutch Governmental Committee on Euthanasia, 1991 ISSUES L. & MED. 339.

See Capron, Euthanasia in The Netherlands: American Observations, 22 HASTINGS CENTER RPT. 30 (1992).

158. Fenigsen, supra note 157, at 343.

Ninety-eight percent of all physicians working in nursing homes were shown to have withheld or withdrawn life prolonging treatment without the patients consent. In hospital settings, it was shown that in 86 percent of all DNR decisions, physicians made them without the patient's knowledge. Id.

159. Fenigsen, supra note 157, at 340, 341.

160. Id.

161. Id. at 341. See also, SHERWIN B. NULAND, HOW WE DIE: REFLECTIONS ON LIFE'S FINAL CHAPTER, Ch. VIII at 155–156, (Knopf 1994).

162. Fenigsen, supra note 157, at 342–343.

163. Id.

164. Id.

Involuntary euthanasia is also administered to newborns with profound disabilities and children with life threatening diseases. Id.

165. Drozdiak, Dutch Remove Barriers to Doctors Carrying Out Euthanasia, WASH. POST, Feb. 10, 1993, at A23.

See Somerville, The Song of Death: The Lyrics of Euthanasia, 9 J. CONTEMP. HEALTH L. & POL'Y 1, 35–40 (1993).

166. Fenigsen, The Netherlands New Regulations Concerning Euthanasia, 9 ISSUES L. & MED. 167 (1993).

167. 35 Am. Medical News 34 (Sept. 14, 1992).

168. Id.; Warden, Euthanasia Around the World, 304 BR. MED. J. 7 (Jan. 4, 1992).

169. Boyd, Majority View of The Institute of Medical Ethics Working Party on The Ethics of Prolonging Life and Assisting Death, 336 THE LANCET 610 (Sept. 8, 1990).

170. Walsh, Michigan Committee Backs Allowing Suicide, WASH. POST, April 26, 1994, at 1. Emphasis provided.

171. Id.

See Consensus Subcommittee Report, Mich. Comm. on Death & Dying, 3/31/94; Annas, Physician-Assisted Suicide: Michigan's Temporary Solution, 328 NEW ENG. J. MED. 1573 (1993).

On December 13, 1994, the Michigan Supreme Court ruled that any legislative authorization validating assisted suicide was unconstitutional. *People of the State of Michigan v. Jack Kevorkian*, 447 MICH. RPTS. 436 (1994), 527 N.W. 2d 714 (1994).

172. Editorial, Mercy for the Dying, N.Y. TIMES, May 28, 1994, at 18. But see Kamisar, Are Laws Against Assisted Suicide Unconstitutional?, 23 HASTINGS CENTER RPT. 32 (1993); Post, Infanticide and Geronticide, 10 AGEING AND SOCIETY 317 (1990).

A New York Federal District court held there was no constitutional right to assisted suicide, even for one who is mentally competent, terminally ill and facing severe suffering. Accordingly, the court held the New York laws that make it a crime to aid a person in committing or attempting to commit suicide. *Quill v. Koppell*, 870 F. Supp. 78 (S.D.N.Y. 1994).

173. Podgers, Matters of Life and Death: Debate Grows Over Euthanasia, 78 AM. BAR. ASSN. J. 60 (May 1992).

In November, 1994, the Oregon Death With Dignity Act was passed by referendum. Its provisions are essentially the same, in effect, as those unsuccessful efforts in the six previously listed states. Brown, Medical Community Still Divided on Oregon's Assisted Suicide Act, WASH. POST, Nov. 13, 1994, at A20. On December 27, 1994, an injunction was issued preventing the state from implementing this new law until its constitutionality could be established. *Gary Lee et al. v. State of Oregon*, 869 F. Supp. 1491 (D. Ore. 1994).

On August 3, 1995, the District Court upheld the previous injunction finding the Act unconstitutional because it violated the Equal Protection Clause of the Constitution's 14th Amendment; this because the coverage of the legislation to include the terminally ill was not rationally related to the legitimate state interest in maintaining life and preventing suicide. 891 F. Supp. 1421 (D. Ore. 1995).

See Rein, Preserving Dignity and Self-Determination of the Elderly: A Proposal for Statutory Refocus and Reform, 60 GEO WASH. L. REV. 1818 (1992).

174. *Compassion in Dying, et. al v. Washington*, 850 F. Supp. 1454 (W.D. Wash. 1994).

See McCarthy, Final Exits: Seattle Group Offers Terminal Patients Advice on Ways to Choose Suicide, WASH. POST HEALTH MAG., Feb. 15, 1994, at 9.

On March 9, 1995, the United States Court of Appeals for the Ninth Circuit reversed this Washington case and in so doing acknowledged that while the right of privacy may encompass freedom from unwanted medical intervention, it did not include a right to have assistance from a second person. The dissent maintained that the right of privacy and self-determination included a right to die with dignity. Compassion in Dying v. Washington, 49 F. 3d 586 (9th Cir. 1995).

Life support systems may be withdrawn from a patient in a persistent vegetative state (who, while competent, never expressed an opinion on the issue) under Pennsylvania law since 1976 if the patient's family or guardian receives written statements from two qualified physicians certifying the patient has no reasonable possibility of recovery. The standard of clear and convincing evidence regarding the patient's wishes was not relevant here. *In re Fiori*, Pa. Superior Ct., No. 00737, Philadelphia, 63 U.S. Law Wk. 2484 (Feb. 14, 1995).

175. *Cruzan v. Director, Missouri Department of Health*, 497 U.S. 261 (1990); *Planned Parenthood of Southeastern Pennsylvania v. Casey*, 114 S. Ct. 909 (1994).

176. *Cruzan*, id.

177. *Planned Parenthood of Southern Pennsylvania*, supra note 175.

178. REV. CODE WASH. § 70.122 et. seq. (1994).

179. *Compassion in Dying*, supra note 174 at 1468.

180. Podgers, supra note 173, at 63.

See, e.g., *McKay v. Bergstedt*, where the Supreme Court of Nevada acknowledged "the right to be free from pain at the time [a life support system] is disconnected is inseparable from his [a] right to refuse medical treatment." 801 P.2d 617, 631 (Nev. 1990); and *State v. McAffe*, 385 S.E.2d 651 (Ga. 1989) where the Georgia Supreme Court allowed a competent patient to remove a respirator and permitted a sedative to be administered to ease a resulting death.

See also, *In re Conroy*, 98 N.J. 321, 486 A.2d 1209 (1985); *In re Storar*, 52 N.Y.2d 363, 420 N.E.2d 64 (1981); *Superintendent of Belcherton State School v. Saikewicz*, 373 Mass. 728, 370 N.E.2d 417 (1977) and *In re Quinlan*, 70 N.J. 10, 355 A.2d 647, *cert. denied, sub. nom.*, *Granger v. New Jersey*, 429 U.S. 922 (1976).

See Fletcher, The Courts and Euthanasia, 15 L. MED. & HEALTH CARE 223 (1987/88) (arguing euthanasia should be decriminalized).

181. Quill, Cassel, & Meier, Care of the Hopelessly Ill-Proposed Clinical Criteria for Physician-Assisted Suicide, 327 NEW ENG. J. MED. 1380, 1381 (1992).

182. Wanzer, Federman, Adelstein, et al., The Physician's Responsibility Toward Hopelessly Ill Patients, 320 NEW ENG. J. MED. 844, 849 (1989); Rhoden, Litigating Life and Death, 120 HARV. L. REV. 375, 442–443 (1988).

183. Id.

See also, Brody, Assisted Death—A Compassionate Response to a Medical Failure, 320 NEW ENG. J. MED. 1384 (1989).

184. Supra note 182.

185. Supra note 181.

186. Id. at 1382.

187. Id.

188. Id.

189. Id.

190. Id.

191. Id.

192. Id.

193. This term would be defined as "an illness in which, on the basis of the best available diagnostic criteria and in the light of available therapies, a reasonable estimation can be made prospectively and with a high probability that a person will die within a relatively short time." Bayer, Callahan, Fletcher, et al., The Care of The Terminally Ill: Morality and Economics, 309 NEW ENG. J. MED. 1490, 1491 (1983).

194. See Barrington, Apologia for Suicide in SUICIDE: THE PHILOSOPHICAL ISSUES at 90, 99, 100, supra note 107. See also, MARGARET P. BATTIN, THE LEAST WORST DEATH, Ch. 9 (Ox. Univ. Press 1994).

In order to ensure these rights and have them protected, a Bill of Rights for Dying Persons has been proposed. See Appendix E.

195. Conard, Elder Choice, 19 AM. J. L. & MED. 233, 234 (1993).

CHAPTER 12

1. Rich, White House to Focus on Seniors' Concerns, WASH. POST HEALTH MAG., April 25, 1995, at 7. See also, Roberts, Generations Living Together, WASH. POST HEALTH MAG., May 9, 1995, at 8.

2. Id.

3. Id.

4. Id. See also, Rich, Delegates Gather for Aging Conference as Social Security, Medicare Face Pressure, WASH. POST, May 3, 1995, at A6; Rich, Conferees Defend Social Security, Medicare, WASH. POST, May 6, 1995, at A7.

5. See generally THE DEPENDENT ELDERLY: AUTONOMY, JUSTICE AND QUALITY OF CARE (Luke Gormally ed.), (Camb. Univ. Press 1992); Gibbs & Sinclair, Residential Care for Elderly People: The Correlates of Quality, 12 AGEING & SOCIETY 463 (1992).

6. ROBERT C. ATCHLEY, SOCIAL FORCES AND AGING 185–87 (6th ed. 1991). See also, Chappell & Blandford, Informal and Formal Care: Exploring the Complementary, 11 AGEING AND SOCIETY 229 (1991).

7. ATCHLEY, id. at Ch. 8.

8. Id. at Ch. 8, p. 397.

9. HARRY R. MOODY, ETHICS IN AN AGING SOCIETY 176–180, (Johns Hopkins Univ. Press 1992).

10. Zweibel, Measuring Quality of Life Near the End of Life, 260 J. AM. MED. ASSN. 839 (1988). See DAVID A. WISE, ISSUES IN THE ECONOMICS OF AGING, Chs. 10, 12, (Univ. Chic. Press 1990).

11. See Kapp, Options for Long-Term Care Financing: A Look to the Future, 42 HASTINGS L. J. 719, 750–52 (1991). See Note, Relative Responsibility Extended: Requirements of Adult Children to Pay for Their Indigent Parents' Medical Needs, 21 FAM. L. Q. 1 (1988).

12. Levy, Supporting the Aged: The Problem of Family Responsibility in AN AGING WORLD, Ch. 18 (John M. Eekelaar & David Pearl eds.), (Ox. Univ. Press 1989).

13. Id. at 263. See also, Callahan, What is a Reasonable Demand on Health Care Resources? Designing a Basic Package of Benefits, 8 J. CONTEMP. HEALTH L. & POL'Y 1, 10–11 (1992).

14. Supra note 12, at 265.

15. ETHICAL CONFLICTS IN THE MANAGEMENT OF HOME CARE: THE CASE MANAGER'S DILEMMA at 142 (Rosalie A. Kane & Arthur L. Caplan eds.), (Springer Pub. 1992).

16. Abrams, Shades of Meaning, 7 FRONTLINES 2, 5 (May, 1990), Center for Health Ethics & Policy, Univ. Colorado, Denver. See generally AN AGING WORLD: DILEMMAS AND CHALLENGES FOR LAW AND SOCIAL POLICY, supra note 12; Editorial, The Final Autonomy, 340 LANCET 757 (Sept. 26, 1992).

17. Kapp, Options for Long-Term Care Financing: A Look to The Future, 42 HASTINGS L. J. 719, 743–746 (1991). See Callahan, Rationing Medical Progress: The Way to Affordable Health Care, 322 NEW ENG. J. MED. 1810 (1990).

18. Cohn, What It Will Take to Cure Health Care, WASH. POST HEALTH MAG., Jan. 26, 1993, at 16, 17. See generally JOHN HOLAHAN et al., BALANCING ACCESS, COSTS AND POLITICS: THE AMERICAN CONTRACT FOR HEALTH SYSTEM REFORM, (Univ. Press Am. 1991).

19. Callahan, Limiting Health Care for the Old in AGING AND ETHICS: PHILOSOPHICAL PROBLEMS IN GERONTOLOGY at 224 (Nancy S. Jecker ed.), (Humana 1991). See Evans, Advanced Medical Technology and Elderly People in TOO OLD FOR HEALTH CARE? at 61–75 (Robert H. Binstock & Stephen G. Post eds.), (Johns Hopkins Univ. Press 1992).

20. Supra note 18. See Callahan, What Is a Reasonable Demand on Health Care Resources? Designing A Basic Package of Benefits, 8 J. CONTEMP. HEALTH L. & POL'Y 1 (1992).

21. K.R. PELLETIER, LONGEVITY: FULFILLING OUR BIOLOGICAL POTENTIAL 8–9, (Dell 1981); Callahan, supra note 19. See THE SECOND FIFTY YEARS: PROMOTING HEALTH AND PREVENTING DISABILITY (Robert L. Berg & Joseph S. Cassells eds.), (Nat'l. Academy Press 1990).

22. PELLETIER, id.

23. Id. at 19.

24. See generally GEORGE P. SMITH, II, BIOETHICS AND THE LAW: MEDICAL, SOCIO-LEGAL AND PHILOSOPHICAL DIRECTIONS FOR A BRAVE NEW WORLD (Univ. Press Am. 1993); GEORGE P. SMITH, II, THE NEW BIOLOGY: LAW, ETHICS AND BIO-TECHNOLOGY (Plenum 1989).

25. PELLETIER, supra note 21, at 21.

26. Greenhouse, Court Order to Treat Baby with Partial Brain Prompts Debate on Costs and Ethics (quoting the former President of The Society of Critical Care Medicine Dr. Raphaely), N.Y.

TIMES, Feb. 20, 1994, at A20. See generally Callahan, Modernizing Mortality: Medical Progress and The Good Society, 20 HASTINGS CENTER RPT. 28 (1990).

27. Soldo, Pellegrino, & Howell, Epilogue: Confronting The Age of Aging, 19 SOCIO-ECONOMIC PLANNING SCIENCES 289 (1985). See generally Symposium, Health Care in America: Armageddon on the Horizon?, 3 STAN. L. & POL'Y REV. 16 (1991).

28. SIMONE de BEAUVOIR, OLD AGE 540, 541 (Patrick O'Brian, transl.), (Putnam 1972). See also, BETTY FRIEDAN, THE FOUNTAIN OF AGE 637, (Simon & Schuster 1993).

29. GEORGE F. WILL, THE MORNING AFTER: AMERICAN SUCCESSES AND EX-CESSES, 1981-86, at 411, (Free Press 1986).

In the final analysis, health should be redefined to exclude a medical or even social mandate to control behavior for the total benefit of one's mortal body. Rather, the goal of good health should be accepted as not freedom from death's inevitability, disease, unhappiness, or stress but rather the development of an ability to cope with them in a competent manner. Fitzgerald, The Tyranny of Health, 331 NEW ENG. J. MED. 196 (1994).

Index